S0-BDS-556

Essentials of
Persuasive Speaking

Theory & Contexts

Essentials of Persuasive Speaking

Theory & Contexts

Rudolph F. Verderber
University of Cincinnati

Wadsworth Publishing Company

Belmont, California

A Division of Wadsworth, Inc.

Speech Editor: Peggy Randall
Editorial Assistant: Sharon Yablon
Production: Cece Munson, The Cooper Company
Designer: Albert Burkhardt
Copy Editor: Carol S. Reitz
Print Buyer: Martha Branch
Cover: Albert Burkhardt
Compositor: Omegatype Typographers
Signing Representative: Steve Simmons

© 1991 by Wadsworth, Inc. All rights reserved. No part of this
book may be reproduced, stored in a retrieval system, or
transcribed, in any form or by any means, electronic, mechanical,
photocopying, recording, or otherwise, without the prior written
permission of the publisher, Wadsworth Publishing Company,
Belmont, California 94002, a division of Wadsworth, Inc.

Printed in the United States of America

2   3   4   5   6   7   8   9   10—95   94   93

Library of Congress Cataloging-in-Publication Data
Verderber, Rudolph F.
    Essentials of persuasive speaking : theory and contexts / by
Rudolph F. Verderber.
        p.   cm.
    Includes bibliographical references and index.
    ISBN 0-534-15030-6
    1. Public speaking. 2. Persuasion (Rhetoric) 3. Forensics
(Public speaking) I. Title. II. Title: Persuasive speaking.
PN4121.V44 1991   90-49775
808.5'1—dc20   CIP

Contents

CHAPTER **3**

Analyzing Audience and Setting   37

CHAPTER **4**

Evidence: The Material of Persuasive Speaking   51

CHAPTER **5**

Reasoning with Your Audience   64

C H A P T E R **9**

Implementing Your Speech Plan: Developing a Persuasive Delivery

P A R T **III**

Modules

M O D U L E **A**

Social Action Campaigning

MODULE **E**

Speech Writing: Preparing and Delivering Manuscripts 221

APPENDIX **A**

Research Tools 233

APPENDIX **B**

Interviewing for Speech Information 237

Preface

As members of a democratic society, we make choices, many of which have a major impact on shaping the nature of our society. For instance, whether we donate money to the free store that supplies food to the needy, whether we support our community's Fine Arts Fund, or whether we vote for a particular political candidate for office may ultimately determine the treatment of the poor, the status of the arts in our community, or the kind of government that rules us. As we recognize the importance of these choices we may begin to see the need to influence the people who are making them. And our most powerful vehicle for shaping and mobilizing public opinion to make "the right choice" is our own persuasive speaking powers.

Despite the importance of persuasion in a democratic society, very few contemporary speech textbooks are devoted solely to the development of persuasive speaking effectiveness. Most speech textbooks focus on the fundamentals of speech preparation that apply to all kinds of speeches. Then they include a chapter, or at most a short unit, applying those fundamental principles to persuasive speaking. A few speech textbooks focus on the theories of persuasion. These, too, may then include a small section on the application of theory to persuasive speaking. This text focuses entirely on persuasive speaking.

Distinguishing Features

Essentials of Persuasive Speaking: Theory and Contexts has many distinguishing features, of which the following four are especially important.

First, the premise that a person earns the right to speak by having logical reasons and sound evidence to justify acceptance of the speech goal. People may have bursts of creative insight that lead them to propose a solution to a problem or a course of action, but in their speeches, they have the responsibility of presenting well supported reasons. Although a speaker may choose to organize the speech in a way that presents reasons indirectly, when a speech has concluded, members of the audience should be aware of the reasons in support of the goal.

Second, guidelines for developing a persuasive strategy based on careful audience analysis. Regardless of the quality of the reasons and evidence that provide the rationale for the speech, they must be adapted to the specific audience. This book features the concept of a speech plan, a written strategy for adapting to a specific audience covering the issues of audience credibility, interest, knowledge, attitude, and motivation. Students learn that even when they plan to present exactly the same arguments to different audiences, the means of developing and organizing those arguments will and should differ.

Third, a campaign approach to persuasion. Although a single, independent speech may result in the audience accepting the speaker's goal, persuasion is more likely to occur as a result of a campaign of speeches over time. As a result, in addition to learning how to prepare and deliver independent speeches, students are encouraged to develop campaigns in which persuasive speeches play a significant role.

Fourth, discussion of the skills necessary to meet different kinds of speaking situations. Although a speech in support of a proposal to limit air pollution has a great deal in common with a speech in support of a candidate for office, a speaker must recognize that the criteria for effectiveness of the two speeches differ. Speakers must recognize the issues that are involved in differing speech situations and speakers must be knowledgable of the available means of persuasion for those differing situations.

Organization

Essentials of Persuasive Speaking consists of the following three parts:

Part I, Orientation, introduces persuasive speaking and discusses major theories of persuasion in order to identify principles upon which sound speech preparation is built.

Part II, Guidelines of Persuasive Speaking, focuses on the preparatory process. It includes writing speech goals, analyzing audiences, discovering material, forming persuasive arguments, organizing speeches, creating a speech plan adapting content to the specific audience, and implementing the speech plan with a persuasive speaking style that uses effective language and delivery.

   Part III, Modules, focuses on persuasive speaking in a social action campaign, in an election campaign, in a sales campaign, and in refutation. The part concludes with a chapter on writing speeches for others.

   Finally, Appendix A provides a summary review of library sources, and Appendix B gives a more detailed account of interviewing for information.

   Although I am responsible for what appears in this book, the content reflects the thoughts of a great number of people. I would like to acknowledge the students who contributed speeches and speech plans. Also, I would like to thank the many instructors who offered feedback and insights through their review of draft versions: John D. Bee, University of Kansas; Carole Blair, University of California, Davis; Barbara Breaden, Lane Community College; Steven R. Brydon, California State University, Chico; Robert Chamberlain, Seattle Pacific University; Lois Einhorn, State University of New York, Binghamton; Ellen D. Hoffman, University of Pittsburgh, Johnstown; and Harold J. Kinzer, Utah State University.

   Finally, I express my gratitude to my wife, Kathie, who provides both valuable insight and inspiration.

Essentials of
Persuasive Speaking

Theory & Contexts

Part I

Orientation

What is persuasive speaking? How does it differ from manipulation or coercion? Can a speaker really make a difference in how people think and behave? What ethical standards, if any, guide the persuasive speaker? In this one-chapter part, I answer these questions and focus on the role of persuasive speaking in a democratic society.

Chapter **1**

Introduction to Persuasive Speaking

Wanted: People who have the creative insight to find solutions to problems and the persuasive speaking skills to affect people's attitudes and move them to action.

This classified ad emphasizes the need for persuasive speakers who can meet the responsibilities posed by a democratic society. Although some people are fond of saying, "We want action, not words," persuasive speaking students are well aware that it is *words* that so affect peoples' attitudes and beliefs that they are driven to action. For instance, scientists and environmentalists presented countless speeches to civic organizations, professional conferences, and legislative assemblies before the public really began to acknowledge the threats posed by pollutants and mount a serious effort to curtail their use.

Unfortunately, of the thousands of formal and informal persuasive speeches that are given daily across the nation, very few are either as successful in achieving their goal or as successful in modeling effective speech skills as they could be. People can *learn* to give effective persuasive speeches, however, and this book is designed to help you meet that goal.

This chapter lays a foundation for your study of persuasive speaking. It defines persuasive speaking and considers persuasive speaking perspectives, the role of persuasive speaking in a democracy, and the responsibilities persuasive speaking carries.

Persuasive Speaking Defined

Persuasive speaking is the art of forming oral arguments and adapting them to specific audiences in a way that is designed to affect their beliefs and/or move them to action. Let's consider the various aspects of this definition.

1. *Persuasive speaking is an art.* Although the basic skills that constitute persuasive speaking can be identified and tested, much of the speaker's effectiveness depends on his or her creative use of those skills.

2. *Persuasive speaking involves the formation of oral arguments.* Persuasive speakers present oral arguments that are composed of reasons and evidence. Although people do not always behave rationally, the speaker has the responsibility to present the strongest arguments possible.

3. *Persuasive speaking involves adapting oral arguments to specific audiences.* Since each audience is unique, composed of individuals with their own specific personalities, oral arguments must be shaped and developed differently for each audience. As a result, an effective persuasive speaker also considers those extralogical means of persuasion necessary to engage the audience emotionally.

4. *Persuasive speaking is purposeful.* Giving a stirring persuasive speech doesn't just happen. Yes, there are stories of people who were so moved by a situation that they rose to deliver inspiring, successful impromptu speeches. But for every story of spontaneous excellence there are hundreds of stories of people spending long hours preparing their speeches. Effective speakers think carefully about exactly what response they want from their audience. Then they find the right material and shape their message in a way that affects an audience's beliefs and moves people to action.

Persuasive Speaking Perspectives

Beginning with Aristotle's *The Rhetoric,* the first comprehensive analysis of persuasive speaking written more than 2000 years ago, persuasive speaking has been taught from a speaker, audience, speech perspective.

Speaker Perspective

Part of your effectiveness depends on you, the speaker. The often-repeated quotation from Ralph Waldo Emerson, "What you are speaks so loudly that I cannot hear what you say," encapsulates the importance of the speaker in the persuasive process: if your listeners don't have or don't develop faith in you, then nothing you say will have much effect on them. Thus, the more believable the source, the more likely there will be a change in attitude.[1] Aristotle called this perception of the speaker *ethos.* Most contemporary books on persuasion call this quality *credibility.*

Although scholars have considered several different dimensions of credibility, I believe the three that have the greatest direct effect on an audience's perception of you are your knowledge/expertise, your trustworthiness, and your personality.

Knowledge/ Expertise.   Your competence includes your qualifications and your knowledge of the subject area. Thus, your knowledge and expertise are often referred to as your track record. If people have good information, are sure of their facts and figures, and have a history of giving good advice, being clear thinkers, and having support for their opinions, they are considered competent. Research has shown that expertise alone can affect persuasiveness. The more "expert" your audience perceives you to be, the more likely they are to accept your information. For instance, one study found that a message advocating a certain number of hours of sleep was more persuasive when the source was a Nobel Prize-winning physiologist than when the source was a YMCA director.[2]

Trustworthiness.   Persuasive messages are likely to be stronger when the audience perceives the source as trustworthy.[3] *Trustworthiness* includes a speaker's mental and ethical traits. Audiences are more likely to trust and believe in a person whom they perceive as honest, industrious, dependable, strong, and steadfast. Audiences often overlook what are otherwise regarded as shortcomings if a person shows character. Just as your persuasiveness increases with the presence of traits that an audience identifies with trustworthiness, a lack of those qualities decreases your persuasiveness. For instance, if your audience perceives you as dishonest, they put much less stock in what you have to say.

In addition to these character traits, audiences consider people trustworthy when they perceive them as having good *intentions.* Audiences are likely to put more faith in a speaker if they believe that the speaker's primary motivations for a specific proposal are its benefits to the public in general or to the audience in particular. If the audience perceives the speaker as being more concerned with special interests, that speaker's credibility is lessened.

Personality.   A third major criterion of credibility has been called personality, the total of your behavioral and emotional tendencies. Sometimes people have a strong emotional reaction to a speaker based solely on a first impression created by the person's physical attractiveness. If a speaker is perceived by an audience as physically attractive, that speaker is more likely to be persuasive. For instance, Shelly Chaiken found that physically attractive students were more effective than less attractive students in getting undergraduate students to sign a petition.[4]

As the speech develops, audiences are likely to take a natural liking or disliking to a person based on his or her enthusiasm, friendliness, warmth, and ready smile. The more likeable or dynamic we perceive speakers to be, the more likely we are to accept their ideas.

Later in this book we will discuss ways that you can increase an audience's perception of your credibility during a speech.

Audience Perspective

Part of your effectiveness depends on your sensitivity to your audience. Effective speakers understand the nature of their audiences and how audiences are reacting to their message.

When people analyze audience reaction to persuasive messages, they are likely to use many different words—some are synonymous. For instance, in reference to listeners' responses to a speech on physical fitness, we can speak of their attitude, their belief, their values, their opinion, their behavioral intentions. Since we will be using these words frequently, let's attempt to clarify them.

Attitude.   We begin our analysis with the word "attitude" because it is used so frequently in persuasive and psychological literature and because it is the least specific of the words used to describe a response. Attitude has been defined in many different ways by scholars through the years. Part of the confusion that hampers people's understanding is that frequently attitude is defined as a tripartite concept that has affective, cognitive, and behavioral aspects. The first of these, the *affective* component, is composed of emotional feelings toward the subject. This aspect of attitude is often indicated by evaluative words like "good" or "bad," "favorable" or "unfavorable." Frequently we hear people say, "He's got a bad attitude toward his schoolwork" or "He's got a good attitude toward teamwork." In these cases we are suggesting that he behaves either favorably or unfavorably toward it. The second aspect of attitude, the *cognitive* component, is composed of intellectual beliefs and ideas about a subject. For example, the belief that men are more aggressive than women or that Orientals are very goal oriented is illustrative of the cognitive component. The *behavioral* component is composed of one's action tendencies toward a subject. For example, thoughts that one would donate money to a charity or take a stand against pornography are behavioral attitudes.

As a result of these three somewhat qualitatively different aspects, many psychologists have called for greater care in using the word "attitude." William McGuire has suggested that because of its broad nature, the word should be qualified whenever it is used.[5] Martin Fishbein and I. Ajzen go one step further and suggest that "attitude" be used only to show the evaluative dimension—that is, to indicate a person's like or dislike of the object.[6] This view seems reasonable, since so many attitude measures focus on liking and disliking. If I asked you, "What's your attitude toward physical fitness?" you might respond, "I'm in favor of it" or "I'm opposed to it" or "I don't feel strongly one way or the other." In keeping with these suggestions, whenever we refer to "attitude" in this text we will be using it as an evaluation. As you will see as we move on in this discussion, we will use the words "belief" and "behavior" or "action" for the other two aspects of attitude.

Our attitudes have three essential characteristics: _direction_ (from favorable to unfavorable), _intensity_ (from strong to weak), and _saliency_ (from very important to not so important). Thus, if I described your attitude toward physical fitness, its direction could be favorable or unfavorable, its intensity could be strong or weak, and its saliency could be important or unimportant.

Belief. As we have mentioned, a _belief_ is an acceptance of truth based on evidence, opinion, and experience; we use the word "belief" to represent the cognitive component of attitude. Although people use the word rather loosely, they are likely to _believe_ that something is true if someone can prove it to their satisfaction. Moreover, people may believe more strongly in some things than in others. For instance, a person may have a strong belief that a good marriage requires trust; the person may have a weak, less important belief that Tylenol is easier on the stomach than aspirin. You should recognize, however, that beliefs are not necessarily true. A person might believe that a crash diet is a safe way to lose weight, even though most scientists believe that it is not.

Beliefs tend to be formed on the basis of reasons and evidence. Most people think of themselves as "rational" beings. As a result, when you ask them why they hold a certain belief, they are likely to supply reasoned statements in support of it. For instance, on the subject of physical fitness, I might believe that keeping in good physical condition increases a person's chances of avoiding heart disease. My belief may be based on some statistics and examples that I have read or observed.

How are beliefs related to attitudes? If I hold a favorable evaluation of physical fitness in general, it is easier for me to hold a belief that being in good physical condition does in fact lower the likelihood of heart disease. In this textbook, we will be interested in designing speeches that establish, reinforce, or change beliefs. In order to do this, we will want to consider audience attitudes toward the subjects of the beliefs we are concerned with. For instance, we will see that if our goal is to persuade an audience to believe that taxes must be increased to finance educational goals, then we will want to examine our audience's attitudes toward taxes and toward education.

Values. *Value,* another word that interacts with attitude and belief, is a perception of the relative worth or importance of something. A value may be seen as a cluster of attitudes or beliefs. This cluster serves as a guideline for measuring the worth of various aspects of our lives. In practice, we hold economic, esthetic, social, political, and religious values. Thus, a person's attitudes and beliefs about physical fitness may lead to *or* grow from a set of esthetic or social values. A person who believes in physical fitness may come to value a trim, solid, healthy body; *or* valuing a trim, solid, healthy body may lead to favorable attitudes and beliefs about physical fitness.

Values tend to be central to a person's cognitive system and as a result are resistant to change. Moreover, values may trigger behavior. For instance, if you value courage, you may be a strong supporter of a politician whom you believe has behaved courageously in backing a measure that could cost him or her the next election.

Opinions. An opinion is a verbal expression of a value, attitude, or belief. Most people use the word "opinion" as a coverall word for any type of response. Thus, if I ask your opinion about physical fitness, you may reply with a *belief,* "I think good physical fitness reduces the risk of heart attacks"; you may reply with an *attitude,* "I am in favor of being fit"; or you may reply with a *value judgment,* "I think physical fitness is a necessity."

Behavior. The final word that we use to describe a response is *behavior,* an action that is related to or a result of an attitude, belief, value, or some combination of these. People who value physical fitness and believe that staying in shape is good for the heart may then *behave* in ways that reflect their positive attitude. For instance, they may "work out" at least three times a week. In this textbook, in addition to presenting speeches that affect beliefs, we will consider speeches that direct behavior.

Let us quickly summarize the relationship among these terms: A person *values* a healthy body. A person may then have a favorable *attitude* toward physical fitness. Given supporting evidence, the person is willing then to *believe* that a good physical condition lowers the likelihood of heart disease. In conversation, the person gives the *opinion* that good physical conditioning is important. As a result of values, attitudes, and beliefs related to physical fitness, the person *may* then engage in specific *behaviors*—the person works out at least three times a week and eats sensibly in order to maintain physical fitness.

The Measure of a Successful Speech.   You may be inclined to think that you either *succeed* or *fail* in your speeches that are designed to affect a belief or move to action. But persuasive effectiveness is not an either/or matter. If you try to persuade a social group that dues should be raised, but at the end of the speech a vote to raise dues fails, it might seem that you have had no persuasive effect. In fact, what happened was probably far more complicated than an either/or assessment. In the first place, any audience of more than one starts with different beliefs about the subject and different attitudes toward various beliefs. Suppose that in an audience of six, two already believe that income taxes need to be raised. If at the end of the speech the same two still believe so and the others do not, then it would appear that no persuasion took place. However, before the speech began those two people's attitudes toward the belief might have been only *somewhat* favorable and by the end of the speech their attitudes might have increased to *highly* favorable. Moreover, a different two of the six may have held very strong beliefs against government funding of social services. If at the end of the speech those two were much less sure of their negative beliefs, persuasion occurred even though four of the six may still be opposed to government support.

Speech Perspective

A third part of your effectiveness depends on the way you use information in your speech. Since your speeches focus on means and methods of affecting attitudes and changing behavior, this section considers a brief analysis of persuasive theory that is relevant to attitude change and motivation.

Theoretical Bases for Changing Attitudes

Since there is no single, universally agreed-upon theory of how audiences process information to form attitudes, this section looks at aspects of three perspectives on attitude change that are especially relevant to persuasive speakers: the learning theory perspective, the social judgment theory perspective, and the consistency theory perspective.

The Learning Theory Perspective of Attitude Change.   One school of thought is that changes in people's attitude come as a result of "a learning experience." This perspective, inspired by the work of Carl Hovland, a professor of psychology at Yale, and his colleagues, suggests that such learning is contingent upon the provision of appropriate rewards.[7] In their work, they maintain that a "major basis for acceptance of a given opinion is provided by arguments or reasons [in a message] which, according to the individual's own thinking habits, constitute 'rational' or 'logical' support for the conclusions."[8] The Yale theorists propose that this learning comes about through an essentially cognitive sequence of attention, comprehension, and acceptance. From a learning theory perspective, then, a persuasive speaker is effective to the extent that the recipients adopt the speaker's arguments as their own cognitive responses. Although recent analysis of the learning theory perspective has shown that the new attitudes and behaviors people adopt are based at least in part on the individual messages *they* generate in response to persuasive speaking messages, research confirms that people's attitudes are affected at least in part by the content of persuasive messages.[9]

In much of Part 2 of this textbook, we will stress means of ensuring that you have good reasons and solid evidence to support your speech goals.

Perceptual Theory Approach to Persuasion. Another school of thought is that attitudes are affected by the meaning that the persuasive communication has for listeners. The most popular perceptual theory is Sherif and Hovland's social judgment theory.[10] Social judgment theory says that people have differing frames of reference for information that they hear. These frames of reference serve as anchor positions to which related messages are compared. As a result, people react to incoming reasons and evidence (about the environment, for instance) by placing the information in one of three categories or *latitudes*: (1) the latitude of acceptance (the position that is most acceptable to them plus all other acceptable positions or statements relative to their attitude), (2) the latitude of rejection (the position that is most objectionable to them plus all other objectionable statements relative to their attitude), and (3) the latitude of noncommitment (the position that is neither accepted nor rejected).

In addition to hypothesizing that people place statements in one of these three categories, social judgment theorists consider the issue of ego involvement—that is, how involved people are with an issue and how important the attitude is to them (salience).

Social judgment theory provides at least three guidelines for the persuasive speaker: (1) the more compatible a person's speech goal is to the listeners' latitude of acceptance, the better the chances are of affecting those listeners' attitudes; (2) the more a person's speech goal appears to contrast with the listeners' latitude of acceptance, the less the chances are of positively affecting those listeners' attitudes; and (3) the more ego involved listeners are in their attitudes, the less likely those listeners' attitudes are changed by any contrasting message.

We will use these guidelines from social judgment theory to help in both phrasing speech goals and selecting information to support speech goals.

Consistency Approach to Persuasion. Consistency theorists hold that a person may adjust a personal attitude in order to maintain internal harmony in the belief system. According to consistency theorists, attitudes change when some fact, behavior, or event produces inconsistency within the system. One of the most popular consistency theories, cognitive dissonance, says that when an inconsistency occurs, listeners have to make some change in their attitude or behavior to return to a state of consistency. For instance, a smoker who hears a speech about new research suggesting that a man loses up to 12 years of his life by smoking may gain consistency by trying to quit smoking *or* by assuring himself that the quality of his life (enhanced by smoking) is more important than extra years of life. Consistency theory provides persuasive speakers with the knowledge that if they can create dissonance, their listeners may resolve their dissonance with changes that are advocated by the speaker.

Theoretical Bases for Motivating Action

Research suggests that sometimes a person's beliefs and attitudes lead directly to behavior; more likely, however, speeches that seek action have to include motivational elements. Typically, "motivation" is seen as a word that describes many forces, with a focus on "forces acting on or within an organism to initiate and direct behavior."[11] Persuasive speakers are more likely to develop motivation for their speech goals if they incorporate methods learned from incentive theory, expectancy-value theory, and basic needs theory.

Incentive Theory. One approach to motivation focuses on the importance of incentives. An *incentive* is usually defined as "a goal objective that motivates."[12] Thus, if a speaker says that in addition to providing a good meal, the Morgan House offers several entrees at a 40-percent discount to diners who place their order before 6:00 P.M., you might see the 40-percent discount as an *incentive* to dining early. A person must keep in mind, however, that incentives differ in value to people from one time to another. For instance, if you have a rather flexible schedule, the 40-percent discount may act as an incentive to dine early, but if your schedule is more complicated or if you want to impress a companion, the 40-percent discount would not be an incentive for you to dine early.

It is generally agreed that "incentives motivate behavior."[13] Let's say that a respected member of a national organization suggests that Susan run for the presidency of that organization because it would give her a great deal of personal status both within her own department and nationally in her field. This incentive of personal status for Susan might be so strong that it overrides even physiological needs for sleep. Such an incentive is not inborn but is learned. Thus, Susan learns that gaining the presidency is an important goal. Thoughts, then, can serve as incentive motivators.

Another factor of motivation is the meaningfulness of an incentive or goal, the importance people ascribe to objects, events, and experiences. Meaningfulness involves an emotional reaction. E. Klinger believes that people pursue those objects, events, and experiences that are emotionally important for them.[14] So, for Susan, becoming president of her national organization is a meaningful goal. An incentive is most powerful when it is a part of a meaningful goal.

Expectancy-Value Theory. Expectancy-value theory is based on the belief that motivated behavior results from a combination of individual *value goals* and the *expectancy* of obtaining a value goal.[15] Expectancy is important because it assumes that behavior is a function of a person's estimation of his or her chances of obtaining the value goal. One of the most prominent individuals working in expectancy-value theory is David McClelland, who argues that a motive is the product of expectancy *times* value.[16]

First, a speaker must understand audience values. McClelland says, "Eventually people develop conscious values that guide their attitudes and behaviors."[17] Although individual values are difficult to predict with any accuracy, we can make predictions about the values of groups of people based on certain similarities. For instance, in Chapter 3 on analyzing audiences, we will discuss analyses of values of various groups and subgroups in the United States.

According to expectancy-value theory, although a goal or incentive may have a very high *value* for a person, if the person has a low *expectancy* of gaining that goal, the person's efforts to attain the goal will be weak. For instance, suppose you are giving a speech to youths in which you are trying to motivate them to strive for high grades in school. Since good grades may be a *valued* goal of students, such a speech may appear to have strong incentive. But if the youths have low expectancies of their abilities to get good grades, they will not be motivated by your appeal. If, in addition to appealing to a desire for good grades, you can show them realistic ways of increasing their expectancies (that is, if you give them pointers about how to improve their study skills so that they can have higher realistic expectancies for achieving good grades), they are likely to be more highly motivated by your appeal.

What, then, according to McClelland, are the motives that are most likely to present strong incentives? In his work he emphasizes motives that can be grouped under the headings of achievement, affiliation, and power.

Achievement motives can be viewed in terms of incentive values of success and failure. Since many people have achievement needs for getting ahead, they are likely to be motivated by appeals that promise them advancement. Thus, a person in an organization may motivate workers with information that shows that hard work will enable them to gain personal recognition in the organization. The example of the speech to motivate youths to strive for good grades is based on achievement motives.

Affiliation motives can be viewed in terms of incentive values of developing relationships with others. Since many people have needs for inclusion with others, they are likely to be motivated by appeals that promise them improved relationships. Thus, a person may motivate a group of workers with information that shows that sharing ideas about how to increase productivity will improve their working relationships with their colleagues.

Power motives can be viewed in terms of controlling or influencing others. Since many people are likely to have needs for greater authority within the organization, they are likely to be motivated by appeals that promise leadership roles. Thus, a person may motivate a group of workers with information that making valuable contributions will increase the likelihood of their becoming a division leader.

Cognitive Motivation: Basic Needs Theory.   Many theorists who take a humanistic approach to psychology have noted the persistent motive within individuals to become competent in coping with their environment.[18] Their theories are cognitive motivation theories. One of the most popular of these, as well as the most relevant to the persuasive speaker, is the basic needs theory of Abraham Maslow. The premise of his theory is that people are more likely to act when the speaker's appeal satisfies a strong unmet need within them. Maslow's hierarchy of needs theory is particularly useful in providing a framework for needs analysis. Maslow divides basic human needs into five categories: physiological needs including food, drink, and life-sustaining temperature; safety needs including security and simple self-preservation; belongingness and love needs including the need to identify with friends, loved ones, and family; esteem needs including the quest for material goods, recognition, and power or influence; and self-actualization needs including the need to develop oneself to meet his or her potential.[19] By placing these needs in a hierarchy, Maslow is suggesting that one set of needs must be met or satisfied before the next set of needs emerges. In theory then, a person will not be motivated to meet an esteem need of gaining recognition until basic physiological, safety, and belongingness or love needs have been met.

What is the value of this analysis to you as a speaker? First, it provides a framework and suggests the kinds of needs you may appeal to in your speeches. Second, it allows you to understand why a line of development works on one audience and fails with another. For instance, if your audience has great physiological needs (if they are hungry or tired), an appeal to the satisfaction of good workmanship, no matter how well done, is unlikely to impress them. Third, and perhaps most crucial, when your proposition conflicts with an operating need, you have to be prepared with a strong alternative in some category or in a higher level category. For instance, if your proposal is going to cost people money (higher taxes), you have to show how the proposal satisfies some other comparable need.

Persuasive Speaking in a Democracy

Persuasive speaking is a companion of democracy. Whereas in a totalitarian state, decisions are made and implemented by representatives of the state, in a democratic society, political, social, educational, and economic decisions are made by the people. The decisions that guide people's lives are hammered out by the clash of ideas. This means that individuals who hold strong beliefs about what is being done or what should be done have a responsibility for stating those beliefs. It was Edmund Burke, the famed British parliamentarian, who observed, "All that it takes for evil to win out is for good people to stand by and do nothing."[20]

An Important Means of Achieving Goals

A frequently heard cry is "What can I do about anything? I'm only one person." Can one person make a difference in society? The answer is an emphatic yes. People who are willing to speak out against an injustice that needs to be righted or a policy that needs to be changed can make a difference if those people are committed to their goals and if they use persuasive speaking skills appropriately.

Sometimes the avenue for change is to use persuasive skills within an existing organizational framework. All organizations, be they business, industrial, educational, political, or social, run on ideas. If you have good ideas and if you have developed the persuasive skills to showcase your ideas, you can gain the leadership positions within the organization necessary to put your ideas into action. An example of a person who has changed the way the American automobile industry does business is Lee Iacocca. Fired from Ford Motor Co., Lee Iacocca became president of Chrysler Corporation, the weak sister of America's "big three" in automobile manufacturing—a company on the verge of bankruptcy whose only reputation was for making bad cars. Not only did Lee Iacocca transform the company into a paying proposition, but he also showed an industry how to make cars that competed with the Japanese. At first his was a lonely voice crying in the wilderness; today he is one of America's most sought-after inspirational speakers.

Sometimes the avenue for change is to use persuasive skills to form an action group. Candy Lightner is primarily responsible for the organization of MADD, Mothers Against Drunk Drivers, an organization that now has more than 320 chapters nationwide. Candy Lightner's daughter was killed in an automobile accident by a man who had a long record of arrests for intoxication and who less than a week earlier had been bailed out on a hit-and-run, drunk-driving charge. When she learned that the man was unlikely to spend any time behind bars, she got MADD. As a result of countless speeches, she rallied thousands to join her in the formation of a new organization dedicated to making changes in the way states treated intoxicated drivers. As a prospective persuasive speaker, you will want to heed her opinion: "I do feel that if you believe in something badly enough, you can make a difference."[21]

Persuasive Speaking Contexts

Persuasive speeches may be individual events or part of a persuasive campaign. Persuasive speaking is perceived as an individual event when it arises directly from an occasion. Suppose, for instance, that at a regular meeting of the nonsalaried employees of Allied Chemicals, a representative of the company announces a new policy governing procedures for filing for sick leave. Phyllis Mitchell might rise to speak in protest of that policy. Many speeches that students give in class are individual events. A speaker has one chance to try to affect class attitude or behavior.

Although persuasion can and does occur on the basis of a single speech, significant social changes, the election of political candidates, and the success of new products are likely to occur as a result of a campaign. For instance, you may wander into the town hall to listen to a candidate running for city council and be persuaded to vote for her solely on the basis of listening to that one speech. But before that candidate can be assured of gaining a seat on the city council, she has to engage in a campaign over time—a campaign that will eventually get a plurality, if not a majority, of voters to support her.

By definition, then, a *campaign* is a series of events, including communication events, that are designed to achieve the election of a person, success of a product, or adoption of a significant change in societal behavior. Candy Lightner's efforts to form MADD and then to build MADD into an organization that has an effect on legislation were part of a campaign. A campaign has some specific purpose, some kind of organizational structure, and a leader or spearheader, and it is characterized by persuasive speaking.

In Part 3 of this text we will present information on each of these three kinds of campaigns.

Persuasive Speaking Carries Responsibilities

People can get so enthralled with the notion that they can influence others' thoughts and behavior that the "power of persuasion" becomes an end in itself. But the power to persuade carries responsibilities. People can be directed to believe and act in ways that benefit or harm society. As a result, those who choose to affect attitudes and behaviors must recognize that awesome responsibility and assure themselves that they behave *responsibly.*

In 1972 the Speech Communication Association, the national association of teachers of speech communication in America, endorsed the Credo for Free and Responsible Communication in a Democratic Society. Two paragraphs of the document lay a foundation for your persuasive speaking responsibilities:

> We accept the responsibility of cultivating by precept and example, in our classrooms and in our communities, enlightened uses of communication; of developing in our students a respect for precision and accuracy in communication, and for reasoning based upon evidence and a judicious discrimination among values.
>
> We encourage our students to accept the role of well-informed and articulate citizens, to defend the communication rights of those with whom they may disagree, and to expose abuses of the communication process.

These paragraphs provide the overall approach to speech responsibilities. Now let us take a look at some specific responsibilities and restraints that speakers must exercise to meet their responsibilities.

You Are Responsible for What You Say. Your audience has the right to hold you accountable for what you say. If, for instance, you say that Peters (your opponent in a hotly contested election) received campaign funds from illegal sources, your audience holds you responsible for the truth and accuracy of that statement.

You uphold this responsibility in at least two ways. First, you should have solid evidence, not personal opinion or hearsay, on which to build your arguments. Before you make any statement about Peters's campaign funds, you are responsible for finding the facts. If you have not found facts to support your claim, it is unethical to present such a claim as if you have the facts.

Second, you should present the facts for your audience to examine. You have the right to advocate a position—however unpopular it may be—but the listener has the right to examine the bases for the conclusions you have drawn. If you state that Peters received funds from illegal sources, you should share with the audience the facts that led you to that conclusion. Although an audience may be willing to trust your judgment on such matters, you owe them, and Peters for that matter, the right to examine the facts for themselves.

You Have a Responsibility to Allow Free Choice on the Part of Your Audience.   Freedom of choice is at the heart of a democratic society. When candidates campaign for office, they recognize that the electorate is free to accept or reject their appeals. When a speaker gives an audience no real choice, then a speech is coercion, not persuasion. For instance, if the president of a corporation gives a speech advocating that company employees volunteer an hour of their own time to solicit donations to the United Way campaign, the speech appears to meet the guidelines of persuasive speaking. But if the president says that those who do not comply will be fired, the speech is really coercion. Although employees appear to have the freedom to disobey, the consequence of loss of job goes beyond what we usually mean by legitimate freedom of choice.

This responsibility also includes speaking to the arguments "on the other side." When there are one or more good reasons in support of that other side, it is your responsibility to deal with them. Later in this book we will discuss ways of refuting such arguments. Not only does such behavior uphold a responsibility but also research suggests that speeches in which the speaker both presents favorable arguments and refutes opposing arguments are likely to be more persuasive than ones in which the speaker ignores arguments of the other side.[22]

You Are Responsible for Restraining Yourself.   First, you must refrain from any communication that may be defined as a clear and present danger. Speeches that present a clear and present danger are those that incite people to panic, to riot, or to overthrow the government. From the time you began studying civics, you learned that a person can't yell "Fire!" in a public place just to see what might happen; that would be speech to incite panic. You could also be prosecuted for giving a speech that incites a mob of students to riot against the administration or a mob of citizens to riot against the government.

Second, you must refrain from using language that defames the character of another person. *Defamation* is harming another person by making statements that convey an unjust unfavorable impression. In a political campaign if Carson calls Simpson a racist, Simpson can sue Carson for defamation. If Carson makes a statement on the basis of hearsay or solely to cast doubt on the political aims of Simpson, then Carson can be held guilty of defamation. If Carson can *prove* that Simpson is a racist, however, Carson will be acquitted. Truth is the best defense of any charge of defamation. So, if you are planning to say anything that could be interpreted as defamation, make sure that you have the evidence to uphold your opinion.

Summary

Persuasive speaking is the art of forming oral arguments and adapting them to specific audiences in a way that is designed to affect people's beliefs and/or move them to action.

Effective persuasive speaking combines speaker, audience, and speech perspectives. Part of your effectiveness as a speaker depends on your *ethos* or *credibility*, a quality that is a product of your knowledge and expertise, your trustworthiness, and your personality. The more credible the audience perceives you to be, the more successful your speeches are likely to be.

Another part of your effectiveness depends on your sensitivity to your audience's attitudes, beliefs, values, opinions, and behaviors in relation to your message. Audience *attitude* refers to whether listeners have favorable, negative, or neutral feelings toward your message. Audience *beliefs* refer to whether listeners accept the truth of your message. Audience *values* mean listeners' perceptions of the relative worth or importance of your message. Audience *opinions* refer to listeners' verbal statements about your message. And audience *behaviors* are listeners' actions as a result of your message.

A third part of your effectiveness depends on the way you use information in your speech. Speeches focus on affecting attitudes and changing behavior. Persuasive speakers can gain insight about attitude changes from aspects of learning theory, social judgment theory, and consistency theory. Learning theorists maintain that audiences "learn" to evaluate, believe, and behave on the basis of reasons and evidence. Social judgment theory focuses on an individual's perception and judgment of a message on the basis of their latitudes of acceptance, rejection, or noncommitment. Consistency theorists hold that a person may adjust a personal attitude in order to maintain internal harmony in the belief system. When a speaker creates dissonance, listeners may resolve that dissonance by accepting the speaker's position.

Although people's beliefs and attitudes may lead directly to behavior, it is more likely that people need to be motivated to act. First, people may be motivated by messages that provide meaningful incentives. Second, people may be motivated by messages that appeal to value goals and people's expectancy of obtaining those goals. Third, people may be motivated by appeals that satisfy physiological, safety, belongingness and love, esteem, and self-actualization needs.

Persuasive speaking is an important means of achieving goals in a democratic society. Sometimes the avenue for change is to use your persuasive skills within an existing organizational framework. Sometimes the avenue for change is to use persuasive skills to form an action group. A persuasive speech may be an individual event or part of a persuasive campaign, a series of events designed to achieve the election of a person, the success of a product, or the adoption of a significant change in societal behavior.

Persuasive speaking carries responsibilities. You are responsible for what you say, you have a responsibility to allow free choice on the part of your audience, and you are responsible for restraining yourself from communication that may be defined as a clear and present danger or from language that will defame the character of another person.

Study Questions

For each of the following, be prepared to give examples in support of your answers.

1. In what ways, if any, do you believe that "purposeful" speaking differs from "manipulative"?
2. Why should you be responsible for presenting logically strong arguments when people do not always behave rationally?
3. List the criteria for speaker credibility. What effect has a speaker's credibility had in changing your attitude or moving you to action? Explain.
4. What, if any, is the difference between changing an audience's attitudes and motivating an audience to act?
5. What are a speaker's ethical responsibilities?

Notes

[1] C. I. Hovland and W. Weiss, "The Influence of Source Credibility on Communication Effectiveness," *Public Opinion Quarterly* 15(1951), 635–650.

[2] R. E. Petty and J. T. Cacioppo, *Attitudes and Persuasion: Classic and Contemporary Approaches* (Dubuque, IA: Wm. C. Brown, 1981).

[3] E. Walster, E. Aronson, and D. Abrahams, "On Increasing the Persuasiveness of a Low Prestige Communicator," *Journal of Experimental Social Psychology* 2(1966), 341.

[4] Shelly Chaiken, "Communicator Physical Attractiveness and Persuasion," *Journal of Personality and Social Psychology* 37(1979), 1394.

[5] William J. McGuire, "The Structure of Individual Attitudes and Attitude Systems," in Anthony R. Pratkanis, Steven J. Breckler, and Anthony G. Greenwald (eds.), *Attitude Structure and Function* (Hillsdale, NJ: Lawrence Erlbaum, 1989), p. 37.

[6] Martin Fishbein and I. Ajzen, "Attitudes and Opinions," *Annual Review of Psychology* 23(1972), 494.

[7] Carl I. Hovland, Irving L. Janis, and Harold H. Kelley, *Communication and Persuasion* (New Haven, CT: Yale University Press, 1953), p. 11; Mary John Smith, *Persuasion and Human Action: A Review and Critique of Social Influence Theories* (Belmont, CA: Wadsworth Publishing Co., 1982), p. 214.

[8]Ibid.

[9]Alice Eagly, "Comprehensibility of Persuasive Arguments As a Determinant of Opinion Change," *Journal of Personality and Social Psychology* 29(1974), 758–773.

[10]Richard E. Petty, Thomas M. Ostrom, and Timothy C. Brock, "Historical Foundations of the Cognitive Response Approach to Attitudes and Persuasion," in Richard E. Petty, Thomas M. Ostrom, and Timothy C. Brock (eds.), *Cognitive Responses in Persuasion* (Hillsdale, NJ: Lawrence Erlbaum, 1981), pp. 11–12.

[11]Herbert L. Petri, *Motivation: Theory and Research*, 2d ed. (Belmont, CA: Wadsworth Publishing Co., 1986), p. 3.

[12]Ibid., p. 163.

[13]Ibid., p. 164.

[14]E. Klinger, *Meaning and Void: Inner Experience and the Incentives in People's Lives* (Minneapolis: University of Minnesota Press, 1977).

[15]Petrie, p. 218.

[16]Katherine Blick Hoyenga and Kermit T. Hoyenga, *Motivational Explanations of Behavior: Evolutionary, Physiological, and Cognitive Ideas* (Pacific Grove, CA: Brooks/Cole Publishing Co., 1984), p. 46.

[17]David McClelland, *Human Motivation* (Glenview, IL: Scott, Foresman & Company, 1985), p. 167.

[18]Petrie, p. 286.

[19]Abraham H. Maslow, *Motivation and Personality* (New York: Harper & Row, 1954), pp. 80–92.

[20]Edmund Burke, letter to William Smith, January 9, 1795.

[21]"You Can Make a Difference," *Time*, January 7, 1985, p. 41.

[22]J. W. Kohler, "Effects on Audience Opinion of One-sided and Two-sided Speeches Supporting and Opposing a Proposition," in Thomas Beisecker and Donn Parson (eds.), *The Process of Social Influence* (Englewood Cliffs, NJ: Prentice-Hall, 1972), pp. 351–369.

Part II

Guidelines to Persuasive Speaking

Persuasive speaking is the art of forming oral arguments and adapting them to a specific audience in a way that is designed to affect people's beliefs or move them to action. In this part we explore the steps in preparing a persuasive speech. The first four steps (writing a persuasive speech goal, analyzing the audience and setting, gathering the best information available, and using the information to form persuasive arguments) provide you with the necessary information to construct a speech that meets audience needs. The next two steps (organizing your reasons to meet audience needs and developing a speech plan) form your basic speech strategy. Whereas the first four steps provide material that can used to form speeches for many different audiences, the next two steps call for you to use your creative talents to adapt the material to the needs of the specific audience for which your speech is being prepared. The final two steps (developing persuasive language and a persuasive delivery) provide the means for implementing your speech plan.

As you gain skill, the first four steps can be done separately or concurrently. Then the strategy steps require that you have a content base and an understanding of your audience so that you can make the choices necessary to assure yourself a high probability of success. After your strategy is determined, you polish your language and practice your delivery.

Chapter **2**

Determining Your Speech Goal *What Interests You.!*

Very soon you are going to be faced with your first in-class speaking assignment. How will you prepare the speech? Whether you are preparing an in-class speech or a speech for a specific real-world audience, my advice to you would be much the same: select a clear speech goal that is adapted to your audience and setting, and gather the necessary information to support that goal. Although this advice is clear enough because it suggests five separate things (topic, goal, audience, setting, and information), it raises the question of whether you should attempt to perform these tasks in some set order or do them concurrently. Although experienced speakers may interchange these steps, in this book I suggest that you begin with selecting a goal (which includes selecting a topic), then analyze the audience and setting, and finally gather the necessary information. As you become comfortable with the material covered in these first four chapters, you can determine the order that seems to work best for you.

In this chapter we consider those matters that are related to goal: selecting a topic, writing a speech goal, classifying the goal, and analyzing the chances of success with that goal.

Selecting a Topic

If you were an environmentalist who had spent the last two years studying the effects of recycling newspapers, aluminum, glass, and plastic, selecting a topic would be no problem. In the real world, people speak on topics that grow from their experience; they don't have to look for topics, they already know what they want to talk about. For you as a student in a communication course, however, what to talk about may pose a very real problem. Regardless of the "artificial" setting, you need to proceed with your preparation as if each speech were a real event.

If you take a minute to think about real-world speakers, you will discover that they all have one thing in common: a driving force to be heard. They have a message! What is your message? Before you get defensive, let me assure you that you have one—you just may not have identified it. For instance, all of us experience things that make us "mad as hell." What kinds of things bother you? Perhaps you're upset that our rivers and streams are turning into cesspools, or that individuals who are given a public trust are doing violence to the very people they serve, or that the greedy are allowed to engage in hostile takeovers only to ruin the companies they take over, or that countless students graduate from high school without being able to read, or that large numbers of people from all walks of life are experiencing the pain and suffering of chemical abuse, or that drunk drivers are committing carnage on our highways and getting away with it.

Getting in touch with what makes you angry is one way to identify topics, but it's not the only way. In addition to battling evil and righting wrongs, persuasive speaking is also about how to make our lives richer, more exciting, or more meaningful. Just as you can identify things that make you mad, you may also be able to identify those things that will "make us better people"—things that would make society healthier, make our world safer, or just make us feel a little better about ourselves. Perhaps you are affiliated with a group that could help a lot more people if it just had more money, or perhaps you have been places and seen sights that would enrich our lives, or perhaps you have read a book that you believe everyone should read or seen a play that just shouldn't be missed.

If this advice has started you thinking but has not yet revealed concrete ideas, try a systematic means of making the search process specific. Take a piece of paper and divide it in half vertically. At the top of the left-hand column write "It really makes me mad that . . . "; at the top of the right-hand column write "Everybody ought to. . . ." Then take some time to brainstorm with your list; that is, write down anything that comes to mind. Don't try to evaluate items; just write them down. Work on the list for a few minutes at a time. Maybe you will need to come back to it two or three times before you get very far. After you have ten or twenty items in each column, take a look at what you've written. Put a check mark by one or two items in each column that you feel especially strong about—these are the topics on which you ought to be giving your speeches!

At this point you might be thinking, "What if my audience doesn't want to hear a speech on this topic?" That's the wrong question! Confronting people with topics they "don't want to hear about" is often a major responsibility of a persuasive speaker. On many of the most difficult social issues, society would never move forward, never break out of its inertia, without people with lofty visions and practical advice forcing it to confront those issues. Your challenge may be to take a topic about which an audience has no belief and help create one, or take a topic about which an audience believes one way and change that belief, or, take a topic about which an audience is passive and get them to do something. The persuasive speaker's goal is to shake people out of their passivity or lethargy, to excite, incite, and at times even inflame. Persuasive speakers use their power to create a need to listen even when people may not want to.

Writing a Speech Goal

Now that you have identified topics that you feel strongly about, you are ready to set about writing a speech goal. How you write your specific goal may well determine the degree of success you attain with the speech. Although any random statement may influence another person's actions (for instance, merely saying "I see the new Penney's store opened in Western Woods" may "persuade" another person to go to Penney's for some clothing need), the successful persuader does not leave the effect of the message to chance. You want a clearly defined persuasive speaking goal.

Your specific goal, or specific purpose, is a single statement that specifies the exact response you want from your audience. For instance, you may have identified such topics as the importance of drug testing by business and industry, or the value of joining Amnesty International, or the need to recycle waste products. Now let's consider a step-by-step procedure for writing these topics as specific speech goals.

1. *Write your goal as a complete sentence that includes a belief you want your audience to hold or an action you want your audience to take.* For instance, corresponding to the three topics mentioned above, you might write: "I want my audience to believe that drug testing by business and industry is an effective

means of dealing with chemical abuse" or "I want the audience to join Amnesty International" or "I want the audience to believe that city governments should solve the problem of waste disposal by establishing recycling programs." All three of these are complete sentences.

2. *Edit the goal to make sure that it is clear enough to be understood by anyone reading it.* Seldom are your first phrasings as clear and concise as the three goals in the preceding paragraph. First drafts are likely to be wordy, unclear, or not quite on target. For instance, a first draft of a waste disposal proposal might be "I want the audience to believe that there ought to be some kind of recycling program that could be used to take some of the pressure off of overextended waste disposal places." This sentence has at least three ideas that are neither specific nor precise: "ought to be some kind of," "to take some of the pressure off," and "overextended waste disposal places." "I want the audience to believe that cities should establish recycling programs to solve the problem of waste disposal" is far more specific. It answers the questions: (1) Who will do something? (cities), (2) What should they do? (establish recycling programs), and (3) For what purpose? (to solve the problem of waste disposal). You might have to write three, four, or even five drafts of the goal before it is really clear enough.

3. *Make sure that the goal contains only one idea.* It's difficult enough to shape audience opinion on one idea without trying to grapple with two. Moreover, if you gain some support for one of the ideas but the audience rejects the other one, they are likely to ignore both. The sentence "I want the audience to believe that cities in the United States should develop recycling programs and should impose deposits on bottles and cans to help solve the problem of waste disposal" has two ideas. After eliminating one of the ideas, the goal could be written as "I want the audience to believe that cities in the United States should develop recycling programs to help solve the problem of waste disposal."

4. *Make sure that the goal is phrased affirmatively.* Beliefs and behaviors are positive concepts. You want to move your audience *toward* something tangible. For instance, instead of saying "I want the audience to believe that cities should not rely on the use of incinerators for waste disposal," you should say "I want the audience to believe that cities should abolish the use of incinerators to solve the problem of waste disposal." The word "abolish" not only suggests an action but also is more precise than "not rely on the use of." In addition, even if you did persuade the audience "not to rely on the use of," what should they do as a result? Again, a well-phrased goal provides the audience with a positive behavior.

5. *Revise the infinitive until it indicates the specific audience reaction desired.* The wordings "to believe," "to attend," and "to do" are infinitives. Rewrite the infinitive until it expresses your goal precisely.

After you have tested the wording, you can move on to classify your goal and determine your chances of success in achieving that goal.

Classifying Speech Goals

After you have written several persuasive speech goals, you will note that they can be grouped by similarities in general purpose and subject matter. By classifying your specific goal you get a better sense of how to proceed to assure yourself that you understand the kind of material you will need to develop that goal.

Classifying by General Purpose *audience centered.*

Classifying by general purpose helps you to clarify your intent. Purpose is an audience-centered analysis of goals. To make such an analysis, you need information about your audience. If you are not sure of your audience's beliefs in reference to your prospective speech goal, you may not be able to complete this step until you have read Chapter 3. Under the heading of general purpose, speeches can reinforce a belief, establish a belief, change a belief, or move an audience to action. Recall from the discussion in the last chapter that a *belief* is an acceptance of truth based on evidence, opinion, and experience. We are likely to *believe* that something is true if someone can prove it to our satisfaction. Also recall that a *behavior* is an action that is related to or a result of an attitude, belief, value, or some combination of these.

Let's consider each of these.

Speeches That Reinforce an Existing Belief. These speeches are given when your audience's commitment to a belief is weak. For instance, suppose you have reason to believe that your audience is somewhat indifferent about people's responsibility to vote. In light of an upcoming election, you decide to give a speech designed to strengthen their belief. You might phrase your speech goal as "I want the audience to reaffirm its belief that every American has a responsibility to vote."

The following are other typical examples of such goals:

I want the audience to reaffirm its belief that America is the land of opportunity.

I want the audience to strengthen its belief in the right of every student to an equal opportunity for an education.

I want the audience to reaffirm its belief in our right to freedom of worship.

Speeches That Seek to Establish a Belief. These speeches are given when your audience doesn't hold a clearly articulated belief on an issue. For instance, suppose you have discovered that recycling is effective in reducing cities' reliance on landfills for waste disposal. Furthermore, you have reason to believe that your audience has no strongly held beliefs about the issue. As a result, you may decide to phrase you speech goal as "I want the audience to believe that the community should start a recycling program."

The following are other typical examples of speech goals that are designed to establish a belief:

> I want the audience to believe that our community should establish an adult literacy program.

> I want the audience to believe that the city should build a downtown entertainment center, mainly to give the children a place to go.

> I want the audience to believe that small schools are better for insecure students than large schools.

Speeches That Seek to Change a Belief. These speeches are given when your audience holds a belief that is different from yours. Suppose that after studying the issue of tax deductions, you believe that allowing homeowners to deduct their interest payments discriminates against people who are forced to or have chosen to live in apartments. Since Americans may deduct house-payment interest on their federal income tax forms (current practice) and since most Americans believe that such a deduction is their right (majority opinion), a speech designed "to have an audience believe that the federal income tax deduction for house-payment interest should be abolished" would seek a change in majority opinion and current practice.

There may be times when the belief of your audience is different from the belief of the majority of Americans or from current practice. For instance, current laws are opposed to teenage drinking of alcoholic beverages; moreover, the majority of Americans believe that drinking alcoholic beverages is bad for teenagers, especially those under age 19. Yet you may be speaking to an audience of 16- to 18-year-olds who believe they should be allowed to drink alcoholic beverages. In this case a speech opposed to teenage drinking would be designed to change the belief of the specific audience.

The following are other typical examples of speech goals that are designed to change a belief:

> I want the audience to believe that the speed limit on all interstate highways should be raised to 70 miles per hour.

> I want the audience to believe that capital punishment should be abolished in all 50 states.

> I want the audience to believe that Social Security benefits should be lowered.

Notice that in these speeches, the response you want is cognitive support. Although the speech may motivate some members of the audience to seek action, the focus of the speech is on the belief itself.

Speeches That Move an Audience to Take Action. These speeches are given when you want the audience to act. Although a portion of the speech may be directed to establishing or changing specific audience beliefs, the emphasis of your speech is on motivating the audience to take action. The following are examples of such goals:

> I want my audience to donate money to this year's Fine Arts Fund.
>
> I want my audience to write to their congressperson to support legislation in favor of gun control.
>
> I want my audience to attend the school's production of A *Chorus Line*.
>
> I want my audience to donate one hour a month to one of the city's established literacy programs to tutor an adult in reading.

You may have noticed that some of the examples under the same heading (for instance, to change a belief) seem to be qualitatively different. Another way to classify speech goals is by subject matter.

Classifying by Subject Matter   *ONE OF 3,*

Classifying by subject matter helps you determine the information necessary to provide logical support for your goal. This classification provides a subject analysis of goals. The subject analysis enables you to focus on the questions that must be answered in order to assure yourself that your speech has a sound content base. Each of the following discussions includes the questions (often called "issues") that are relevant to a particular type of speech goal. The subject matter of persuasive speeches may (1) state a fact (past, present, or future), (2) evaluate a person, place, thing, or action, or (3) propose a policy or action.

Speeches Affecting Audience Beliefs about Statements of Fact. Either statements of fact are true or they are not. Specific goals about statements of fact are a mainstay in courts of law; they also occur in deliberations about politics, education, the environment, and other contexts. The following are typical speech goals that take a position on statements of fact:

> I want the jury to believe that Jones is guilty of murder in the first degree.
>
> I want my audience to believe that the greenhouse effect is a reality.
>
> I want my audience to believe that SAT tests are inaccurate predictors of college success.

When your goal is to reinforce, establish, or change an audience's belief about a statement of fact, your material must answer at least two questions: (1) What is the definition of the subject complement? (guilty of murder, a reality, inaccurate predictors) and (2) What facts are available to support the assertion that the subject of the sentence meets that definition? Suppose that you were trying to establish that Jones is guilty of murder. After you had defined murder as "a premeditated act of killing," you would look for information to show Jones's premeditation.

Speeches Affecting Audience Beliefs about Statements of Evaluation.   A speaker's goal may be to reinforce, establish, or change an audience's evaluation of a person, place, thing, or action—that is, to show whether the person, place, thing, or action is good or bad. The following are typical speech goals of evaluation:

✓ I want my audience to believe that small schools provide a better education for most students than large schools.

I want my audience to believe that drug testing is an ineffective means of controlling drug abuse in the workplace.

I want my audience to believe that Smith is the best qualified candidate for city council.

When your goal is to reinforce, establish, or change an audience's evaluation of a person, place, thing, or action, your material must answer at least two questions: (1) By what criteria is the evaluative word or phrase measured? (better education, ineffective means of controlling drug abuse, best qualified candidate) and (2) What facts are available to establish that the subject meets those criteria?

Suppose you were trying to establish that Smith is the best qualified candidate for city council. If you had determined that experience in government, sensitivity to the needs of the community, and honesty were three of the most important qualifications, then you would look for information that Smith's behavior meets those criteria.

Speeches Affecting Audience Beliefs about Statements of Policy or Action.   A speaker's goal may be to reinforce, establish, or change an audience's belief about a proposed action or an attempt to move an audience to action. Policy speeches are most likely to be heard in settings where lawmakers give speeches in favor of or opposed to suggested legislation. The following are typical speech goals advocating policies:

I want the audience to believe that work on nuclear power plants should be halted.

I want my audience to vote to increase the budget for women's athletics.

I want my audience to believe that Social Security benefits should be lowered.

When your goal is to reinforce, establish, or change an audience's belief about a proposed policy or action, your material must answer at least three questions: (1) Is there a problem or a need for a change in policy or action?, (2) Will the proposed policy or action solve that problem or meet that need?, and (3) Is the proposed policy or action the best way of solving the problem or meeting the need? Suppose you were attempting to get your audience to believe that Social Security benefits should be lowered. After you had found information to show that the current level of Social Security benefits was causing a major problem, you would look for information to show that lowering benefits not only would solve the problem but also would be the best way of solving the problem.

Notice that both types of speech goals that have been given as examples meet the same tests. Also notice that the examples given can be classified either way. For instance, the speech goal phrased "I want my audience to believe that drug testing is an effective means of controlling drug abuse in the workplace" may be classified by purpose as one that establishes or changes audience belief (depending on the audience) and may be classified by subject as one that affects audience beliefs about a statement of evaluation. Thus, you could say that the goal is designed to change audience beliefs about a statement of evaluation.

Determining the Chances of Achieving Your Goal

Whether you revise your goal and how you proceed to establish your goal depend in part on your assessment of the chances of achieving your goal. As with analyzing speech goals by purpose, determining the chances of achieving your goal requires information about your audience. In this section we look at the criteria for determining the chances of achieving your goal. Then in the next chapter we will discuss aspects of audience interest, knowledge, and attitude that help you make the prediction.

Your speech goal and the information you present are perceived differently depending on the perceptual frame of reference in which that information is placed. For instance, the information that a policy is supported by the city's conservative majority is perceived differently depending on whether the listener is politically conservative or liberal.

Using the language of social judgment theory that we introduced in the last chapter, you need to consider whether your audience is likely to perceive your goal as being within their latitude of acceptance, latitude of rejection, or latitude of noncommitment.

Recall that people's latitude of acceptance consists of the position that is most acceptable to them plus all other acceptable positions or statements relative to their attitude. Environmentalists, for example, are likely to hold a frame of reference that says that "The environment is being seriously attacked by human carelessness." As a result of this belief, other statements such as "The greenhouse effect has begun" or "Plastic containers are a leading contributor to pollution" are acceptable to them, or in social judgment language, such beliefs are within their latitude of acceptance.

If you suggest ideas that are close to your listeners' position, they are likely to assimilate them, that is, they are likely to see them as within their latitude of acceptance. Your listeners' tendency to assimilate facilitates your persuasive efforts. For instance, if the majority of your listeners have a frame of reference that says that a community has a responsibility to provide cultural opportunities for the members of that community, then a request to support the Fine Arts Fund is likely to be accepted by them, since it fits into their latitude of acceptance. As a result, you could predict a high probability of success for achieving your speech goal with that audience.

Recall that people's latitude of rejection consists of the position that is most objectionable to them plus all other objectionable statements relative to their attitude. To continue our example, for environmentalists, the most objectionable belief might be "Some pollution is the price we must pay for progress." As a result of their negative position on this belief, other statements such as "The greenhouse effect is vastly overrated" or "Environmentalists are always crying wolf" are also regarded as objectionable, or in social judgment language, such beliefs are in their latitude of rejection.

If you make statements that are different from the your listeners' position, they are likely to accent the contrasts so much that they place them in their latitude of rejection. This tendency to contrast apparently different statements hinders your efforts to persuade. For instance, if a majority of your listeners believe that any community endeavor should be self-sustaining, then the plea for support for the Fine Arts Fund would likely fall within their latitude of rejection. As a result, you could predict a low probability of success for achieving your speech goal with that audience.

Finally, recall that people's latitude of noncommitment consists of statements they hold as neutral. Their noncommitment may be due to lack of information on the statements or a disregard for the importance of the statements. For environmentalists, then, the statement "Scrubbers on fuel processing plants are expensive" could not be evaluated with available information or might be regarded as inconsequential to their attitude.

If you make statements for which your listeners have no frame of reference, then they are likely to be neutral on that issue. For instance, if a majority of your listeners are neither in favor of nor opposed to organizations soliciting for support, then the plea for support for the Fine Arts Fund would likely fall into their latitude of noncommitment. As a result, you could predict that they would be open to persuasion.

In addition to hypothesizing that people place statements in one of these three categories, you want to consider your audience's *ego involvement* with the goal. That is, you want to determine how involved people are with an issue and how important their attitude is to them (salience). For instance, environmentalists might be so ego involved in their attitude toward environmental issues that they are unable to examine conflicting information rationally.

Social judgment theory provides the following two guidelines:[1]

1. If you determine that your listeners have moderate or low ego involvement in a subject, you have a better opportunity to persuade them. As a result of such ego involvement, their latitude of acceptance of your position is increased. You can predict a greater likelihood of success for your speech if it is directed toward people who are minimally or moderately involved with the subject or people for whom your ideas are within their latitude of acceptance. In such situations you want to go forward with your speech goal as you have written it.

2. If you determine that your listeners have a high ego involvement in the subject, you will have difficulty changing their attitudes. Their high ego involvement increases their latitude of rejection of your position on the subject. When you believe that you are facing this prospect for the majority of your audience, you may want to reshape your goal in such a way that it gives you a greater chance of success. Or, if you believe it is important to pursue the goal regardless of the audience's position, then you may want to consider how you can approach the audience so that you do not make them more defensive.

Summary

To have any chance of giving an effective speech you must have something to talk about that you are deeply committed to. One way to get in touch with such topics is to brainstorm a list based on things that make you angry and things that you think will improve the quality of life.

Your specific goal, or specific purpose, is a single statement that specifies the exact response you want from your audience. Write your goal as a complete sentence and then write at least three variations to make sure that the intention of the goal is clear enough to be understood by anyone reading it. Make sure that the goal contains only one idea, that it is phrased affirmatively, and that the infinitive indicates the specific audience reaction you desire.

If you classify by general purpose, you can identify your goal as one that reinforces a belief, establishes a belief, changes a belief, or moves an audience to action. If you classify by subject matter, you can identify your goal as one that affects beliefs about statements of fact, beliefs about statements of evaluation, or beliefs about statements of policy or action.

When your goal is to reinforce, establish, or change an audience's belief about a statement of fact, your material must define the subject complement and support the assertion that the subject of the sentence meets the definition. When your goal is to reinforce, establish, or change an audience's evaluation of a person, place, thing, or action, your material must determine the criteria by which the evaluative word or phrase is measured and support the assertion that the subject of the sentence meets those criteria. When your goal is to reinforce, establish, or change an audience's belief about a proposed policy or action, your material must identify the problem or need for a change in policy or action, show that the proposed policy or action will solve that problem or meet that need, and show that the proposed policy or action is the best way to solve the problem or meet the need.

Whether you revise your goal and how you proceed to establish your goal depend in part on your assessment of the chances of achieving your goal. Using the language of social judgment theory, you need to consider whether your audience is likely to perceive your goal as being within their latitude of acceptance, latitude of rejection, or latitude of noncommitment. You also want to consider your audience's *ego involvement* with the goal. From this perspective, then, if you determine that your listeners have moderate or low ego involvement in the subject, you have a better opportunity to persuade them; if you determine that your listeners have a high ego involvement in the subject, you may have difficulty changing their attitudes. As a result, you may want to reshape your goal in such a way that it gives you a greater chance of success.

Skill Development Exercises

1. From a recent issue of *Vital Speeches* select the three speeches that are *most* persuasive to you. Following the guidelines for writing speech goals, write what you believe are the speech goals of each of the speeches.
2. Rewrite the following speech goals to conform with accepted guidelines:
   a. I want the audience to believe that the University of Cincinnati Department of Communication would be very wise to construct a policy whereby persuasive speaking be required for all its majors.
   b. I want to try to see to it that everyone goes away from the speech with renewed support for the old idea that everyone should vote.

c.   I want the audience to believe that the Cincinnati Bengals are the best football team in the National Football League and that they are more than likely to be the champion of the Central Division.

d.   I want the audience to believe that the people of Ohio should not get in the way of efforts to legalize casino gambling.

e.   I want the audience to believe that beyond a shadow of a doubt that scoundrel Pat Quinzy is the one who embezzled the money from the First National Bank.

Speech Preparation Exercises

1.   Write at least ten words or phrases under the following two headings. Then select one of the words or phrases for the topic of your first speech assignment.

It makes me mad that: Everybody ought to:

2.   Using the topic you have selected, write a specific speech goal to use for your first speech assignment.

a.   Identify it by general purpose. Does it reaffirm a belief? Create a belief? Change a belief? Move an audience to action?

b.   Identify it by subject matter. Does it affect audience beliefs about statements of fact? About statements of evaluation? About statements of policy?

3.   In order for your speech to have a sound logical structure, what questions (issues) must your material answer? (Recall that there are different sets of questions for each type of speech goal.)

Study Questions

For each of the following, be prepared to give examples in support of your answers.

1.   Why are "things that make you angry" good topics for persuasive speeches?

2.   What is the difference between classifying goals by general purpose and by content?

3.   Suppose you heard a speech in which the speaker was advocating the registration of handguns. Would that goal be within your latitude of acceptance, your latitude of noncommitment, or your latitude of rejection? Why?

4. What effect does an audience's "ego involvement" have in determining the chances of success for a persuasive speech?

Note

[1]C. Sherif, M. Sherif, and R. Nebergall, *Attitude and Attitude Change: The Social Judgment-Involvement Approach* (Philadelphia, PA: Saunders, 1965), pp. 176–177.

Chapter 3

Analyzing Audience and Setting

Now that you have a clearly written speech goal, you need to turn your attention to the audience. As we have said, with practice you may be able to conduct an analysis of the audience and occasion while you are determining your speech goal. For now, however, we treat the analysis of audience and occasion as a second step of preparation.

Analyzing the Specific Audience

Audience analysis is the study of the audience's composition, knowledge, interests, and attitudes. You use the results of this analysis to guide you in forming a persuasive speech strategy. This section considers how you get audience information, what kind of audience information you need, and how you use the information to make predictions about potential audience interest, knowledge, and attitude.

Getting Audience Information

An audience analysis is composed of specific information that you gather or infer about your audience in one of three ways:

1. If you are a member of the group that makes up the audience to which you are speaking, you can get information directly from experience you have had with the group. For instance, you are a member of the group of people who will be hearing your classroom speeches; in a real-life situation, you may be a member of a community action group to which you will give your speech.

2. If you are not a member of the group that makes up the audience, you can get information from the person who scheduled you to speak. If your speech is to the Westwood PTA (Parent-Teacher Association), you could get information about members of the PTA who usually attend meetings from the person who contacted you (perhaps the PTA president or social chair).

3. If the contact person cannot answer all of your questions satisfactorily, you need to make informed guesses based on indirect information. If you were scheduled to speak at a community town meeting, you could get demographic information indirectly by observing or studying housing, voting patterns, and other such behaviors.

Kinds of Audience Information You Need

Now let's consider the kinds of information you need in order to make predictions about audience interests, knowledge, and attitudes. The point of this section is that you may be able to make valid predictions about your audience based on the types of information listed here.

Education. You need to know how well educated members of your audience are. You want data to confirm whether most members of the audience are high school educated, college educated, or post-college educated, or whether the educational levels of the audience are mixed. Studies of education levels reveal several kinds of information that you can use to help make your predictions. For instance, a study of nine American lifestyles found that highly educated Americans tend to be more concerned with current issues, more tolerant of social change, and more liberal about such issues as women's and gay rights and abortion than less educated Americans.[1] In addition, the higher the education level of the audience, the more likely they will be able to process complex arguments and to differentiate among similar positions.

Age. You need to know both the average age and the approximate age range of the audience. If age is a distinguishing feature, you can turn to public opinion surveys for generalizations about interests and attitudes based on age.

For instance, a 1986 study of college-age students reported in *USA Today* showed students of the 1980s as very optimistic. Do parallel studies of students of the 1990s report that same optimism? Age also provides a primary key to determining an audience's life experiences. When you have an accurate picture of average age, you can select examples that are most relevant to that age. Suppose you are planning to use examples of popular music in your speech to help you relate to the audience. Obviously, you want to pick different examples for an older audience than for a younger audience. In a speech to an audience of teenagers you would most likely get only blank stares with allusions to the music of Glenn Miller and Tommy Dorsey; likewise in a speech to an audience of mostly older people you might be met with bewilderment and perhaps even hostility if your only references were to heavy metal and hard rock performers such as Guns and Roses.

Gender.   You want to determine whether your audience is primarily male, primarily female, or reasonably balanced. Gender becomes especially important if the audience is primarily male or female. Although sex differences are less marked than they once were (for example, women can no longer be stereotyped as housewives and men can no longer be stereotyped as breadwinners), men and women still have different perspectives on many issues. Men still tend to show greater interest in sports than women; women show a greater interest in relationships and "people issues" than men.[2] If the audience is composed of mostly men and you are a woman (or vice versa), you need to make sure that your language and illustrations relate to the differing orientation.

Occupation.   You need to know whether the majority of your audience has the same or similar occupations or occupational status. If the majority of your audience has a single occupation such as nursing, banking, drill press operating, teaching, or sales, it is easier to make accurate predictions about attitudes or issues related to their occupation. For instance, an audience of nurses is likely to be supportive of health care issues. In addition, they have an interest in and understanding of medical examples.

Income.   You need to know whether the majority of your audience is at about the same income level. If you have information to confirm that the average income of the audience is high, low, or average, you can make predictions about how the audience might react to speeches that have an economic focus. There is no sense in trying to convince an audience with well below average incomes of the value of investments, purchases, or recreational opportunities that require substantial resources. On the other hand, people with lower incomes are sometimes more sympathetic than people with higher incomes to appeals to support the needy, even if the level of support they can afford is marginal.

Whether any audience considers money an obstacle may well depend on their financial circumstances.

Race, Religion, and Nationality. You need to know the ranges of race, religion, and nationality of your audience. Information of this kind may both affect the kinds of material you use to illustrate or support your arguments and provide a basis for making predictions about how they might stand on an issue. For instance, a predominantly Catholic audience is likely to be against abortion on demand.

Geographic Uniqueness. You need to know whether the majority of your audience is from the same state, city, neighborhood, or other definable area. The knowledge that an audience shares a geographic bond can help you select meaningful examples. For instance, it is much easier to paint a vivid picture of the harms of littering or pollution if you are able to personalize the issue by relating these harms to your audience's city or neighborhood. Most people are more inclined to support a project to improve the environment if they see the problem as in "their backyard."

Group Affiliation. You need to know whether the members of your audience belong to the same group or organization. Group affiliation is a bonding element. If you have evidence to verify that most members of the audience belong to the same group, then you can predict with more certainty the kinds of information they will perceive as relevant to them. If your listeners are all members of the PTA, you may assume that they will be supportive of educational issues. Group affiliation can be especially important when determining the kinds of developmental material that will appeal to the audience. For instance, members of an engineering society will respond more favorably to mechanical analogies than they might to historical or literary parallels. Similarly, audiences composed of National Rifle Association (NRA) members are likely to oppose any attempt to argue in favor of gun control.

Drawing an Audience Profile

As you study information about your audience's age, education, gender, occupation, income, race, religion, nationality, geographic uniqueness, and group affiliation, you can determine how they are alike and how they differ. From these likes and differences, you can construct an audience profile that identifies the *significant features* of the audience that will help you make predictions about audience interests, knowledge, and attitude. The following list gives two sets of audience information to show the importance of differences in audience profile.

	A	B
Age	18–22	40–60
Education	College students	Mixed
Gender	Mixed	Predominantly male
Occupation	Students	Mixed
Race	Mixed, but mostly Caucasian	Mixed, but mostly Caucasian
Religion and nationality	Mixed	Mostly Catholic
Geographic area	Mostly midwestern	Mostly Cincinnati
Group affiliation	General college student	Mixed

For audience A the predominate features are age (18–22), education, occupation, and group affiliation (college students). With audience A, then, you are facing a relatively homogeneous audience of college students. In contrast, for audience B the predominate features are age, gender, religion, and geography. With audience B you are facing an older, primarily male audience of Catholic Cincinnatians. In both cases predictions about the audience's interests, level of knowledge, and attitude will be based on these key features. Because the audience profiles differ, your predictions about them will differ as well. Moreover, as you are planning developmental material for the speech you will need to select a different kind of material for audience A than for audience B because their interests and their knowledge levels are different.

Making Predictions about Audience Reactions

The next step in your audience analysis is to use the significant information to assess the likelihood of audience interest, level of audience knowledge, and attitudes about your topic in general and your specific speech goal in particular.

Audience Interest. You need to assess whether the audience is likely to have an interest in your topic. Occasionally a topic creates an interest with all members of the audience. Suppose you are planning to give a speech on the topic of cholesterol with a tentative goal of convincing members of the audience of the need to lower their intake of fats. If your speech is for audience B (mostly men between the ages of 40 and 60), you may predict that they would have greater initial interest than if your speech is for audience A (18- to 22-year-old college students). Why? Because the cholesterol and heart attack connection is more prevalent and of greater immediate concern to older men. Young people, as a group, tend to take warnings about such things as cholesterol levels and other potential health risks far less seriously. But, even though the audience is less likely to have an immediate interest, you still have the possibility of building interest by the way you develop your speech.

In most speeches, the amount of audience interest depends on what the speaker does with the topic. Even if you are talking about the need for recycling programs to a group of environmentalists, they can lose interest if your material isn't new to them or explained creatively.

Audience Understanding. You need to assess whether the level of audience knowledge is sufficient for them to understand the oral arguments you present in your speech. Consider whether this particular audience has enough background information to understand your speech. If not, you have to consider how much background information you need to present. Also consider whether their level of knowledge is appropriate for them to understand any technical information you might need to present. If not, you have to consider ways of simplifying technical information.

For some speeches special background knowledge is unnecessary. Since most people are familiar with automobiles, for example, you may predict that an audience has enough background information to understand the content of a speech explaining special features of new models. For other topics some basic orientation information may be necessary before the speech makes sense. For instance, before most audiences will understand the importance of quality circles in increasing morale and productivity in assembly plants, you have to explain the meaning of quality circles (plant committees of eight to ten workers who meet weekly to uncover problems and present their ideas to managers) and how they function in an industrial setting.

Even if the audience has background knowledge, they still might not have the information necessary to understand technical explanations. For the automobile speech, you may decide that the audience does not have enough information to understand technical discussions of engineering. In this case you must determine whether that technical information is necessary. If it is, you have to determine how you can discuss it so that the audience will understand.

Audience Attitude. Especially when the response you are seeking is changing a belief or moving to action, you need to know the direction and strength of audience attitudes about your topic in general and your specific goal in particular. On the basis of the data you have collected, you need to predict whether your listeners will be favorably disposed toward your topic and goal, whether they will be neutral (perhaps apathetic), or whether they will be unfavorably disposed—perhaps even hostile.

As discussed in Chapter 1, audience attitudes are expressed by opinions. These opinions may be distributed along a continuum from highly in favor to

Figure 3-1   *An Opinion Continuum*

		Mildly	Neutral, no opinion, uninformed		Mildly in favor		Highly in favor
Hostile	Opposed	Opposed				In favor	

hostile. (See Figure 3-1.) Even though any given audience may have one or a few individuals' opinions at nearly every point of the distribution, audience opinion will tend to cluster at a particular point on the continuum. That point represents the general audience attitude on that topic. Except for polling the audience, there is no way of being sure about your assessment.

First, you can make reasonably accurate estimates based on the demographic information you have collected. For instance, skilled workers are likely to look at minimum wage proposals differently from business executives; men look at women's rights proposals differently from women; a meeting of the local Right to Life chapter looks at abortion differently from a meeting of NOW (National Organization of Women); members of the NRA are likely to be opposed to proposals that restrict the purchase and use of firearms. The more data you have about your audience and the more experience you have in analyzing audiences, the better are your chances of judging their attitudes accurately.

Second, you can find survey information that may be directly related to your topic. Here is where your creativity is most needed. Suppose you are giving a speech on pesticides. How can you find out what people think about their use? You can begin by locating sources that report information from professional polling agencies. For instance, most libraries carry the *Gallup Report*, a monthly magazine that provides survey information gathered through Gallup polls. From this and similar sources you can get up-to-date surveys of opinions on a variety of topics. Next, you can scour magazine sources (*Readers' Guide to Periodical Literature* and *The Social Sciences Index*) on your topic, looking for audience poll information.[3] All three popular weekly news magazines (*Newsweek*, *Time*, and *U.S. News & World Report*) commission polls by professional polling agencies when they believe their topic is a "hot one." For instance, an article in *Newsweek* on food safety featured a poll that showed that 73 percent of Americans polled believed that the United States should use fewer pesticides and chemicals on foods.[4]

Third, you can draw inferences from studies of people's values. Table 3-1 shows the results from Milton Rokeach's 1971 study of adult male and female

Table 3-1 *Value Rankings for American Men and Women*

Values	Rokeach, 1971		Linder and Bauer, 1983	
	Men	Women	Men	Women
Terminal values				
A world at peace	1	1	12	10
Family security	2	2	9	3
Freedom	3	3	2	4
A comfortable life	4	13	11	14
Happiness	5	5	4	2
Self-respect	6	6	1	1
A sense of accomplishment	7	10	8	7
Wisdom	8	7	6	9
Equality	9	8	13	11
National security	10	11	18	18
True friendship	11	9	5	6
Salvation	12	4	17	12
Inner harmony	13	12	3	4
Mature love	14	14	7	8
A world of beauty	15	15	16	13
Social recognition	16	17	15	17
Pleasure	17	16	14	16
An exciting life	18	18	10	15
Instrumental values				
Honest	1	1		
Ambitious	2	4		
Responsible	3	3		
Broad-minded	4	5		
Courageous	5	6		
Forgiving	6	2		
Helpful	7	7		
Capable	8	12		
Clean	9	8		
Self-controlled	10	11		
Independent	11	14		
Cheerful	12	10		
Polite	13	13		
Loving	14	9		
Intellectual	15	16		
Logical	16	17		
Obedient	17	15		
Imaginative	18	18		

terminal and *instrumental* values[5] and results from Fredric Linder and David Bauer's study of undergraduate college men and women's *terminal* values done in 1983.[6] Figure 3-2 reports the results of a more recent study of personal preferences on dominant personal and social values.[7] From this information you can identify the values that have been frequently tested and you can see that perceptions of values can and do change over time depending on many different factors. The value of *a world at peace*, for instance, was first important to American adults in 1971, during the height of the Vietnam War, but it was ranked tenth to twelfth in importance to undergraduate men and women in 1983, a time of relative world peace. Also, remember that the results might be different depending on whether you are studying the values of people on the basis of sex, age, race, education, or some other variable. If you keep your eyes open, you can find more recent analyses that discuss perceived changes in values.

What importance does this information about values have to you in analyzing audiences? By understanding people's general value orientation, you can analyze your subject in terms of those values. For instance, if your speech goal has a strong "responsibility" orientation, you may be able to assume that your audience will be sympathetic toward your appeals.

You are likely to be able to classify most of your audiences as predominantly one of the following: no opinion—either no information or no interest, in favor—already holding a particular belief, or opposed—holding an opposite point of view. These classifications may overlap. Since you have neither the time nor the opportunity to present a line of development that is adapted to all possible attitudes within the audience, you should assess the prevailing attitude and work from there.

Chapter 7 on the speech plan considers ways of developing strategies that enable you to adapt to various attitudes.

Figure 3-3 is a checklist you may use to help you analyze an audience.

Figure 3-2 *Dominant Personal and Social Values*

1. Moral integrity (honesty)
2. Personal freedom
3. Patriotism
4. Work (your job)
5. Being practical and efficient
6. Political democracy
7. Helping others
8. Achievement (getting ahead)
9. National progress
10. Material comfort
11. Leisure (recreation)
12. Equality (racial)
13. Individualism (nonconformity)
14. Equality (sexual)

Figure 3-3 *Audience Analysis Checklist*

Complete the following statements about your audience.

INFORMATION

1. The audience education level is ＿＿ high school, ＿＿ college, ＿＿ post-college.
2. The age range is from ＿＿ to ＿＿ . The average age is about ＿＿ .
3. The audience is approximately ＿＿ percent males and ＿＿ percent females.
4. My estimate of the income level of the audience is ＿＿ below average, ＿＿ average, ＿＿ above average.
5. The audience is basically ＿＿ the same race or ＿＿ a mixture of races.
6. The audience is basically ＿＿ the same religion or ＿＿ a mixture of religions.
7. The audience is basically ＿＿ the same nationality or ＿＿ a mixture of nationalities.
8. The audience is basically from the same ＿＿ state, ＿＿ city, ＿＿ neighborhood, ＿＿ other definable area.

PREDICTIONS

1. Audience interest in this topic is likely to be ＿＿ high, ＿＿ moderate, ＿＿ low.
2. Audience understanding of the topic will be ＿＿ great, ＿＿ moderate, ＿＿ little.
3. Audience attitude about the topic will be ＿＿ in favor, ＿＿ neutral, ＿＿ opposed.

Analyzing the Setting

While you are analyzing your audience, you also want to analyze the setting by answering the following questions:

When will the speech be given? This question includes whether the speech is a part of some special occasion, at what time of day it occurs, and where on the program it occurs.

What hour of the day will the speech be given? The time of day the speech is delivered can affect how it is received. For instance, if you are scheduled to speak after a meal, your audience might be lethargic, mellow, or even on the verge of sleep. As a result, you want to insert more "attention getters" to counter potential lapses of attention.

Where will your speech occur on the program? This question is equally important. If you are the featured speaker, you have an obvious advantage: you are the focal point of audience attention. In the classroom, however, yours will be one of many speeches, and your place on the schedule may affect how you are received. In your classroom speech you are guaranteed enough speaking time, but going first or last still makes a difference. If you go first, you may have to be prepared to meet the distraction of a few class members strolling in late; if you speak last, you must counter the tendency of the audience to be a bit weary from listening to several speeches in a row.

What are the time limits for the speech? The amount of time you have to speak greatly affects the scope of your speech and how you develop the speech. Keep in mind that the time limits for your classroom speeches are going to be quite short. Students often get overly ambitious about what they can accomplish in a short speech. In a five-minute speech you might be able to support two reasons for your speech goal, but you just don't have time to support four or five reasons. Problems with time limits are not peculiar to classroom speeches. Any speech setting includes actual or implied time limits. For instance, a Sunday sermon is usually limited to about 20 minutes; a keynote speech for a convention may be limited to 30 minutes; a political campaign speech may be limited to 45 minutes or an hour. Whatever the time limit, speakers must consider realistically how much can be covered within that time limit. Although you want your topic to have depth, you need to avoid covering too broad an area.

What are the expectations for the speech? Every occasion provides some special expectations. For your classroom speeches one of the major expectations is meeting the assignment. Whether the assignment is made by general purpose (to create audience belief) or by content (to affect audience belief about a policy), your goal should reflect the nature of that assignment.

Meeting expectations is equally if not more important for real-life speeches. For instance, if you attend an Episcopalian Sunday service, you expect the minister to have a religious theme; if you attend a campaign rally, you expect a speech revealing the candidate's stand on issues or platform.

Where will the speech be given? The room in which you are scheduled to speak affects your presentation. If you are fortunate, your classroom is large enough to seat the class comfortably. But classrooms vary in size, lighting, seating arrangements, and the like. Giving a speech in a room that is long and narrow creates different problems from speaking in one that is short and wide. In a long narrow room you must talk louder to reach the back row, but your eye contact can be more limited to a narrow range. If a room is dimly lit, you must try to get the lights turned up. You have to meet the demands of any situation.

Outside of the school setting you may encounter even greater variations. You need such specific information about the room in which you are scheduled to speak as seating capacity, shape, number of rows, nature of lighting, existence of a speaking stage or platform, and distance between speaker and first row before you make final speech plans. If possible, visit the place and see it for yourself. In most instances you have some kind of speaking stand, but you can never count on it. You must be prepared for the situation as it exists.

What facilities are necessary to give the speech? For some speeches you may need a microphone, a chalkboard, or an overhead or slide projector and screen. If the person who has contacted you to speak has any control over the setting,

Figure 3-4   *Setting Analysis Checklist*

1. Answer the following questions about the setting.
   a. When will the speech be given? _____
   b. Where will the speech be given? _____
   c. What size audience is expected? _____
   d. What facilities are necessary to give the speech? _____
   _____
   e. What are the time limits for the speech? _____
   f. What is the specific assignment? _____
2. What is the most important factor you must take into account to meet the demands of the setting? _____
   _____

make sure you explain what you need. But always have alternative plans in case what you asked for does not arrive.

How large will the audience be? The size of the audience will help you decide how formal to be in your presentation. If you are anticipating an audience of 25 to 35, you gear yourself for a relatively informal setting where you are close to all members of the audience. With a small audience you can talk in a normal voice and feel free to move about as you are talking. In contrast, if you anticipate an audience of 200 or more, in addition to needing a loudspeaker, your delivery, language, and even the nature of your development are more formal.

Figure 3-4 is a checklist you may use to evaluate the setting for your speech.

Summary

I, K, A

After you have determined your speech goal, you begin to analyze your audience and setting. Audience analysis is the study of audience composition, interests, knowledge, and attitudes.

You get information directly from experience you have had with the group, from the member of the group who scheduled you to speak, or indirectly from observation of and inferences about the kinds of people who are likely to attend the speech. The kinds of information you gather relate to education, age, gender, occupation, income, race, religion, nationality, geographic uniqueness, and group affiliation.

Attitudes are expressed by opinions. Your goal is to determine whether your audience has no opinion about, is in favor of, or is opposed to your goal. In addition to information from your demographic analysis, you can get information from public opinion sources and from inferences based on studies of audience values.

You also analyze the speech setting based on answers to such questions as when the speech will be given, where it will be given, time limits, size of audience, and specific features of the assignment.

Skill Development Exercises

1. Examine advertisements from five different magazines. On the basis of the content of the advertisements, indicate the specific audiences anticipated for those magazines.
2. From a recent issue of *Vital Speeches* select the three speeches that are *most* persuasive to you. What, if any, evidence exists to suggest that the speakers analyzed their audiences during preparation for their speeches?
3. Listen to a speech (a sermon, a campaign speech, etc.). Make notes that show in what way, if any, the speaker recognized the distinguishing characteristics of the audience. For that same speech indicate what the speaker did to adapt to the particular setting.
4. Suppose you are invited to speak to two groups. You are a member of the first group and you are familiar with the second group. (Choose from among such groups as a church group, a college social group, a community action group, the employees at the company for which you work, and a community political organization.) Using a topic of your choice, first complete the audience analysis checklist in Figure 3-3 for each audience. Then discuss the significant factors that you believe most contrast the two audiences.

Speech Preparation Exercises

1. Using the speech goal you have selected for your first speech, complete the audience analysis checklist in Figure 3-3 for your classroom audience.
2. Using the same speech goal, complete the setting analysis checklist in Figure 3-4 for your classroom audience.

Study Questions

For each of the following, be prepared to give examples in support of your answers.

1. Why is it important to have information about your audience if you hope to succeed?

2. Of the various kinds of information you can get about your audience (education, age, etc.), which do you regard as most important in making predictions about your audience?
3. What do you hope to achieve from making predictions about your audience?
4. What effect does an analysis of setting have on speech preparation?

Notes

[1]Arnold Mitchell, *The Nine American Lifestyles: Who We Are and Where We're Going* (New York: Macmillan, 1983).

[2]A. Haas and M. Sherman, "Reported Topics of Conversation Among Same-Sex Adults," *Communication Quarterly* 30(1982), 332–342.

[3]For more information about these and similar sources, see Appendix A.

[4]"Anxiety in the Market," *Newsweek*, March 27, 1989, p. 22.

[5]Based on Milton Rokeach, "Change and Stability in American Value Systems, 1968–1971," *Public Opinion Quarterly* 38(Summer 1974), 229.

[6]Fredric Linder and David Bauer, "Perception of Values Among Male and Female Undergraduate Students," *Perceptual and Motor Skills* 56(1983), 60.

[7]From a study done by sociologists James Christianson and Choon Yang and reported in Everette E. Dennis, "American Media and American Values," *Vital Speeches*, March 15, 1988, p. 350.

Chapter **4**

Evidence:
The Material
of Persuasive
Speaking

Whatever your speech goal, you need *evidence,* information that supports your oral arguments. If you are trying to convince a community to establish recycling programs, you need evidence to show that there are major environmental problems with the way most cities are disposing of their wastes and that recycling is an effective means of solving those problems.

Finding evidence comes through painstaking and sometimes laborious hard-nosed research. Although some people can rely on others to find information for them, most of us don't have that luxury. This chapter considers sources of information you can use as evidence and the kinds of evidence you need to form persuasive arguments.

Sources of Information

The material of persuasive speaking is all around you, but you must know where to look and how to gather it. Amassing the necessary information requires observation, interviews, surveys, and library research to supplement your own experience.

Your Experiential Base of Information

When Edmund Burke, the famous British statesman, was asked how long it took to prepare his famous speech "On Conciliation," he said, "I've been preparing for my entire life." The same can be said by any responsible speaker, for preparation is on ongoing activity. When Lee Iacocca gives a speech in support of Chrysler-made cars, his preparation includes his years of experience in the automotive industry. When you are speaking on topics that are within your field of experience, that experience provides a framework for analyzing the information and a perspective for using that information in the speech.

Observation

When your topic is outside of your direct experience, you can use personal observation to help you "get a feel" for the topic. For instance, you can be more effective in getting an audience to see the blight of a landfill dump, the poverty of a slum area, or the effects of pollution on our water system if you have seen these for yourself.

You may even be able to become a "participant observer." For instance, in preparation for your speech on recycling waste, you could join a team of people who pick up recyclable material or perhaps work at a recycling center for a few days. Whatever your topic, you can increase your field of experience by observing firsthand.

Interviews

Much like an effective newspaper reporter, you are likely to get some of your best and most quotable information on your topics from interviews. To begin, you need to identify and then make an appointment to talk with someone who has firsthand experience with the topic. For a speech on recycling waste, you could arrange an interview with a city official in the Department of Sanitation, with a person who works at a private recycling center, or with workers at incineration centers or landfills.

To make the most of your interview, you need to write a list of good questions. The better your questions, the more likely you are to get the information you need without wasting the time of the person who is willing to talk with you. For detailed information on planning and conducting meaningful interviews, see Appendix B.

Surveys

A variation of the interview is the survey. A *survey* is a list of one or more questions that can be asked of a large number of people. For instance, if you want to know what peoples' attitudes are toward drug testing, banning automatic rifles, or increasing property taxes, you can take a survey.

Sometimes a survey can be taken on one question. If you were preparing for a speech on waste recycling, you could ask:

> If the city adopted a voluntary program of waste product recycling, what would be your attitude toward placing paper, glass, and plastic products in separate containers for pickup on regular garbage removal days? Please indicate your reaction to this proposal.
>
> ___ highly in favor ___ in favor ___ neutral ___ opposed ___ highly opposed

A survey can, of course, contain many questions. The shorter the survey, however, the more likely you are to get a large number of responses.

In addition to considering what you will ask, you will want to make sure that you have polled enough people and that you have sampled different segments of the population before you attempt to draw any significant conclusions from your poll. For instance, for a poll of college students you should sample freshmen, sophomores, juniors, and seniors, an equal number of men and women, and people of all races.

Library Research

For many of your speeches, the bulk of your information is going to come from library research. By now you may see yourself as being quite good at finding library material through your library's card catalog and the *Readers' Guide to Periodical Literature*, basic sources that you have used many times for research papers. To locate all the material in your library that is relevant to your topic, however, you are going to have to learn to use a wider variety of research indexes and sources. For a review and to increase your awareness of the specialized sources that professional researchers access, I have listed many of those research sources in Appendix A.

Evaluating Sources

Since you are likely to find a wealth of books, newspaper and magazine articles, and government documents for most of your topics, you need a method of reviewing and evaluating them. Good researchers are aware that "all sources are not created equal." A skill that can help you review and evaluate is *skimming*, rapidly going through the work to determine what is covered and how.

Whether you are reviewing a book, a magazine article, or a monograph, spend a minute or two finding out what it covers. Does it really present information on the part of the topic you are exploring? Does it contain documented statistics, examples, or quotable opinions? Is the author qualified to draw valid conclusions? If you are reviewing a book, read the table of contents carefully, look at the index, and skim pertinent chapters, asking these same questions. While skimming you can decide which sources should be read in full, which should be read in part, and which should be abandoned. Minutes spent in evaluation can save you hours of reading.

What to Look for in Your Sources

As you read, you should be looking for factual statements and expert opinions that you can use as evidence in your speeches.

Factual Statements

Factual statements are objective statements about things that exist or occurrences that can be documented. "Compact disks are 'read' with a laser beam," "The Macintosh II computer comes with a hard disk drive," and "Chickenpox vaccines are now available to the public" are all statements of fact about things that exist. "Six persons died and over 600 were injured in Santa Cruz County during the October earthquake," "Johannes Gutenberg invented printing from movable type in the 1400s," and "Romanian reform leaders executed ousted ruler Nicolae Ceausescu and his wife Elena on December 25, 1989" are all statements of fact about occurrences that can be documented.

Objects and occurrences do not achieve "factual" status until they are in some way verified. Factual statements come from direct or indirect observation. Direct factual evidence is material that you gain through your own experience and observations. For instance, if you counted and identified all the cars that were parked in Lot #1 and you found that of the 312 cars that were parked, 163 were manufactured by foreign companies, the statement "Over half the cars parked in Lot #1 at 11:00 A.M. today (163 of 312) were manufactured by foreign automobile companies" would be a direct factual statement. On the other hand, indirect factual evidence is that which you get from reported observations in written sources. For instance, if the Division of Parking on campus took a count of cars parked in Lot #1 and the count was reported in yesterday's issue of *The News Record,* the student newspaper on campus, then the newspaper account would be indirect factual evidence.

In your research you are likely to obtain descriptive historical statements, examples and illustrations, and statistics.

Descriptive Historical Statements.   *Descriptive historical statements* are statements that confirm the existence of an entity or an occurrence. For

instance, the statement "The Japanese bombed Pearl Harbor on December 7, 1941" is a historical statement of an occurrence; "The person who assassinated John F. Kennedy was Lee Harvey Oswald" is a historical statement of identification. Statements such as these provide background information for your topics as well as information from which arguments can be formed. If you were researching the problem of waste disposal, you would look for background information confirming which waste products can be recycled and dates when recycling programs were begun.

Examples and Illustrations.   *Examples* are specific instances that are or can be used as proof for general statements. For instance, "Ford Escorts' frequency-of-repair records for the last two years are much closer to the records of cars made by Nissan and Toyota than they were in the past" is a specific example that may be used to support the generalization "American cars are beginning to rival the quality of foreign cars."

An *illustration* is an example in story form. In her speech on confronting misperceptions, Patti Gillespie makes the following point:

> I recently heard a male senior professor say with considerable pride that on his faculty there were now an equal number of men and women. His observation was quickly affirmed by one of the junior men in the department. Because I knew the department and could not get the figures to tally, I asked that we go through the faculty list together. Both men were surprised when we discovered that, by actual count, the current faculty consisted of nine men and five women, that is almost two men for each woman.[1]

In a shorter form, the example could be stated, "In one department two male faculty members asserted that their faculty was composed of an equal number of men and women, when in reality there were almost twice as many men." Notice that in the storylike illustration form, the individual item is both more powerful and more interesting.

Statistics.   *Statistics* are numerical facts. Statistical statements, such as "Seven out of every ten local citizens voted in the last election" or "The cost of living rose 4.5 percent in 1988," pack a great deal of information into a small package.

As you research your topic, you are likely to find a great deal of statistical information. For instance, a person researching waste products might come across the following information:

> Recycling is gaining popularity, but currently only 11 percent of U.S. solid waste lives again as something else. And still the volume of garbage keeps growing—up by 80 percent since 1960, expected to mount an additional 20 percent by 2000. Not including sludge and construction wastes, Americans collectively toss out

160 million tons each year—enough to spread 30 stories high over 1000 football fields, enough to fill a bumper-to-bumper convoy of garbage trucks halfway to the moon.[2]

Testing Evidence

Before you accept factual evidence such as historical statements, examples, or statistics, ask the following questions:

Is the Evidence from a Primary or a Secondary Source?   Primary sources are those sources that gathered or first reported the information. Secondary sources use information from primary sources. Each year the Department of Labor compiles statistics about unemployment rates. If the statistics you found about unemployment came directly from the Department of Labor reports, your evidence would be from a primary source; if you got your statistics from a *Time* magazine article about unemployment, you would be using a secondary source. So what's the difference? When you use primary sources you get the information as it was originally compiled. When you use secondary sources, you may be getting only part of the information; moreover, you are relying on that source to report the information accurately.

To illustrate the questions raised by using secondary source material, let's consider an item from a major article on air pollution in the July 24, 1989, issue of *Newsweek.* The item said, "Last year it [the USX Clairton Coke Works] pumped nearly 6 million pounds of toxic chemicals into the Pennsylvania sky." We can cite *Newsweek* as a secondary source for the amount of toxic chemicals USX sent into the air. But since the statement is unattributed, we don't know the primary source for the amount. In addition, we don't know whether "6 million pounds" is an accurate measurement, a reasonable guess, or an extrapolation based on one day, one week, or one month of tests. Although you will use secondary sources for your evidence, you need to be aware of their weaknesses.

Is the Source of the Evidence Reliable? Just because data appear in print does not make them good evidence. If the source itself is unreliable, biased, or fraudulent, no reliable conclusion can be drawn. Evidence from agencies that are responsible for compiling data is likely to be the best. If evidence comes from a secondary source, like *Newsweek,* you want to make sure that the source has a reputation for reliability. Although *Newsweek, Time,* and *U.S. News & World Report* are regarded as a reliable news magazines, *The National Enquirer* and other similar tabloids are not. When evidence comes from a source that is usually considered unreliable or in some way suspect, you want to make sure that you get corroboration for the evidence.

Is the Evidence Accurate? If we find evidence that the United States is recycling only 11 percent of its solid waste or that the volume of waste is up 80 percent since 1960, how do we know this evidence is accurate? Although the evidence may come from a good source, it still may not be accurate. Before using evidence that is going to play a major role in proving a point, you should look for corroborating evidence from other sources. Whenever possible you should try to double check evidence, especially when the evidence seems particularly startling.

If you can't verify "facts," you must either exclude them or be prepared to announce the source of unverified "factual statements" in your speech. You might say, "According to Bill Silber, president of the Animal Protection League, evidence exists to show that animal experimentation is not necessary for commercial product testing." It would also be wise to make an additional statement such as "Since this is the only source I can find for this information, I think we should treat this as tentative until corroborating material is presented."

Determining the accuracy of factual statements can be a long and tedious job. In most instances accuracy can be reasonably assessed by checking the fact against the original source, if one is given, or against material from another article or book on the same subject. Although checking accuracy may seem a waste of time, you will be surprised at the difference in "facts" reported in two or more sources. If at least two sources say essentially the same thing, you can be a little more confident.

Is the Evidence Recent? Since situations change, sometimes rapidly, you must know when the evidence was true. Five-year-old evidence may not be true today. Furthermore, even a current article from last week's news magazine may be using old information. The statement "Currently only 11 percent of U.S. solid waste lives again as something else" was true for 1989. If in 1992 you want to make an accurate statement about the amount of solid waste that is recycled, you should get more recent information.

Is the Evidence Significant? Significance is a major test for statistical evidence. Statistics are significant when the percentage base is reasonable and when the interpretation is within the limits of the statistics. For instance, a statistic that 60 percent of landfills studied are in violation of government standards sounds damning. But if only five landfills across the country were studied and three of them are in violation, this is not as meaningful as if 500 were studied and 300 were in violation. If only five were studied, then the statement is too strong an interpretation for the statistic.

By themselves statistics are hard to interpret. For instance, the statement that Americans toss out 160 million tons of garbage a year doesn't really tell us much. When we see that the figure is up 80 percent since 1960 (a time period in which the population has increased by only about 20 percent), the figure takes on additional meaning. Then when we learn that the average U.S. citizen produces twice as much waste as a citizen of Japan, the next highest nation in waste, we begin to get a more complete picture.

Expert Opinion

A second kind of research material that you will use in your speeches is expert opinion. *Expert opinions* are interpretations of facts made by authorities in a particular subject area. For instance, after reviewing the numbers of landfills in operation in the United States and the numbers that have closed in the last five years, an authority may give an opinion on how many landfills are likely to close in each of the next few years and the viability of landfills in meeting waste disposal needs.

Although you cannot rely entirely on opinions for evidence in your speeches, expert opinion can be used to interpret and give weight to facts you have discovered. Moreover, in situations where you can't get facts, where facts are inconclusive, or where facts need to be supplemented, you have to support your claims with expert opinion.

Opinions may often be classified as being either inferences or judgments. An *inference* is a conclusion or generalization based on what has been observed. Let's clarify the distinction between an inference and a verifiable factual statement with an example. When Ellen says, "Rainfall for the last two years in Ohio has been below average," she is relating factual information—it can be verified. If, however, Ellen adds, "According to Paul Jorgenson, a biologist, 'We're in a pattern of drought brought on by the greenhouse effect,' " she is citing an opinion that is an inference. The expert is concluding—without actually knowing—that the two years of drought are a product of the greenhouse effect. Other interpretations, or inferences, could be drawn from the fact about the drought. Perhaps another expert would say that this is a normal statistical pattern that suggests that two years of below-average rainfall simply means we are due for a year that has above-average rainfall.

A *judgment* is an expression of approval or disapproval. If Ellen's expert went on to say, "It is really a shame that our awareness of the greenhouse effect has resulted in so little action to do something about it," the expert would be making a judgment.

If you plan to use expert opinions in your speech, instead of passing them off as facts, you should say something that suggests the level of confidence that should be attached to the statement. You may well say, "The temperatures throughout the last half of the 1980s were much higher than average. Many scientists believe that these higher-than-average temperatures represent the first stages of the greenhouse effect, but the significance of these temperatures is still in doubt."

In order to test opinions you have found, you should ask the following questions:

Is the Source an Expert? The quality of an opinion depends on whether the source, the person giving the opinion, is an expert or not. If a coworker at a department store gives an opinion about the relationship between drug abuse and birth defects, the statement is not evidence; the opinion is not expert. If, on the other hand, a neonatologist who has studied the relationship between drug use and birth defects says that birth defects are observed in higher numbers when the mothers are drug users, the opinion is expert. Of course, opinions are most trustworthy when they are accompanied by factual statements. If the physician can give information from tests conducted to support the opinion, that opinion is worth even more.

How do you choose experts? How do you tell an expert from a "quack"? *Experts* are those who have earned a reputation for knowledge on the subject. The opinions of these people on subjects on which they have earned their reputations are expert opinions. Thus, in a court of law an attorney may call on a handwriting expert to give an opinion on whether the signature on a document was written by the person named. Yet even experts hold opinions that turn out to be off base. The best indicator of the trustworthiness of an expert is that person's record. The higher the percentage of the person's claims that turn out to be true, the more trustworthy is that person's opinion.

Is the Source Biased? You may find an opinion from an expert source that is still not good evidence because the source is biased. For instance, if a space biologist is known to have a bias toward the probability of life forms like our own on other planets, that expert's opinions in that specific area reflects the bias. If you think an expert opinion may be biased, you should look for other experts' opinions for corroboration.

Is the Expert's Opinion Consistent with Known Facts? Expert opinions range from those with such a high degree of probability that they can be treated as factual to those that are mere speculation. If an environmental expert is asked for an opinion about what the effects of a consistently rising temperature would be on the oceans in the year 2025, the expert's opinion can be treated with a high degree of confidence, because there are accurate ways of determining the melting of the ice caps given a certain rise in temperature over time. On the other hand, if you ask the same expert to predict whether these conditions will in fact be the case in 2025, the opinion must be treated with a much lower degree of confidence, since at this time no one can accurately predict whether or not global temperature will continue to rise at a given rate over the next 30 years or so.

Visual Representations

So far the discussion of evidence has focused on the verbal, but evidence can be expressed visually as well. As you research you are likely to find material presented in charts, diagrams, maps, and drawings.

The major rationale for the use of visual material in any speech is that information is more likely to be understood and retained when oral expression is supplemented with visual aids. Whether a picture is worth a thousand words or not, research has shown that people learn considerably more when ideas appeal to both the eye and the ear than when they appeal to the ear alone.[3]

Visual aids are used in two ways in a speech: (1) visual aids may be used as a means of showing verbal information so that as a speech progresses members of the audience gain visual as well as auditory impressions; and (2) visual aids may be used to create moods, emotions, and attitudes that supplement or take the place of verbal information.

Regardless of the evidence, you have a choice of representing that evidence visually as well as verbally in your speeches.

Recording Data

As you do research you need to record evidence carefully so that you can build a file of evidence to use later in your speeches.

What should you record? Record any factual statements and authoritative opinions that relate to your speech goal. Since this evidence will be used to form arguments, you can never be sure which material will prove to be most valuable.

How should you record? It is best to record each fact or expert opinion along with the necessary bibliographical documentation separately on a note card. (I like to use 4 x 6 cards because they are large enough to hold most items but small enough to be handled easily.) Record the source with enough detail so that you or anyone looking for the information can find it. Figure 4-1 provides a sample of the way to record information. Notice that the label for the evidence is put in the upper left-hand corner of the card. The body of the card includes a lead sentence that suggests the nature of the evidence. Only one item of evidence is included on the card. The bibliographical documentation is placed after the evidence on the lower right-hand side. Also notice that the bibliographical entry is abbreviated. For instance, the label "FB Cook, 172" refers to the full biblio-

Figure 4-1   *Note Card*

Landfill Problems
  Half the dumps that are open operate illegally; that is, they fail to meet state or federal regulations.

FB Cook, 172

---

graphical citation: James Cook, "Not in Anybody's Backyard," *Forbes*, November 28, 1988, p. 172.

Although photocopying can assist you in preparing note cards, photocopying does not replace making note cards. If you photocopy, you may then be able to cut out information and paste it to a card to save time in writing or typing, but each individual item must be entered separately.

As your stack of information grows to 50 or 100 cards, you will need to work out a method of organizing them. After you collect several cards on the same subject, you might find it useful to make a heading card with a tab on the upper left-hand corner. For instance, if you have seven evidence cards on the topic of waste disposal that all provide information on "Size of the Problem," then the heading card should be tabbed "Size." Each of the evidence cards dealing with the size of the problem can be collected under that heading. If the same item seems to belong to two headings, make another copy of that card and sort it accordingly. When you have finished, you will have a stack of cards that are easily resorted after a final editing.

How do you know when you are "finished"? In some cases "finished" means finding every bit of available information; in some cases it means finding the facts that enable you to put together a coherent discussion of the topic; in some cases it means using up the time allotted to the research portion of your preparation.

Citing Sources in Speeches

In your speeches, as in any communication in which you are using ideas that are not your own, you should attempt to work the source of your material into the context. Stating sources not only helps the audience evaluate the content but also adds to your credibility as a speaker. In a written report, ideas taken from other sources are designated by footnotes; in a speech, these notations must be included as tag statements. Your citation need not be a complete representation of all the bibliographical information. Figure 4-2 lists several acceptable ways of citing your sources.

Although you do not want to clutter your speech with bibliographical citations, you do want to make sure that you have properly credited the sources

Figure 4-2

In the feature article in the November 27 issue of *Newsweek*, . . .
As Senator Jones was quoted in an article on nuclear waste in Thursday's *New York Times*, . . .
John Villforth, an FDA administrator, reported in a May 1986 FDA *Consumer* that . . .
A General Accounting Office study published in December 1986 found that . . .
But according to Ellen Silvergel, chief toxic scientist for the Environmental Defense Fund, in a June 29, 1987, issue of the *Washington Post*, . . .
The December 1987 issue of *Discover* explains that . . .
Last Wednesday when I asked Mary Goodwin, the planning director for Cincinnati's waste disposal, how the city was faring in finding markets for recyclable material it had collected, she said . . .

---

of your most important information. If you practice these and similar short citations, you will find that they soon come naturally.

Summary

Effective speaking requires high-quality information. You need to know where to look for information, what kind of information to look for, how to record information, and how you can use information in your speeches.

To find material, you need to explore your own knowledge as well as observe, interview, survey, and read.

In the sources you find you will be looking for factual statements and expert opinions. Factual statements are about things that have an actual, concrete existence or report actual, documentable occurrences. Factual evidence is tested on the basis of type of source (primary or secondary), reliability of source, accuracy of evidence, recency of evidence, and meaningfulness of evidence. Expert opinions are interpretations of facts made by authorities in that particular subject area. Opinion evidence is tested on the basis of the expertise of the source, bias of the source, and consistency with known facts.

When you find material that you want to consider using in your speech, you should record each bit of data along with necessary bibliographical documentation on a separate note card.

When you use evidence in your speeches, you should cite the sources.

Skill Development Exercises

1. From a recent issue of *Vital Speeches* select the three speeches that are *most* persuasive to you. From each speech, find examples of using the following

sources of information: personal knowledge, observations, interviews, and written sources. Which of the four were the major sources for each of the speeches?
2. From these speeches select the two best examples of (a) expert opinion, (b) example or illustration, and (c) statistics.
3. For either the *Index to Behavioral Sciences* or the *Index to Humanities*, two sources that people tend to be less familiar with than either the *Readers' Guide* or *The Magazine Index*, spend some time familiarizing yourself with the kinds of magazines and journals that are indexed. Indicate five different persuasive speech topics for which you believe these indexes would lead you to relevant information.

Speech Preparation Exercises

1. List three written sources that you believe would provide information for the speech goal you have selected for your first speech.
2. From the sources you have identified write three note cards (one giving an example, one giving a quotation, and one giving a set of statistics) that are relevant to your speech goal. Be sure to cite the author, title, source, date, and page number of the article or book. Also make sure that you have properly labeled the card.

Study Questions

For each of the following, be prepared to give examples in support of your answers.

1. What kinds of information can you hope to get from interviews and/or observation that you can't get from written sources?
2. Contrast factual statements with expert opinions. What are the advantages of each?
3. Why are primary sources superior to secondary sources?

Notes

[1] Patti Gillespie, "Campus Stories, or the Cat Beyond the Canvas," *Vital Speeches*, February 1, 1988, p. 237.
[2] "Buried Alive," *Newsweek*, November 27, 1989, p. 67.
[3] Bernadette M. Gadzella and Deborah A. Whitehead, "Effects of Auditory and Visual Modalities in Recall of Words," *Perceptual and Motor Skills* 40 (February 1975), 260.

Chapter **5**

Reasoning with Your Audience

Landfills, the primary source of the majority of our waste disposal, can no longer be depended upon to meet our waste disposal needs. In just the last ten years, according to an article in the November 28, 1988, issue of *Forbes*, 70 percent of landfill sites in the United States, some 14,000, have closed. Moreover, of the 5500 that remain, the Environmental Protection Agency (EPA) estimates that another 2275 will close in the next five years.

What you've just read is an example of a speaker's reasoning with an audience. Reasoning with audiences, presenting oral arguments, is an integral part of persuasive speaking. As we saw in our brief analysis of theory, audiences "learn" attitudes through reasons and evidence. This chapter develops the premise that you are more likely to persuade an audience when the body of your speech is composed of logical reasons and good evidence in support of your speech goal. This chapter defines reasoning, analyzes the basic elements of reasoning, discusses the selection of good reasons, and then considers how to build a master outline of potential reasons and evidence to use as a foundation for your persuasive speeches.

Reasoning

Reasoning occurs in speeches when you give reasons or facts in support of other statements. Reasoning is used to form oral arguments. An *oral argument* may be a single unit of reasoning or a series of interlinked reasons in support of a speech goal. Stephen Toulmin, a contemporary philosopher, has developed a theoretical view of reasoning that you can use to help understand how reasoning works.[1] He says that a unit of reasoning, an oral argument, consists of six elements: claim, grounds, warrant, backing, qualifier, and rebuttal. As you will see, some of these elements are part of the oral argument, some are implied, and some are constructed by the speaker or by members of the audience to test the soundness of the reasoning. We base our analysis of reasoning on the Toulmin model not only because it gives insight into how reasoning works with an audience but also because it provides a visual means for testing the strength of your reasoning.

To define these six elements in a meaningful way, let's analyze the reasoning of the chapter opening example:

> Landfills, the primary source of the majority of our waste disposal, can no longer be depended upon to meet our waste disposal needs. In just the last ten years, according to an article in the November 28, 1988, issue of *Forbes,* 70 percent of landfill sites in the United States, some 14,000, have closed. Moreover, of the 5500 that remain, the EPA estimates that another 2275 will close in next five years.

- **Claim.** The *claim* (or conclusion) is the assertion to be proven. In the example, the claim is the statement "Landfills, the primary source of the majority of our waste disposal, can no longer be depended upon to meet our waste disposal needs."
- **Grounds.** The *grounds* are the reasons and evidence that are given in support of the claim. Grounds answer the question "On what basis can we make such a statement?" The statistics "70 percent of landfill sites . . . , some 14,000, have closed" and "of the remaining 5500 that remain, . . . 2275 will close in the next five years," are the grounds for the claim.
- **Warrant.** A *warrant* is a verbal statement that explains the reasoning—the relationship between the grounds and the claim. It shows how the claim follows from the grounds that have been presented. The warrant is the element of the Toulmin analysis that explains the kind of reasoning that is taking place. Although in most speeches warrants are implied rather than stated, evaluation of reasoning requires a verbal statement of the warrant. One way of stating the warrant for the landfill argument would be: "When statistics show that the majority of landfills are closed,

it follows that they can no longer be depended upon to meet our needs." When we verbalize the reasoning (state the warrant), we hope that the warrant represents good reasoning. But the only way we know whether the reasoning is good is to put it to the test. By stating the warrant, we put the reasoning in a testable form.

- **Backing.** *Backing* is the support for the warrant. Recall that the warrant upon which the reasoning is based for the landfill argument may be stated "When statistics show that the majority of landfills are closed, it follows that they can no longer be depended upon to meet our needs." Backing for the warrant could then be stated "When statistics meet tests of statistical analysis and are well documented, they are valid for warranting arguments."

- **Rebuttal.** *Rebuttal* shows the circumstances under which the claim would not follow from the grounds. In rebuttal, the person who formed the argument questions the claim. In this case, a person would ask, "Is it not possible that additional landfills could be built?" It is through rebuttal that a speaker develops the means for testing the soundness of the reasoning and predicting the probability of the claim.

- **Qualifier.** The *qualifier* indicates the level of probability of the claim. Since speakers are unlikely to be able to demonstrate a certainty for their claims, they want to present enough support to suggest a high probability. In our example, the speaker is attempting to show the high probability that we can no longer rely on landfills to meet our waste disposal needs. But the degree of probability is based not just on "high hopes" but on factors that may alter the validity of the reasoning. You determine probability by weighing the warrant against the rebuttal statements. In this case, if it is possible that additional landfills can be built, then the level of probability for the claim would be significantly lower than if there were now severe restrictions on getting licenses for landfills.

Since one of the strengths of the Toulmin method is the graphic layout of the elements, let's consider how this reasoning might be diagrammed. (The initials in parentheses stand for the elements of the Toulmin model.)

(Q) It is highly probably that

(G) 70 percent of landfill sites, some 14,000, have closed. Of the remaining 5500, another 2275 will close in the next five years.

(C) Landfills can no longer be depended upon to meet our needs.

(W) When statistics show that landfills are closing, it follows that they can no longer be depended upon.

(R) Unless new landfills can be built.

Backing (B) When statistics meet tests of statistical analysis and are
well documented, they are valid for warranting arguments.

Finally, let's see how the reasoning looks in outline form, the form that
you will use for your speech preparation:

Claim: I. Landfills can no longer be depended upon to meet our waste disposal
needs.
   A. Of the current landfill sites, 14,000 (70 percent) have closed.
   B. 2275 of the remaining 5500 will close in the next five years.

As you can see, the outline provides the logical skeleton of the unit of
argument. The length of the oral presentation of such an oral argument will
depend on how much the speaker elaborates on the points.

In the remainder of the discussion we will focus on four of the elements:
the three essentials for forming an oral argument (a claim, grounds, and a warrant
that describes the reasoning) and the rebuttal, the part that raises the questions
that test the soundness of the oral argument.

Types of Reasoning

Although reasoning (an oral argument) always includes a claim and
grounds in support of the claim, there are many different types of relationships
(warrants) between claims and their support. Even though the number of kinds
of reasoning that are actually used is too large to discuss in a single chapter, a
small number of forms represent a majority of the kinds of reasoning that you are
likely to use in your speeches: reasoning from example, reasoning from statistics,
reasoning from analogy, reasoning from causation, reasoning from sign, reasoning from definition, and reasoning from authority.

Reasoning from Example

When you *reason from example* you move directly from one or more
individual examples to a claim. Since you are likely to have discovered numerous
examples in your research, you may want to draw a conclusion directly from
those examples. For instance, the claim, "Bob Jones will vote for Todd Forbes,
the Republican candidate for Congress" can be supported with the examples that
in 1984, 1986, and 1988 Bob Jones voted for the Republican candidate. The
rationale (or in Toulmin's language, the *warrant*) for the logic of the reasoning
may be stated as follows: since Jones voted Republican each of the last three
times, he is likely to vote Republican this time. In this instance, the conclusion
is supported with three cases—enough to be used as a basis for a prediction. But

see how much stronger the argument would be if we could say, "Bob Jones has voted for the Republican candidate for Congress each of the last seven times." The more cases that can be cited without an exception, the more likely, or probable, the conclusion.

Let's see how a speaker might use reasoning from example to support recycling. Because recycling has worked to reduce waste when it was adopted in Minneapolis, Pittsburgh, and Cincinnati, we might draw the conclusion that recycling would work in all major cities. The warrant for such reasoning might be stated, "Since recycling has worked in three representative major cities that have recently adopted it, recycling is likely to work in all cities." In outline form we could represent the reasoning as follows:

Recycling would work in all major cities.
  I.   Recycling has worked in Minneapolis.
  II. Recycling has worked in Pittsburgh.
  III. Recycling has worked in Cincinnati.

After you have reasoned from example, you should test the strength of the reasoning by asking the following questions:

1. *Are enough instances cited?* For instance, are three cities enough to show that recycling has worked in all cities that have adopted it? The instances cited should represent most or all possibilities; enough must be cited to satisfy listeners that the instances are not isolated or handpicked. The reasoning implies that these three examples are enough to generalize about all cities. When there are many possibilities, the more cases that can be cited without an exception, the more likely, or probable, the claim.

One of the most common fallacies of reasoning, *hasty generalization,* is based on conclusions being drawn from an insufficient number of examples. If a speaker presents a claim with few (if any) examples, you can question the soundness of the reasoning on that basis alone.

2. *Are the instances typical?* Since the examples offered are supposed to represent most or all of the possibilities, you must question whether the examples are typical. For the recycling claim, you would ask, "Are the three cities cited typical of all cities?" *Typical* means that the instances cited are similar to or representative of most or all within the category. If the instances are not typical, they do not support the generalization. Since these three cities are all in the Midwest, there is a good chance that they do not meet the test of being typical.

3. *Are negative instances accounted for?* In looking at material we may find one or more exceptions to the generalization. If the exceptions are minor or infrequent, then they do not necessarily invalidate the generalization. If, how-

ever, the exceptions prove to be more than rare or isolated instances, the validity of the generalization is open to serious question. If we found examples of cities that had bad experiences with recycling, those examples would negate the three examples cited. If you believe that negative instances are not accounted for, then you can question the logic of the reasoning on that basis.

Reasoning from Statistics

Another form of reasoning that is closely related to reasoning from example is reasoning from statistics. *Statistics* are nothing more than large numbers of examples. When you *reason from statistics* you move directly from one or more sets of statistics to a claim. Since you are likely to have discovered numerous statistics in your research, you may want to draw a conclusion directly from them. For instance, if you want to support the claim that Heather Gamble will win the election, you can cite the evidence that in the most recent poll, 63 percent of those asked said they were planning to vote for Heather.

The reasoning represented in the chapter opening is from statistics. Recall that the reasoning went as follows: Landfills can no longer be depended upon to meet our waste disposal needs. Seventy percent of landfill sites in the United States, some 14,000, have closed. Of the remaining 5500, another 2275 will close in next five years. In outline form, the reasoning looks like this:

Major U.S. cities should adopt a waste recycling program.
  I. The majority of landfills will soon be closed.
    A. Seventy percent have closed in the last ten years.
    B. Of the 5500 that remain, 2275 will close in the next five years.

After you have reasoned from statistics, you should test the strength of the reasoning by asking the following questions:

1. *Are the statistics accurate?* If the statistics are not valid, if they cannot be verified, then no valid conclusion can be drawn from them.

2. *Do the statistics represent a broad enough base?* For instance, showing that 70 percent of 15,000 landfills have closed is more meaningful than showing that 70 percent of ten landfills have closed. No valid conclusion can be drawn from a sample that is too small to be representative.

3. *Are the statistics representative?* Even if a large number of landfills have been studied, if they are all in one section of the country or in the same type of situation, then no valid conclusion can be drawn. For instance, if the statistics represent a sample from the densely populated northeastern states, then you can't properly conclude that what was true of landfills from that section will be true of landfills across the United States.

Reasoning from Analogy

When you *reason from analogy* you move directly from a single example that is significantly similar to the subject of the claim. Suppose we want to claim that Northwest High School should conduct a lottery to raise enough money to buy band uniforms. We could support the claim with a single analogous example: Country Day, a school that is similar to Northwest in significant ways, conducted a lottery and raised enough money to purchase uniforms for its entire band.

The rationale for such reasoning might be stated as follows: Since Country Day, a school similar to Northwest High in key ways (private, fewer than 1000 students, family income moderate to high), had great success with its lottery, Northwest is likely to achieve the same success.

Notice that an *analogy* is a comparative generalization. You reason that what is true in one situation will be true in a different, but similar (analogous), situation.

Let's consider how we could reason from analogy in support of recycling. "All major cities in the United States should adopt recycling. Look at Japan. Since all major cities in Japan have adopted recycling, the volume of waste being sent to landfills has decreased by more than 40 percent." Again, in outline form, the argument would look like this:

All major U.S. cities should adopt a waste recycling program.
  I. Recycling programs are working in the cities of Japan.
      A. Japanese cities have lowered their volume of waste being sent to landfills by more than 40 percent.

The implied warrant is: Since recycling is working in Japan, recycling is likely to work well in the United States.

After you have formed an argument from analogy, you should test its strength by asking the following questions:

1. *Are the subjects being compared similar in all important ways?* If the subjects do not have significant similarities, then they are not comparable. If you believe that the subjects being compared are not really similar in important ways, then you can question the reasoning on that basis. For instance, in our example, is Japan similar to the United States in significant ways? Is it similar in size, number of cities, size of cities, and so forth? Since Japan and Japanese cities are much different from U.S. cities, there may be some question of whether they are truly analogous.

2. *Are any of the ways that the subjects are dissimilar important to the outcome?* If dissimilarities exist that outweigh the subjects' similarities, then conclusions drawn from the comparisons may be invalid. If you believe that the ways the subjects are dissimilar have not been considered, then you can question the reasoning on that basis. If the differences between Japanese cities and U.S. cities

are important to a prediction about the effectiveness of recycling, then the analogy might be questionable.

Reasoning from Causation   *One or more examples.*

When you *reason from causation* you are stating a claim that is supported on the basis of a special connection between one or more examples and the claim. Reasoning from causation says that one or more examples cited always (or at least usually) produce a predictable effect. For instance, you could develop reasoning based on the causal relationship between mortgage interest rates and house sales: House sales are bound to increase during the next three months. Recently mortgage interest rates have dropped markedly. The warrant for the claim can be stated: "Since in the past large drops in mortgage rates have spurred (caused) an increase in housing sales, housing sales are likely to increase markedly in the next three months."

Let's see how you could reason from causation to support recycling. "Major cities should adopt recycling programs because environmental cleanup efforts have been more successful in cities that have adopted recycling." The warrant for such reasoning could be stated as follows: "Since recycling has caused people to engage in environmental cleanup in cities where it has been adopted, it should be adopted in all cities." Now let's look at that argument in outline form:

All major cities should adopt recycling programs.

I. Environmental cleanup efforts have increased markedly in cities that have adopted recycling programs.

You should test the strength of reasoning from causation by asking the following questions:

1. *Are the data alone sufficient cause to bring about the particular conclusion?* Is the adoption of recycling enough to spur environmental cleanup? If the data are truly important, it means that if we eliminate the data, we eliminate the effect. If the effect can occur without the data, then we can question the causal relationship. If you believe that the data alone are not important or significant enough to bring about the conclusion, then you can question the reasoning on that basis.

2. *Do some other data that accompany the data cited cause the effect?* Are there some other factors (pride, government support, and so forth) that are more important for the increase in cleanup efforts? If the accompanying data appear to be equal or more important in bringing about the effect, then we can question the causal relationship between cited data and conclusion. If you believe that some other data really caused the effect, then you can question the reasoning on that basis.

3. *Is the relationship between cause and effect consistent?* If there are times when the effect has not followed the cause, then you can question whether a causal relationship exists. If you believe that the relationship between the cause and effect is not consistent, then you can question the reasoning on that basis.

Reasoning from Sign

When you *reason from sign* you are stating a claim that is supported by one or more examples that act as indicators of the subject in the proposition. When certain events, characteristics, or situations always or usually accompany something, we say that these events, characteristics, or situations are *signs*. For instance, your doctor may argue that you have an allergic reaction because you have hives and are running a slight fever. The rationale for the argument might be stated as follows: Hives and a slight fever are indicators (signs) of an allergic reaction.

Signs are often confused with causes; signs are indicators, or effects, but not causes. A rash is an indication or an effect of an allergic reaction, but rashes do not cause allergies.

Let's see how an argument from sign could be used in support of the claim that landfills are nearly full. A person could say, "Landfill managers are scurrying to purchase new sites and are contracting with other counties in the state to ship large portions of waste to them." The warrant for such an argument could be stated "Scurrying to purchase new sites and contracting to ship waste to locations outside of the city are signs that landfills are nearly full." In outline form, the argument would look like this:

I. Our landfills are nearly full.
   A. Managers are scurrying to purchase new sites.
   B. Managers are contracting to ship waste outside of the city.

After you have formed an argument from sign, you should test its strength by asking the following questions:

1. *Do the signs cited always or usually indicate the conclusion drawn?* For instance, are landfill managers' efforts to seek new sites and to ship waste outside the city signs that current landfills are getting full? If the data can occur independent of the conclusion, then they are not necessarily indicators. If you believe that the data cited do not usually indicate the conclusion, then you can question the reasoning on that basis.

2. *Are sufficient signs present?* Events or situations are often indicated by several signs. If enough signs are not present, then the conclusion may not follow. For instance, if you believe that the two signs, scurrying for new sites and

contracting with other counties to receive portions of waste, are not sufficient to validate the claim, then you can question the reasoning on that basis.

3. *Are contradictory signs in evidence?* If signs are present that usually indicate different conclusions, then the stated conclusion may not be valid. If you believe that contradictory signs are in evidence, then you can question the reasoning on that basis.

Reasoning from Definition

When you *reason from definition* you are stating a claim that is supported by one or more examples that usually characterize the subject of the claim. For instance, you may wish to argue that Heather Collins is an excellent leader. In support of the claim, you argue that Heather uses good judgment, that her goals are in the best interests of the group, and that she is decisive. The rationale of such an argument might be stated as follows: "Showing good judgment, considering the best interests of the group, and being decisive are characteristics most often associated with leadership."

Let's see how reasoning from definition can be used in support of the claim that "our city should establish a waste recycling program." A speaker might reason as follows: "Recycling is a cost-effective method of dealing with waste because recycling is efficient, it is practical, and it is productive." The rationale of such an argument might be stated as follows: "Efficiency, practicality, and productivity are characteristics most often associated with the cost effectiveness of a public program." In outline form, the argument would look like this:

I. Recycling is a cost-effective method of dealing with waste.
   A. Recycling is efficient.
   B. Recycling is practical.
   C. Recycling is productive.

After you have formed a unit of reasoning from definition, you should test its strength by asking the following questions:

1. *Are the characteristics mentioned the most important ones in determining the definition?* For instance, are efficiency, practicality, and productivity the most important criteria for measuring cost effectiveness? If other criteria are considered to be more important, then the reasoning is questionable.

2. *Is an important aspect of the definition omitted in the statement of the characteristics?* Even if the three criteria mentioned are important, are other criteria, such as beneficiality, even more important? If a more important criterion is not mentioned, then the reasoning may be questionable.

3. *Are the characteristics cited best described by some other term?* For instance, are the three criteria mentioned normally more true of stinginess than

of cost effectiveness? If the characteristics or criteria are most often associated with another trait, than the reasoning may be questionable.

Reasoning from Authority

When you *reason from authority* you are stating a claim that is supported by one or more expert opinions. Reasoning from authority says that one or more expert opinions are enough to establish the claim. For instance, you could form the following argument based on authority: "The United States has to limit the number of throwaway items. According to Norman Nosenchuck, director of the New York State Division of Solid Waste, 'We have been a throwaway society—we simply have to change our ways.' " The rationale for such reasoning might be stated as follows: "If an authority on waste disposal favors limiting throwaway items, it should be done." In outline form, the reasoning would look like this:

I. The United States has to limit the number of throwaway items.
    A. The director of the New York State Division of Solid Waste says, "We have been a throwaway society—we simply have to change our ways."

After you have formed an argument from authority, you should test its strength by asking the following questions:

1. *Is the source a recognized authority?* For instance, a solid waste director is an authority on matters of solid waste.
2. *Is the opinion supported by other authorities?* The more authorities that support an idea, the stronger the support. If you find other authorities that disagree with the claim, then you can question the claim on that basis.

So far we have considered reasoning that explains the relationship between a single claim and its evidence. In the next chapter on organizing your speech, we will consider the relationship between a group of reasons and a claim.

Finding Reasons

You might still want to know how you go about finding reasons. You can find some reasons by asking *why* people should believe or act on the claim. If you want to persuade your listeners to increase their level of exercise, begin by asking yourself why. From your background information you might be able to supply the following three reasons: (1) to help them control their weight, (2) to help them strengthen their cardiovascular system, and (3) to help them feel better. For most of your speeches, however, you need to supplement your background information with reasons you discover by observing, interviewing, and reading.

Ordinarily, you find as many reasons as you can and then choose the best ones.

For example, for the speech goal "I want the audience to believe that the United States should overhaul the welfare system," you might think of or find at least six reasons:

I. The welfare system costs too much.
II. The welfare system is inequitable.
III. The welfare system does not help those who need help most.
IV. The welfare system has been grossly abused.
V. The welfare system does not encourage seeking work.
VI. The welfare system does not encourage self-support.

Once you have compiled a list of possible reasons, select the best ones (probably no more than three or four) on the basis of the following criteria:

1. *Choose reasons that provide the best support for your speech goal.* Sometimes statements look like reasons but don't supply much proof. For instance, "The welfare system is supported by socialists" may sound like a reason for overhauling it, but it doesn't really offer much proof that the system needs overhauling. Who is supporting the system is not relevant to a decision about whether a system should be overhauled. Moreover, even when you have three or four reasons, together they might not really form a powerful argument. In the next chapter on organizing reasons, we will consider overall patterns of reasons that are logically sound as well as psychologically appealing to audiences.

2. *Choose reasons that can be supported.* Some reasons that sound impressive cannot be supported with facts. A reason that cannot be supported should not be used in the speech. For example, the fourth reason, "The welfare system has been grossly abused," sounds like a good one, but if you cannot find facts to support it, you should not use it in your speech. You'll be surprised how many reasons mentioned in various sources have to be dropped from consideration for a speech because they can't be supported.

3. *Choose reasons that will have an impact on the intended audience.* A reason may give strong logical support for some belief or action, but if it doesn't adapt to the needs, interests, attitudes, or values of the audience, it will have little impact. Suppose that in a speech designed to motivate your audience to eat at the Sternwheeler Restaurant, you have a great deal of factual evidence to back up the reason "The seafood is excellent." Even though you have a good reason and good support, it would be a poor reason to use in the speech if the majority of the audience did not like seafood!

Although you cannot always be sure about the potential impact of a reason, you can make a reasonable estimate of its possible impact based on your general audience analysis. For instance, on the topic of eating out, a college audience is much more likely to weigh price than is an audience of business executives. As a result, the reason "The prices are reasonable" is likely to have a greater impact on a college audience than on an audience of executives. As we emphasize in this book, your entire strategy for selecting and presenting information is based on audience considerations.

Constructing a Master Outline

In the last chapter we discussed how you can organize note cards under headings. Now that we have studied the reasoning process, you are in a position to edit your cards and form a master outline. This editing process can be accomplished by (1) writing each heading in reason form so that it may be treated as a claim with the supporting material playing the role of grounds, (2) reorganizing the reasons, and (3) typing essential material from each evidence card into outline form.

If you were affirming the speech goal "I want the audience to believe that cities should establish recycling programs to solve their problem of waste disposal," you might have 73 note cards that you have organized under the following headings:

> Benefits of recycling
> Landfills running out of room
> Recycling is practical
> Problem of waste disposal
> Incineration problems
> Recycling to reduce amount of waste

Now you are ready to begin the editing process:

1. Phrase Headings as Reasons. The next step is to phrase each heading so that it can be used as a reason in support of your major claim. For instance, if your major claim was phrased, "Cities should establish recycling programs," you might phrase each of the headings as complete-sentence minor claims, or reasons. Why should cities establish recycling programs? Because:

> Recycling has many benefits.
> Landfills, the primary means of dealing with waste in most cities, are no
> longer capable of handling the amount of waste accumulated.
> Recycling is a practical alternative.
> Waste disposal is becoming a major problem in American cities.

Incineration, a promising alternative, has proven to be environmentally
   unsound.
Recycling will solve the waste problem in cities.

2. Reorganize the Reasons. The third step is to reorganize the reasons
(minor claims) so that they provide a logical basis for your argument. In this
section we recommend an initial organization following a problem-solution
order. Although you may decide to use any of several orders of main points
in your speech, at this stage of preparation, by reordering the main points in
problem-solution order, you can see whether you have arguments that both
justify a need for some change and justify the value of the proposed solution.
We will discuss the parts of a problem-solution analysis in greater detail next
chapter.

PROBLEM

1. Waste disposal is becoming a major problem in American cities.
2. Landfills, the primary means of dealing with waste in most cities, are no
   longer capable of handling the amount of waste accumulated.
3. Incineration, a promising alternative, has proven to be environmentally
   unsound.
   RECYCLING SOLUTION
4. Recycling will solve the waste problem in cities.
5. Recycling is a practical alternative.
6. Recycling has many benefits.

Under each reason, then, you place the evidence you have to form six
oral arguments that you can use in your speech. After you have edited the
reasons, you should test them to make sure they are sound. If the reasoning does
not meet the tests, then you should try to get more evidence, change the form
of the argument, or drop it from consideration. For instance, the fourth reason,
"Recycling will solve the waste problem in cities," sounds like a good one. But
if it turns out that you have only two note cards to support this reason and neither
represents very good data, you should either look for more data or drop the
reason.

3. Prepare a Complete Outline. At this stage your outline includes your
speech goal, each of the reasons complete with evidence, and a bibliography.
Although your specific speech outline includes an introduction and a conclusion, neither is necessary for your master outline.

To help you with the form of a draft of your outline, refer to Figure 5-1. Although we will discuss outlining guidelines in the next chapter, as you go over Figure 5-1 you will notice that each of the reasons or minor claims is designated with a Roman numeral, each item of evidence includes only essential material from the note card, and that evidence is designated by some abbreviation rather than complete bibliographical data. For instance, in the bibliography the *Fortune* article is shown as follows:

> Rice, Faye, "Where Will We Put All the Garbage?" *Fortune,* April 11, 1988, pp. 96–100. (Fn)

The symbol (Fn) is the symbol for that particular entry. If there were two articles from *Fortune,* one might be (FnR) for *Fortune* article authored by Rice. The other might be (FnC) or some other designation. Also notice that in the outline, in addition to the article designator, the page number is included: (Fn, 97) for *Fortune,* p. 97. By using this method you have a complete record of where every item came from, but you will not have the cumbersome task of filling in entire bibliographical entries for each item.

Is building such a master outline merely a classroom academic exercise? Busy work? No. The best analogy for this master outline is a lawyer's brief. When lawyers are called upon to plead a case before a judge or a referee, they may be required to submit a brief before any trial is scheduled. Even when the briefs are not required, lawyers still prepare them to make sure that they have in fact covered all points of law necessary to give the best support for their client.

Although many speakers try to combine the process of preparing the master outline with preparing the outline for a specific speech, I believe this is a major mistake. Why? Because the two documents serve two different purposes. By completing a master outline you assure yourself that you have enough information to establish the probability of your proposition. If you haven't found enough information to support the proposal, then you need to find more information or change the direction of your proposal.

If you went directly to preparing a speech outline, you might be able to develop a rather persuasive appeal, but if you could not prove that what you were advocating met the major logical tests that you can apply during the master brief stage of preparation, your proposal would be a poor one. What's wrong with that? If your audience was persuaded, the adoption of your proposal could prove to be a costly mistake.

How detailed is the master outline? It should contain enough reasons to establish the logic of the proposal and enough evidence to support each reason. Of course length also depends on the complexity of the topic. A reasonably complete master outline on a very limited topic such as parking on campus will be much shorter than a content outline on poverty in America.

Figure 5-1   *Master Outline*

Speech goal (major claim): I want the audience to believe that city governments should institute recycling programs to help deal with the problem of waste disposal.

Supporting claims (reasons) with data. (Note how the following master outline offers reasons in support of the proposal.)

I. The waste disposal problem is increasing in size.
   A. The United States generates more solid waste every year—16 percent more last year than ten years ago. Fb, 172
   B. The volume of trash is now more than 160 million tons a year. US, 60
   C. Our production of refuse will rise to 193 million tons by the end of the century. US, 60
   D. Every American produces some 3.5 pounds of refuse per day. US, 60
   E. In Philadelphia, disposal costs per ton have nearly tripled since 1983. Fn, 96
   F. In New Jersey, half of all household waste is now trucked to out-of-state landfills up to 500 miles away. Fn, 96
   G. Collection and dumping costs for a household in Union County near New York City have gone from $70 to $240 in the past 12 months. Fn, 96
   H. The following numbers are pounds of garbage, yearly total per person (excluding industrial waste) according to National Solid Wastes Management Association: Portugal 334; West Germany 744; Japan 757; United States 1547. Fn, 98
II. Current solutions for handling waste disposal are not working.
   A. Landfills are not working.
      1. The United States lost 70 percent of its landfill sites in the last ten years; 14,000 have closed and only 5500 remain. Fb, 172
      2. The number dropped from an estimated 10,000 in 1980 to 6500 in 1988. Fn, 96
      3. EPA estimates 2275 will close in the next five years. Fb, 172
      4. Although new sites are available, they are getting harder to access. Fb, 172
         a. Orange County's expansion of landfill was stopped by the Department of Environmental Conservation because there was an aquifer under the site. Fb, 172
      5. All but four states are running out of landfill space. Fn, 96
         a. New Jersey already exports 52 percent of its waste. Fb, 172

Figure 5-1 *(continued)*

---

    6. Half the dumps that are open operate illegally, failing to meet state or federal regulations. Fb, 172

      a. Paul Montrone: State keeps them open because "there's no place to put the garbage." Fb, 172

      b. New York's landfill, the largest in the world, is an "environmental monstrosity." Fb, 172

  B. Incineration is not working.

    1. 80 percent of the 160 million tons we generate still goes into landfills. Fb, 172

    2. Plan economics of incinerators have become less favorable. Fb, 173

    3. Environmentalists question incinerator safety. Fb, 173

    4. Incinerator foes point to potential air and water pollution; unless fire is kept above a certain temperature such household items as solvents and plastics can produce highly toxic chemicals called dioxins. Fn, 98

    5. Incinerators leave millions of tons of ash that must be buried; toxic metals such as lead and mercury are more concentrated in ash than in original garbage. Fn, 98

  C. Costs of alternatives are rising.

    1. The costs are estimated to increase from \$10–\$12 per ton to \$70–\$120 per ton. Fb, 172

III. Recycling is receiving wide support.

  A. Currently there are 600 city programs. Fb, 174

  B. Currently 30 states call for recycling and 10 require it. US, 61

  C. In just two years, the rural town of North Stonington, CT, has reduced the volume of waste that goes to landfill by two-thirds. US, 61

  D. The low-income city of Camden, NJ, has one of the best recycling programs in the country. US, 61

  E. Rhode Island, which is now recycling about 200 of the 4000 tons it produces each day, is soon expected to be recycling up to 1000 tons per day. US, 61

IV. Recycling has proven effective in Japan for helping to solve the problem of waste disposal.

  A. The Japanese are recycling some 40 percent of their waste and sending only 27 percent to landfills. Fb, 174

  B. According to Allen Hershkowitz, author of a book on subject, 50 percent of Japan's household and commercial waste is recycled. (In the United States 86 percent winds up in landfills.) Fn, 98

Figure 5-1   *(continued)*

C. The Japanese have shown willingness to separate trash into three, four, and more categories. Fb, 174

V. Recyclers are now able to make money.

A. In a six-month period Dade County firefighters have raised $4990 for a burn center at James M. Jackson Memorial Hospital. T, 95

B. On Chicago's South Side, some 20 neighborhood can pickers process more than 12,000 tons of scrap paper and metal each year at the Resource Center, one of the nation's largest nonprofit recycling operations. T, 95

C. Alberta Freeman, 55, of New Orleans, and family pickup up cans— last year they cleared some $500. T, 95

D. Sam Hailey, Palm Beach County, FL, has collected 944,000 cans to earn $10,000 in 12 years. T, 95

E. Reynolds Metals paid nearly $93 million to recyclers while taking in 305 million pounds of aluminum, enough to make nearly 8 billion cans. T, 95

VI. Uses for recycled material are expanding.

A. As more trash is being recycled, more of it is finding new uses. N, 37

B. A subsidiary of Chicago's Eaglebrook Plastics helps turn milk cartons into grist to make items ranging from park benches to hammock spreaders. N, 37

C. Tires are crushed into "crumb rubber" that can be used in road pavement or rubber substitutes. N, 37

D. Last year 33.3 billion aluminum beverage cans were recovered. T, 95.

E. Recycling success is based on economics. Herschel Cutler, executive director of the Institute of Scrip Recycling Industries: "If the market value is sufficiently high, the stuff will recycle." Fb, 174

1. Most success has come with iron, steel, paper, aluminum, and glass—nearly 20 million tons per year out of a total of 160 million. Fb, 174

2. Ten states have helped by leveling deposits on beverage bottles. This has pushed recycling up to 50 percent in those states. Fb, 174

3. Paper is a big market. This year 26.5 million tons will be recycled—30 percent of the total. Fb, 176

Sources:

"A Lot of Rubbish." *U.S. News & World Report*, December 25, 1989–January 1, 1990, pp. 60–61. (US)

"Buried Alive." *Newsweek*, November 27, 1989, pp. 67–76. (N)

Cook, James. "Not in Anybody's Backyard." *Forbes*, November 28, 1988, pp. 172–182. (Fb)

Figure 5-1   *(continued)*

Lester, Stephen, Will Collette, Brian Lipsett, Barbara Sullivan, and Iris Rothman. *Recycling . . . The Answer to Our Garbage Problems* (Arlington, VA: Citizens Clearinghouse for Hazardous Wastes, Inc., 1987). (R)

Rice, Faye. "Where Will We Put All the Garbage?" *Fortune*, April 11, 1988, pp. 96–100. (Fn)

Schwartz, John. "Turning Trash into Hard Cash." *Newsweek*, March 14, 1988, pp. 36–37. (N)

Thompson, Terri, and Mimi Bluestone. "Garbage: It Isn't the Other Guy's Problem Anymore." *Business Week*, May 25, 1987. (BW)

Trippett, Frank. "Give Me Your Wretched Refuse." *Time*, November 23, 1987, p. 95. (T)

[handwritten: PERSUASIVE SPEAKING]

Summary

[handwritten: 1) Reasoning with audiences, presenting oral arguments.]

Reasoning with audiences, presenting oral arguments, is an integral part of persuasive speaking. A unit of reasoning (an oral argument) is composed of six elements: the *claim* is an assertion to be proven; *grounds* are evidence and reasons that provide the basis for a claim; a *warrant* is a verbal statement that explains the reasoning—the relationship between the data and the claim; *backing* is the support for the warrant; *rebuttal* shows the circumstances under which the claim would not follow; and the *qualifier* indicates the level of probability of the claim.

Although forms of reasoning are composed of claims and grounds, there are different relationships between these elements. *[handwritten: EXAMPLE, Support your claim]* When you reason from example, you support your claim with a series of examples or cases. To determine the strength of reasoning from example, you question the number and typicality of the instances and whether negative instances are accounted for.

[handwritten: STATES, Move to a claim] When you reason from statistics, you move directly from one or more sets of statistics to a claim. To determine the strength of reasoning from statistics, you question whether the statistics are accurate, whether the statistics represent a broad enough base, and whether the statistics are representative.

[handwritten: ANALOGY, 1 EXAMPLE] When you reason from analogy, you support your claim with a single example that is significantly similar to the subject of the claim. To determine the strength of reasoning from analogy, you question the similarity of the subjects and whether any dissimilarities have been omitted.

When you reason from causation, you support your claim with one or more examples that show a special direct connection between the examples and the claim. To determine the strength of reasoning from causation, you question whether data are sufficient to bring about the effect, whether some other data may have caused the effect, and whether the relationships between cause and effect are consistent.

When you reason from sign, you support your claim with one or more examples that act as indicators of the subject in the proposition. To determine the strength of reasoning from sign, you question the number of signs, the relationship of the signs to the conclusion, and the omission of contradictory signs.

(6)   When you reason from definition, you support your claim with one or more examples that usually characterize the subject of the claim. To determine the strength of reasoning from definition, you question whether the characteristics mentioned are the most important ones in determining the definition, whether an important aspect of the definition is omitted in the statement of the characteristics, and whether the characteristics are best described by some other term.

(7)   When you reason from authority, you support your claim with one or more expert opinions. To determine the strength of reasoning from authority, you question whether the source is a recognized authority and whether the opinion is supported by other authorities.

You can find some reasons by asking why people should believe or act on the claim. You want to choose the reasons that provide the best support for your speech goal, that can be supported, and that have an impact on the intended audience.

At this stage you begin to construct the master outline by editing the note cards you have organized. To do so you (1) write each heading in reason form so that it can be treated as a claim with the supporting material playing the role of data, (2) reorganize the reasons, and (3) type essential material from each evidence card into outline form.

Skill Development Exercises

1. From a recent issue of *Vital Speeches* select the three speeches that are *most* persuasive to you. Indicate what you believe are the three strongest arguments in these speeches. For each of the three arguments construct a complete Toulmin diagram including claim, grounds, warrant, backing, rebuttal, and qualifier. Based on your Toulmin analysis, which appears to be the strongest argument? Why?
2. From these same speeches list the reasons that each speaker presents in support of his or her goals. Are the reasons well supported? Are the reasons adapted to the specific audience? Explain.

Speech Preparation Exercises

1. Organize your note cards under their respective headings.
2. Write each heading in reason form so that it may be treated as a claim with the supporting material playing the role of data.

3. Reorganize the reasons.
4. Type essential material from each evidence card into outline form.
5. Include a complete bibliography.

Study Questions

For each of the following, be prepared to give examples in support of your answers.

1. What is meant by "reasoning"? How does it differ from "arguing"?
2. What is the relationship among grounds, warrant, and claim?
3. What are "good reasons"? What is your basis for evaluation?

Note

[1]The analysis was first presented in Stephen Toulmin, *The Uses of Argument* (Cambridge: Cambridge University Press, 1958). The model was somewhat revised and was applied more directly to argumentation in Stephen Toulmin, Richard Rieke, and Allan Janic, *An Introduction to Reasoning* (New York: Macmillan Publishing Co., 1979).

Chapter **6**

Organizing Your Persuasive Speech

At this stage of preparation you have a master outline of reasons and evidence and you have assured yourself that the reasoning represented by each unit is sound. Now you begin to develop a strategy for your speech. The first part of this strategy is to select the reasons that form the oral argument that will be most effective in adapting to the interests, knowledge, and attitude of your audience. This chapter analyzes several typical organization structures of speeches, considers means of beginning and ending your speech, and presents guidelines for writing your full speech outline.

The Structure of Your Speech

The body of your speech is made up of the reasons you select, organized in a way that forms an oral argument that you believe is most likely to help you achieve your goal. Although you may have two to ten reasons that you could use in your speech, the reasons you select are more likely to achieve your goal when they are organized in ways that form one of the following oral argument patterns.

Problem-Solution Pattern

The most basic, and perhaps most logically sound structure for a speech is the problem-solution pattern. As the name suggests, this pattern involves reasons showing that a problem exists and reasons showing that your proposal will solve those problems.

Let's consider why this pattern may be the most logically sound. For any policy proposal there are three questions, or issues, that must be addressed to satisfy the audience that you have considered the essentials of problem solving.

1. *Are there problems, harms, or ills within the system that establish a need for a change from the present policy?* Since we assume that existing policies should be continued until and unless a good case is built against them, there must be some good reason for change. For instance, Congress won't vote to raise taxes until members are assured that there is a pressing need for the additional income. Reasons that establish a need—the existence of a serious problem—may show the size of the problem, the symptoms of the problem, the causes of the problem, and the inability of current laws or procedures to solve the problem. For a speech on recycling, you would begin with reasons showing that the problem is growing not only because of increased amounts of refuse but also because of failures of landfills and incineration to meet the problem.

2. *Will the suggested proposal meet the need or eliminate the problems that have been cited?* A proposal is a good one only if it meets the needs or corrects the problems you cite. For instance, you must show that recycling *can* reduce the amount of refuse that must be disposed of.

3. *Does the proposal represent the best solution?* A proposal is usually evaluated on two criteria: practicality and beneficiality. If a proposal can be adopted without serious upheaval, then it may be practical. For instance, building a bridge over a river is usually chosen instead of tunnelling under a river because a bridge is more practical than a tunnel. In your speech you will present information to show that such things as costs, time, materials, and labor are practical. The second criterion for evaluating a proposal is beneficiality. Any proposal will have either positive consequences (benefits) or negative consequences (disadvantages). For a proposal to be adopted, you must show that its benefits or advantages will be greater than its disadvantages. For instance, when an expressway is being advocated, the speaker must show that the benefits of moving large numbers of cars through an area outweighs the costs of dislocating people and businesses in the path.

The problem-solution pattern provides a viable argument for audiences who are mildly in favor, uninformed, neutral, apathetic, or mildly opposed, a range of attitudes that are likely to be prevalent with most of your speech audiences.

Let's see how a problem-solution organization would look:

Speech goal: I want the audience to believe that cities should establish recycling programs to solve the problem of waste disposal.
  I. Waste disposal has become a major problem in most American cities.
 II. Recycling would help to solve the problem.
III. Recycling is the best solution to the problem.

When you form a speech using the problem-solution organization, the warrant for the reasoning that shows the relationship between the reasons and the major claim (the goal of the speech) may be stated as follows: When a problem is presented that is not or cannot be solved with current measures and the proposal can solve the problem practically and beneficially, then the proposal should be adopted.

Comparative-Advantages Pattern

A second organizational structure that is logically and motivationally appealing to an audience is the comparative-advantages pattern. This pattern focuses on the superiority of your proposed course of action. You are not emphasizing the role of the proposal as a solution to a problem as much as you are emphasizing the proposal as a better alternative.

As we saw in the problem-solution organization, one strategy for motivating an audience to adopt a new proposal is to show that a problem is so severe that some action must be taken, and of the possible actions, the one advocated by the speaker is the best one. But what if the audience doesn't sense any particular problem, or what if the audience accepts the problem but is faced with several alternatives, each of which has some appeal? In this case, the best strategy might be to focus the speech on the comparative advantages of the particular solution you suggest.

The comparative-advantages pattern may work for any audience attitude except hostile. A comparative-advantages organization of reasons for recycling might look like this:

Speech goal: I want the audience to believe that cities should establish recycling programs to solve the problem of waste disposal.
  I. Recycling saves resources.
 II. Recycling is easy.
III. Recycling can be initiated almost immediately.

When you form a speech using the comparative-advantages organization, the warrant for the reasoning that shows the relationship between the reasons and the major claim (the goal of the speech) may be stated as follows: When reasons are presented that show that a proposal is a significant improvement over what is being done, then it should be adopted.

Criteria-Satisfaction Pattern

Although the previous two patterns have a wide range of audience appeal, neither is designed for an audience that has a negative attitude toward your proposal. When you are dealing with audiences that are opposed to your ideas, you need a pattern of organization that will not aggravate the hostility. The criteria-satisfaction pattern can work well with the hostile audience. The pattern focuses on common ground—an identification between speaker and audience that lays a groundwork for acceptance of the proposal.

The criteria-satisfaction pattern works especially well when you want to establish a value judgment. For instance, suppose you are trying to get agreement that Jones is the best qualified candidate for office. By what criteria do we measure best qualified? Most people are likely to agree that a qualified candidate is one who has relevant experience, has a history of being forward thinking, and listens to his or her constituency. In the early part of the speech, then, you can focus on criteria with which an audience agree. Then, when you get to the point where you offer Jones as the best candidate, you can show how Jones meets the criteria that the audience has agreed with.

The criteria-satisfaction pattern also works with a policy proposal. For instance, a criteria-satisfaction organization for the recycling proposition might look like this:

Speech goal: I want the audience to believe that cities should establish recycling programs to solve the problem of waste disposal.
  I. We all want to improve our environment.
     A. We all want to help save our forests.
     B. We all want to find ways of limiting the eyesores of landfills.
 II. Establishing recycling programs will improve our environment.
     A. Recycling could cut our consumption of forest timber by 30 percent.
     B. Recycling could cut the amount of waste sent to landfills by 50 percent.

When you form a speech using the criteria satisfaction organization, the warrant for the reasoning that shows the relationship between the reasons and the major claim (the goal of the speech) may be stated as follows: When a proposal meets a set of agreed-upon criteria, it should be adopted.

Residues Pattern

The residues pattern, sometimes called a negative pattern, is also effective for hostile audiences. The feature of this pattern is to focus on the shortcomings of all the potential solutions to a problem except the one offered.

Speech goal: I want the audience to believe that cities should establish recycling programs to solve the problem of waste disposal.
  I. Landfills are no longer able to solve the problems of waste disposal.
 II. Incinerators won't work because of environmental hazards.
III. Recycling is the only other available solution.

When you form a speech using the residues pattern, the warrant for the reasoning that shows the relationship between the reasons and the major claim (the goal of the speech) may be stated as follows: When all the other proposals for solving a problem are impractical or create serious disadvantages, the solution offered in the proposal should be adopted.

Motivational Pattern

The final pattern we consider is the one favored by many authors because it combines problem solving and motivation for any audience, including one that may be opposed to your proposal. This is called the motivational pattern. Much of the thinking behind motivational patterns is credited to Allan Monroe, a professor at Purdue University.[1] Most motivational patterns consider a unified sequence that replaces the normal introduction, body, conclusion model. The Monroe plan uses the steps of (1) attention, (2) need, (3) satisfaction, (4) visualization, and (5) action. For the proposition, "I want the audience to believe that cities should establish recycling programs to solve the problem of waste disposal," the motivated sequence might look like this:

  I. The great majority of the nearly 200 million tons of trash a year is disposed of in landfills.
 II. Landfills are stretched to the breaking point.
III. Recycling can dramatically reduce the amount of waste sent to landfills.
 IV. Think of the contribution you can be making to the ecology of your city.
  V. Here are a set of labels you can use on containers to help you get started with recycling today.

Since motivational patterns are variations of problem-solution patterns, the warrant is much the same. In this case, the warrant might be stated: When the current means are not solving the problem, a new solution that does solve the problem should be adopted.

Speech Introductions

Although the body is the main part of any speech, success in achieving your goal in persuasive speeches may be increased considerably with well-constructed introductions and conclusions. Since the introduction is of major importance in forming a successful speech strategy, you need to work on it with great care. In this section we consider the goals and types of introductions.

Goals of Introductions

Why is the introduction so important to an effective speech? (1) It gains initial attention, (2) it sets the tone for the speech, (3) it creates a bond of goodwill between you and your audience, and (4) it leads into the content of your speech. Let's look at each of these goals separately.

1. *Getting attention.* Even when you perceive that the audience has an initial interest in your speech, you want to start your speech in a way that gains attention. Some speakers fail to realize that attention must be accompanied by involvement or else it may be short-lived. For instance, you may get momentary attention by pounding on the stand, by shouting "Listen!," or by telling a joke, but if the content of the attention-getting device does not relate to the subject matter of the speech, you may lose audience attention as soon as the impact of the attention-getter has faded. The attention-getter is composed of one or more sentences that direct audience attention to the body of the speech.

2. *Setting the tone.* In addition to getting attention, the first few sentences of your speech usually set the tone for the speech. You should know what kind of tone you want to set; then the opening should be in keeping with that tone. If you want to set a lighthearted tone, then a humorous opening is appropriate; if you want to set a serious tone, then the opening of the speech should be serious. A speaker who starts with a rib-tickling ribald story is putting the audience in a lighthearted, devil-may-care mood. If that speaker then says, "Now let's turn to the subject of abortion (or nuclear war, or drug abuse)," the speech may be doomed from the start.

3. *Creating a bond of goodwill.* The opening is also your first opportunity to present yourself in the way that you want your audience to see you. Since you want the audience to believe that you have their best interests at heart, you need to begin to create a feeling of goodwill between you and your audience at the beginning. You may create goodwill with a separate statement, but in most speeches it is conveyed through the sincerity of your voice and your apparent concern for the audience as people shown by personal pronouns and direct form of address.

4. *Leading into the content.* Finally, it is through the introduction that you lead the audience's attention to the goal of your speech. With all but hostile audiences you are likely to reveal the goal of your speech in the introduction. Occasionally you may want to proceed less directly and keep the audience in suspense until their attention is firmly established. In either case you should have good reason for proceeding as you do.

How long should the introduction be? For a speech in which you are already likely to have the audience's attention, the introduction can be as short as a few lines. If developing audience's interest is vital to your success, however, you may want an introduction that is the equivalent of 10 percent of your speech or longer.

Typical Introductions

Ways to begin your speech are limited only by your imagination. Try three to five different introductions in practice and pick the one that seems best suited to fit your purpose and meet the needs that you identified in your analyses of audience and occasion. Let's look at some representative approaches that work for short and long speeches, including startling statements, questions, stories, personal references, quotations, and suspense. Most of the examples represent introductions that could be used for speeches as short as five minutes.

Startling Statement.   Especially in a short speech, the kind you are likely to give in your first assignment, you must grab listeners' attention and focus on the topic quickly. One excellent way to do this is to open with a startling statement that overrides the various competing thoughts in your listeners' minds. For instance, you could begin a speech on literacy with the following opening:

> In 1988 of the 3.8 million high school graduates in our country, 700,000 could not read. The severity of illiteracy in this country is alarming.

Question.   Asking a question is another way to get your listeners to think about your ideas. Like the startling statement, this opening is adaptable to the short speech. Whether the question method works depends on how the audience perceives it. The question has to have enough importance to be meaningful to the audience. Notice how you could begin a speech against the legalization of drugs with a series of short questions:

> Would you feel safe riding on an airplane if you knew that the pilot was high on drugs? Would you feel comfortable taking advice from a stockbroker who had just sniffed cocaine? How would you feel riding on a rollercoaster knowing that

the person who tested it for safety was smoking marijuana prior to conducting the test? These are all scary thoughts. But with the legalization of drugs, scenarios like these could become commonplace.

Anecdote, Illustration, Example.   All these story-type openings allow you to begin your speech dramatically. But keep in mind that a good opening must lead into the speech as well as get attention. If your anecdote does both, you probably have an unbeatable opening. If your story is not related to the subject, save it for another occasion. Because most good stories take time to tell, they are usually more appropriate for long speeches; however, you will occasionally come across a short one that is just right for your speech. How do you like this opening for a speech on the need for service?

> After a leading department store chain advertised a special sale on its new top-of-the-line vacuum cleaners, my friend Ken called to buy one. The sales clerk had never heard of the product and was unaware of the sale. Her boss suggested that Ken call around to the other branch stores to find the item, but she refused to do the calling herself on the grounds that she was "too busy for that kind of service." Undaunted, Ken asked for the customer service department, where a representative offered to order the vacuum cleaner but said it would have to be picked up at a distant storage warehouse. Ken then asked to speak with the store manager, who said he would look into it and get right back to Ken. He didn't. Instead, four days later, a sales clerk from the store called Ken's wife independently to inquire whether she might be interested in a vacuum cleaner. Folks, this is not a way to run a business![2]

Personal Reference.   Although any good opening should engage the audience, the personal reference is directed solely to that end. In addition to getting attention, a personal reference can be especially good for building goodwill between you and your audience. A personal reference opening like this one on exercising is suitable for a speech of any length:

> Say, were you panting when you got to the top of those four flights of stairs this morning? I'll bet there were a few of you who vowed you're never going to take a class on the top floor of this building again. But did you ever stop to think that maybe the problem isn't that this class is on the top floor? It just might be that you are not getting enough exercise.

Quotation.   A particularly vivid or thought-provoking quotation makes an excellent introduction to a speech of any length. Use your imagination to develop the quotation so that it yields maximum benefits, as in the following:

> George Bernard Shaw once wrote, "The road to hell is paved with good intentions." Probably no statement better describes the state of the tort system in this country. With the best of intentions, the scales of a system designed to

render justice have been tipped. The balance has moved so far toward the desire to compensate all injuries and all losses that the overall cost to society has become too high. We have reached a point where exposure to liability is becoming almost limitless and incalculable, making everyone—governments, businesses and individuals—a victim.[3]

Suspense. An extremely effective way of gaining attention is through suspense. If you can start your speech in a way that gets the audience to ask, "What is she leading up to?" you may well get them hooked for the entire speech. The suspense opening is especially valuable when the topic is one that the audience might not ordinarily be willing to listen to if started in a less dramatic way. Consider the attention-getting value of the following:

> It costs the United States more than $116 billion per year. It has cost the loss of more jobs than a recession. It accounts for nearly 100,000 deaths a year. I'm not talking about cocaine abuse—the problem is alcoholism.

Speech Conclusions

Shakespeare wrote, "All's well that ends well," and nothing could be truer of a persuasive speech. The conclusion offers you one last chance to hit home with your point. Too often speakers either end so abruptly that the audience is startled or ramble on aimlessly until they exhaust both the topic and the audience. A poor conclusion can destroy much of the impact of an otherwise effective speech.

What is a conclusion supposed to do, and how can you make your conclusion do it? A conclusion has two major goals: (1) wrapping the speech up in a way that reminds the audience of what you have said and (2) hitting home in such a way that the audience will remember your words or consider your appeal. Look at it this way: You may have talked for five minutes or 55 minutes, but when you get near the end you have only one last chance to put the focus where you want it. So, even though the conclusion will be a relatively short part of the speech—seldom more than 5 percent (35 to 40 words of a five-minute speech)—it is worth the time and effort to make it an effective one.

Let's look at several of the most common types of conclusions.

Summary. By far the easiest way to end a speech is by summarizing the main points. Thus, the shortest appropriate ending for a speech on the tyranny of identification numbers would be: "So, the number system needs to be revised to prevent criminal use, to protect innocent bystanders, and to bring consumers and suppliers to a more personal level." Such an ending restates the reasons, which are, after all, the key ideas of the speech.

Because the conclusion may be important for heightening the emotional impact of the speech, even when you are using a summary you may want to add something to it to give it greater impact. The following are several ways of supplementing, or taking the place of, the summary.

Story.   Storylike material works just as well for the speech conclusion as for the speech introduction. In his speech, "Profitable Banking in the 1980s," Edward Crutchfield, Jr., ends with a personal experience showing that bankers must be ready to meet competition that can come from any direction:

> I played a little football once for Davidson—a small men's college about 20 miles north of Charlotte. One particularly memorable game for me was one in which I was blindsided on an off-tackle trap. Even though that was 17 years ago, I can still recall the sound of cracking bones ringing in my ears. Well, 17 years and 3 operations later my back is fine. But I learned something important about competition that day. Don't always assume that your competition is straight in front of you. It's easy enough to be blindsided by a competitor who comes at you from a very different direction.[4]

Appeal to Action.   The appeal to action is a common way to end a persuasive speech. The appeal describes the behavior that you want your listeners to follow after they have heard the arguments. Notice how Marion Ross, professor of economics at Mills College, ends her speech on living a full and creative life with a figurative appeal to her students:

> We, the faculty, want you to grow wings that won't melt in the sun as did those of Icarus. We want to give you the materials to make your own wings, and we are bold enough to say the thoughts of great thinkers, works of great art and, in some cases, musings of tinkerers of the past are wrought of gold. They won't melt. Use them. It is you who must take these materials, forge them with your own energy and burnish them with your own imagination to make your own wings.[5]

Emotional Impact.   No conclusion is more impressive than one that drives home the most important points with real emotional impact. Consider the powerful way General Douglas MacArthur finished his speech when he ended his military career:

> But I still remember the refrain of one of the most popular barrack ballads of that day, which proclaimed most proudly that "Old soldiers never die; they just fade away."
>
> And like the old soldier of that ballad, I now close my military career and just fade away—an old soldier who tried to do his duty as God gave him the light to see that duty.
>
> Goodby.[6]

Writing a Title

For most of your classroom speeches you will not need a title unless your professor requires one. You will be called upon to speak, you will walk to the front of the class, and you will begin. But in most real-life situations you will want a title. A title is probably necessary when you are going to be formally introduced, when the speech will be publicized, or when the speech is going to be published. Especially when the group that invited you is trying to motivate people to attend the speech, a good title may play an important role in attracting an audience for the speech. A title should be brief, descriptive of the content, and, if possible, creative.

Three kinds of titles are the simple statement of subject, the question, and the creative title. For many speeches, the title may be a shortened version of your speech goal. For instance, if your goal is "to convince the audience that business and industry should take a more active role in reducing illiteracy," the title may be "Reducing Illiteracy." Sometimes you can put the title in question form. For instance, you might title the speech on reducing illiteracy, "Can the Increase in Illiteracy Be Reversed?" In some cases, you may want to create a catchy title to help the group that has engaged you build an audience—for instance, "Bringing Light to Darkness: Eliminating Illiteracy." Under these circumstances, you may want to go through a brainstorming process to find a title.

The following groups of titles illustrate the three types:

SHORTENED PURPOSE

Problem Students
Selling Safety
Precursors to Peace
Environmental Myths and Hoaxes
The Housing Crisis

QUESTION

Too Much of a Good Thing?
Do We Need a Department of Play?
Are Farmers on the Way Out?
Shock Waves and Shortages Ahead?
Is Industrial Policy the Answer?

CREATIVE

Dirty Business: Money Laundering and the War on Drugs
Are We Up a Creek Without a Paddle? Canada's Language Crisis
Freeze or Freedom: On the Limits of Morals and Worth of Politics
I Touch the Future: I Teach

Once you have your goal written, you can write a title. When you are trying to be creative, you may find a title right away or not until the last minute.

The Complete Outline

From the beginning of this text, I have illustrated various principles via outlining and suggested that you prepare your speeches via the outlining method. Now that you have considered the three parts of your speech, introduction, body, and conclusion, you are ready to examine the entirety of your speech. To do so, I suggest you write a complete outline.

Do "real speakers" prepare outlines? Most of them do. Of course, there are some speakers who use alternate means of planning speeches and testing structures that work for them. A few speakers are able to accomplish the entire preparation process in their heads and never put a word on paper, but they are few indeed. Most speakers have learned that they can save themselves a lot of trouble if they outline their speeches during some stage of speech preparation.

Guidelines for Outlining

A sentence outline is a short representation of the speech that is used to test the logic, organization, development, and overall strength of the structure before any practice begins. Although some speakers prefer to construct topic or phrase outlines during the preparation stage, the complete-sentence outline is the preferred form because it helps the speaker make sure that the speech is logically sound.

Although many books suggest slightly different guidelines for outline preparation, the following one is in keeping with the best information available about outlining. The following rules focus on issues that most textbooks stress. After the rules I offer an annotated sample outline that incorporates those rules.

1. Head your outline with a title (optional) and a well-worded specific purpose.

2. Divide your outline into three parts: introduction, body, and conclusion. Speakers usually outline the body of the speech first and then fill in the introduction and the conclusion.

3. Use a standard set of symbols. Main points are usually indicated by Roman numerals, major subdivisions by capital letters, minor subheads by Arabic numerals, and further subdivisions by lowercase letters. Although you can show a greater breakdown, you rarely need to subdivide an outline

further. Thus, an outline of a body of a speech with two main points might look like this:

Body
  I.
      A.
          1.
          2.
      B.
  II.
      A.
      B.
          1.
             a.
             b.
          2.

4. Write reasons and major subdivisions as complete sentences. By using complete sentences you are able to see (1) whether each reason really develops the speech goal and (2) whether the wording is clear. Although a phrase or key-word outline is best when the outline is to be used as speaker's notes, for the planning stage (the blueprint of the speech) complete sentences are best. For instance, read the first draft of three reasons in support of the goal "The U.S. military should permit women to participate in combat."

   I. By not allowing women the military creates a problem that is really a violation of their rights.
  II. A lot more women than people think are really in good enough shape to do military combat.
 III. And, a lot of times that women have found themselves in combat situations they have done a reasonably good job.

The wordings of these reasons are so general and so cluttered with excess verbiage that listeners are unlikely to understand them or be able to recall them. Notice how much clearer the reasons are when they are revised:

   I. Excluding women from combat is a violation of their rights.
  II. Women are capable of fighting.
 III. When women have been pressed into combat, they have performed well.

5. Each main point and major subdivision should contain a single idea. This rule assures you that development will be relevant to the point. Contrast the following:

INCORRECT	CORRECT
I. Carter Johnson is well qualified and has the support of his party.	I. Carter Johnson is well qualified. II. Carter Johnson has the support of his party.

Using the main point in the incorrect example will lead to confusion, for the development cannot relate to both ideas at once. If your outline follows the correct procedure, you can be confident that your supporting material is relevant to the main point and that the audience will see and understand the relationship.

6. Minor points should relate to or support major points. This guideline ensures the correct subordination of ideas. Consider the following example:

I. Donating blood hurts less than getting an ordinary shot.
    A. A shot hurts because of the injection of fluid.
    B. When you donate blood, nothing is injected into your system.
    C. Donating takes only 30 minutes.

Points A and B are directly related to the main point because both deal with pain. Point C should be placed elsewhere in the outline because it deals with time.

7. The number of words in the outline should equal no more than one-third the total number to be used in the speech. An outline is a skeleton of the speech and should be a representation of that speech, not a manuscript with letters and numbers. One way of determining the suitable length of an outline is to determine the length of the speech, and multiply that length by 160 (an average number of words spoken each minute), and divide that total by 3. So, for a ten-minute speech (about 1600 words), a 530-word outline is about right.

Sample Outline

The following sample outline illustrates the principles in practice. In the analysis written in the margin, I have tried to summarize and emphasize each of the various rules as well as make suggestions about some other facets of the outlining procedure.

Speech goal: I want my audience to donate blood to the Hoxworth Blood Center on a regular basis.

Analysis

By writing the speech goal before the outline of the speech, the speaker can refer to the goal to test whether the reasons presented are relevant.

Introduction

I. Last week you read about how the life of Todd Jenkins was saved by a blood transfusion.

II. People like Todd all over the city rely on the kindness of others to supply the blood that they might need one day.

Body

I. Blood donations are needed more than ever to help save lives.
   A. This year the Cincinnati area alone will need more than 14,000 gallons of blood—that's 110,000 donors.
   B. The demand is growing yearly because of the increase of such blood-related diseases as AIDS.

II. The knowledge that you have donated raises your self-esteem.
   A. Giving blood helps you feel as if you have accomplished something important that day.
   B. Hoxworth Blood Center gives you a sticker to wear that says, "Be nice to me, I gave blood today."

III. Donating blood is much less of a problem than most nondonors think.
   A. Donating blood is a nearly painless activity.
      1. Donating blood hurts less than getting an ordinary shot.
         a. A shot hurts not because of the penetration of your skin, but because of the injection of fluid.
         b. When you donate blood, nothing is injected into your system.
      2. The slight weakness most people experience is gone by that evening.
   B. It is not really time consuming.
      1. The process takes only about 30 minutes.
      2. You can donate blood no more than once every two months.

The heading Introduction *sets this section apart as a separate unit. The introduction gets attention, sets the tone, gains goodwill, and leads into the body. The heading* Body *sets this section apart as a separate unit. Each main point is a reason stated as a complete, substantive sentence. The first reason focuses on why people are asked to give blood. The two subdivisions, shown by consistent symbols (A and B) indicating the equal weight of the points, considers need and demand. The second reason provides motivation for taking the time to give blood. Notice that each reason considers only one idea. The degree of subordination is at the discretion of the speaker. After the first two stages of subordination, words and phrases may be used in place of complete sentences. The third reason attempts to deal with one of the major excuses people use for not giving blood. Throughout the outline, notice that each reason gives direct support to the specific goal. Moreover, each of the subordinate statements provides proof for the reason. The speech follows a modified problem-solution pattern: The first reason shows that a need for blood exists; the second reason offers a benefit; and the third reason deals with the practicality of giving.*

The heading Conclusion sets this section apart as a separate unit. The conclusion summarizes the three reasons and provides the information necessary to follow through with the goal.

In any speech where research was done, a bibliography of sources should be included.

Conclusion

I. Blood is desperately needed, you'll feel better about yourself, and it really doesn't hurt that much.
II. Call the Hoxworth Blood Center at 569–1175 to set up an appointment.

Sources:

Interview with Cindy Ayers, Communications Department, Hoxworth Blood Center.
Personal experience as a donor.

Summary

After you have a master outline of reasons and evidence, you begin to consider how you will organize your speech.

The body of your speech is composed of the reasons you select, organized in a way that forms an oral argument that you believe is most likely to help achieve your goal. Depending on how you view your audience's attitude you may decide to organize your information following a problem-solution pattern, a comparative-advantages pattern, a criteria-satisfaction pattern, a residues pattern, or a motivational pattern.

The introduction to your speech is designed to get attention, set the tone of your speech, and lead into the reasons. Speech openings take many different forms including startling statements, questions, quotations, storylike openings, and suspense.

The conclusion is your final opportunity to drive your points home. Although you may end your speech with a simple summary of reasons, your speeches are likely to have much greater impact if you supplement the summary with an appeal for action or an ending that arouses the emotions.

Most public speeches have a title that is a shortened form of the speech goal, a question, or a creative, attention-getting teaser for the speech.

By writing your speech in outline form you are able to make sure that it is logically developed.

Skill Development Exercises

1. From a recent issue of *Vital Speeches* select the three speeches that are *most* persuasive to you. Identify what appear to be the main points in each of the speeches and then determine the organizational pattern they follow (or seem to come closest to following). Are the organizational patterns clear? Do they seem to be appropriate for achieving the speech goal? For the speech with the weakest organization, suggest a pattern that you believe would have been better.
2. Determine the weakest introduction and the weakest conclusion from the three speeches. Then create an introduction and a conclusion that you believe would have improved the speech. Be prepared to share them with your class.

Speech Preparation Exercises

1. List the major reasons you are considering for your speech. Attempt to cast the reasons in (a) a problem-solution pattern, (b) a comparative-advantages pattern, and (c) a criteria-satisfaction pattern. Which would be the most effective? Why?
2. Create three different openings for your speech. Which do you like the best? Why?
3. Create three different conclusions for your speech. Which do you like the best? Why?
4. Create three titles for your speech. Which do you like the best? Why?

Study Questions

For each of the following, be prepared to give examples in support of your answers.

1. Suppose you are giving a speech in support of requiring a course in persuasive speaking for all students. In what ways would your speech differ if you use a comparative-advantages organization rather than a problem-solution organization?
2. Suppose you are anticipating a highly negative audience for your speech. Which organizational pattern do you believe would give you the greatest opportunity for success? Why?
3. Why does the text say that getting attention is the first goal of a persuasive speech introduction?
4. Under what circumstances do you believe that the conclusion of a speech is likely to have a major persuasive effect?
5. Discuss why the text suggests that the main points of persuasive speeches be written on the speech outline as complete sentences.

Notes

[1]Monroe's motivated sequence was featured in Allan Monroe, *Principles and Types of Speech* (Glenview, IL: Scott, Foresman & Company, 1935). Monroe and recent coauthors have featured this organizational pattern through all 11 editions of the textbook.

[2]Adapted from Thomas R. Horten, "Our No-Service Economy," *Vital Speeches*, March 1, 1988, p. 306.

[3]William M. McCormick, "The American Tort System," *Vital Speeches*, February 15, 1986, p. 267.

[4]Edward E. Crutchfield, Jr., "A System That Works," *Vital Speeches*, June 15, 1980, p. 537.

[5]Marion Ross, "Go, Oh Thoughts, on Wings of Gold," *Vital Speeches*, February 15, 1989, p. 284.

[6]Douglas MacArthur, "Address to Congress," in William Linsley, *Speech Criticism: Methods and Materials* (Dubuque, IA: Brown, 1968), p. 344.

Chapter **7**

Forming Your Persuasive Speech Plan

Let's pause for a moment to consider what you have accomplished in your persuasive speech preparation: (1) You have a clearly written *tentative* speech goal, tentative in that you reserve the option to make a minor modification or a major revision of that goal as you determine your speech strategy. (2) You have identified the significant features of your audience, and you have made predictions about the degree of audience interest in your topic, the extent of the audience's knowledge of your topic, and the attitude of the audience toward your goal. (3) You have a master card file of information organized under a number of clearly stated reasons that you can draw from to support your goal. (4) You have command of several organizational patterns for your reasons. Now you are ready for the most creative part of your preparation: forming your speech plan. A *speech plan* is a detailed strategy for adapting your speech to your specific audience. A speaker writes a different speech plan for each audience.

In this chapter I discuss the specifics of forming your speech plan: determining specific strategies for adapting the content to the audience's interest level, knowledge level, and attitude that you have predicted; developing strategies for increasing your credibility with your audience; determining strategies for motivating your audience; and finally, committing yourself to a complete speech outline that incorporates your strategies and follows a pattern that is most likely to help you achieve your goal.

Strategies for Increasing Audience Interest

From information that you have gained from your audience analysis, you can determine whether the majority of the members of your audience are interested in your topic. This section considers strategies for getting, maintaining, and building audience interest.

Strategies for increasing audience interest are based on means of showing the relevance of your information. One way to do this is to show that the information is timely, that there is a sense of urgency about your proposal. The importance of timeliness to persuasion was demonstrated dramatically by the increase in the number of people in all parts of the United States who purchased earthquake insurance right after the October 17, 1989, earthquake in the San Francisco Bay area. The reality of the earthquake, along with scientific information showing that quakes of equal size or larger could occur anywhere in the United States at any time, motivated people to buy earthquake coverage.

When your topic isn't timely, you must use your creativity to increase the perception of urgency. Suppose you are proposing that the United States needs to substantially increase its oil reserves. Since people may not see the immediate urgency for action on long-range energy sources, they are not going to feel a need to take direct action. One way of creating urgency is to dramatize the effects of failing to look ahead. For instance, you might describe the events of the early 1970s when OPEC decreased our oil supplies. By painting pictures of the long lines at gas stations and the rush of people to trade in their gas-guzzling giant cars for smaller, more gasoline-efficient models while taking a beating in trade-in losses, you might be able to rekindle that sense of urgency. You might even be able to show how recent smaller oil crises affect our economy today.

A second way of showing relevance is through proximity, the physical closeness of an event. Audiences are more interested in topics that they perceive as being in "their own backyard." For instance, speakers against nuclear power have a much easier time getting Cincinnati audiences to consider their arguments when they use supporting evidence from the Fernald plant on the outskirts of town rather than evidence from the uranium-processing plant outside of Richland, Washington.

When the proposal does not appear to affect the immediate surroundings, you may still be able to create proximity. Speakers were able to increase the perception of proximity of the overthrow of Eastern European governments in late 1989 by showing American audiences how these events had a direct effect on our foreign policy and military security.

A third way of showing relevance is through direct personal effect. Audiences are more likely to show interest in your topic if they perceive it as personal. For instance, you are likely to get the attention of homeowners with a speech about property taxes because property taxes affect them directly. With many of your topics you should be able to establish direct ties quite easily.

If the topic is removed from personal experience, you must find some personal link. For instance, even though the problem of substance abuse—alcohol and drugs—has been growing over the years, speakers weren't able to focus the interest of many audiences on this problem until they demonstrated that substance abuse affects or may affect some member of the family. When you perceive that an audience doesn't see the personal ties, you have to establish them or risk the loss of interest.

In each of these cases, relevance is heightened through the use of vivid examples, illustrations, and personal experiences.

In your speech plan, then, you will write a paragraph on how you plan to get, maintain, or build audience interest in the topic. In addition to any other means, you will show how you plan to increase the audience's perception of the timeliness, proximity, and personal effect of the information.

Strategies for Adapting to Audience Knowledge

From information that you have gained from your audience analysis, you can determine whether the majority of the members of your audience have enough background information to understand your speech arguments. This section considers strategies for building an audience's background information and for adapting arguments to the audience's level of understanding.

Providing Background Information

When you believe that your audience's information level is not high enough for them to understand your reasons and evidence, you need to increase their knowledge with background information. Suppose that at a local PTA meeting you are advocating the adoption of a policy of year-around schooling for public elementary and secondary education. Since you can predict that even an audience of people interested in educational issues is unfamiliar with specific year-around schooling plans, you need to explain the concept completely. Moreover, you probably want to familiarize the audience with U.S. cities where year-around schools are in operation as well as other countries where year-around schooling is the norm.

The need for orienting your audience, giving background information, is more important early in the history of discussion of a particular topic. For instance, it's only been in the last few years that most people can honestly say that they have heard much about the greenhouse effect. Although scattered information has been available on this topic for many years, prior to 1989 most people just hadn't paid much attention to the information or were completely unaware of it. During those years, any speaker talking on the topic to a general audience would have had to educate the audience about the concept. Now, however, speakers who talk about the greenhouse effect can assume a much greater general understanding of the concept. Still, savvy speakers may remind the audience that the greenhouse effect refers to the theory of global warming.

You want to present background information in ways that won't insult the intelligence of your audience. For instance, since a general definition of "year-around schooling" seems self-evident, instead of acting as if no one in the audience could possibly know what you are talking about, you could use such statements as "As you are probably aware" or "As we have come to find out." Speaking this way, you suggest that your audience knows but may just need some reminders. Those who are familiar with the concept won't feel insulted and those who are not familiar with the concept will get the necessary information.

Another important consideration in providing background information is the pressure of time. For nearly any speech you have some time limit. In a classroom speech, you may be limited to five to ten minutes for the entire speech, an amount of time that won't allow for a complete orientation. Even when you have as long as an hour to speak, you must still use time for orienting your audience wisely. The tighter the time constraints and the more complicated your information, the more careful you have to be in making decisions about the nature and amount of background information. Focus on information that is absolutely necessary to audience understanding. If you spend five minutes of a seven-minute speech giving background information, you won't have enough time to develop your arguments.

Facilitating Understanding

How well your audience understands your arguments and evidence depends on the care you have taken in defining terms and using examples and comparisons. As you consider your speech development, ask the following questions.

Have I defined all key terms carefully? Defining is stating the meaning of a word in the particular context in which you are using it. Unless you are able to define words clearly, your audience is not going to fully understand your meaning.

Suppose you are advocating the responsibility of business and industries in lowering the rate of illiteracy in the workplace. Although most members of the audience are likely to be aware that "illiteracy" means unable to read, they are not likely to have a clear idea of what you mean by "illiteracy" in your speech. Are you talking only about people who are totally unable to read? Or are you talking about people who have some basic reading skills but are unable to read well enough to understand the kinds of written directions and instructions that are necessary for them to function on the job? Unless the audience is sure of what you mean, they are not going to be able to either understand your information or retain it. Since in almost any speech you use terms that are fundamental to the audience's understanding of the speech, you must make sure that you define those terms.

Have I supported every generalization with at least one specific example? *Examples* are specific instances that explain or support a general statement. They help audiences give a specific meaning to ideas. Suppose that in your speech advocating the responsibility of business in lowering the rate of illiteracy in the workplace you state that some businesses are already assuming this responsibility. Left at that, members of the audience are not going to know either what it means to "take the responsibility" or the kind of money involved in taking that responsibility. If, however, you add, "For instance, Aetna Life and Casualty recently spent $750,000 to teach 500 of its new employees basic reading, writing, and arithmetic each year; American Express spends $10 million annually to teach its new workers basic English and social skills; and Domino's Pizza of Ann Arbor, Michigan, spends $50,000 a year on a reading program, heavily seasoned with lessons on cuisine chemistry," members of the audience will understand the nature of the responsibility and some of the costs involved.

Have I compared or contrasted my new information with information the audience already understands? A *comparison* explains how two things are similar, whereas a *contrast* focuses on their differences. Suppose you are giving a speech advocating that your company adopt a new word processing package. As you are explaining the superiority of the new program, you might say, "Version 5 maintains the option of changing typefaces and formats with key strokes. But, in contrast to Version 4, Version 5 reduces the number of key strokes necessary to accomplish the function. You'll recall that to start the process you used to have to hold down both the Shift and Command keys while you struck the letter S. Well, with the new version. . . ." Through this contrast the audience is reminded of information it already has and the differences with the new version are explained.

In short, the decision rule is to be prepared to define, exemplify, and compare at any place where there appears to be any difficulty. This decision rule is based on a sound psychological principle; the more different kinds of explanations you give, the more people will understand. In your speeches you need to present your information in ways that will adapt to different learning styles.

In your speech plan, then, you will write a paragraph on how you plan to give the audience necessary background information, if it is needed, and how you will discuss information in terms that members of the audience will understand.

Strategies for Adapting to Audience Attitudes

From information that you have gained from your audience analysis, you can determine whether the majority of the members of your audience are in favor of, have no opinion about, or are opposed to your speech goal. In this section we consider strategies for dealing with each of these possibilities. Since it is easier to show strategies in terms of a specific example, suppose that the original wording of your goal is "I want the audience to believe that they should alter their intake of saturated fats in order to lower their overall cholesterol level."

In Favor

Your greatest opportunity for achieving your goal is with an audience that is already favorably disposed toward the goal—an audience for which your proposal is within their latitude of acceptance.

Although speaking to an audience that is in favor of your goal at the outset sounds like an ideal situation, it carries many hazards. A favorable audience is seldom interested in a rehash of familiar material. For instance, if members of your audience are in favor of lowering their cholesterol levels, you make a mistake by staying with the goal of convincing them of the importance of lowering their cholesterol level. What keeps people who have a favorable attitude from acting is their lack of agreement on *what* to do. Your job is to provide a specific course of action they can rally around. When you believe your audience is on your side, try to crystallize their attitudes, recommit them to a particular direction, or suggest a specific course of action to serve as a rallying point. If you can focus the speech on a specific way of reducing saturated fat intake, you can perhaps get audience attitudes going in the same direction. The presentation of a well-thought-out, specific solution increases the likelihood of audience action.

For an audience favorable to a speech on lowering cholesterol levels, rather than limiting yourself to the goal "I want my audience to believe that they should alter their intake of saturated fats to lower their overall cholesterol level," you might modify the goal to read, "I want my audience to try to lower their intake of saturated fats by at least 10 percent to lower their overall cholesterol level." Although the change is relatively small, it gives you a chance to take advantage of an already positive situation.

Even when the audience is on your side, they may perceive what you want them to do as impractical. Then they are likely to ignore your appeal regardless of its merits. For instance, if your goal is to have the class write letter to their congressperson, the act of writing that letter may seem impractical even to an audience of partisans. If, on the other hand, you suggest writing a short message on a postcard *and* you can give your audience addressed postcards, they may be more inclined to write if they agree with the merits of your appeal.

No Opinion

The next easiest audience to affect is one that has yet to form an opinion on the topic. An audience that has not formed an opinion may be uninformed, neutral, or apathetic.

If you believe that your audience has no opinion because it is *uninformed,* your strategy should involve giving enough information to help them understand the subject before you develop your persuasive appeals directed toward establishing a belief or moving to action. For instance, if you believe your audience has no opinion about lowering their cholesterol level because they are uninformed, then only small numbers of your audience will know what cholesterol is, how it is formed, and what effects it has on blood composition. Even those who know what cholesterol is may not know enough about it to form an opinion about its effects. In the early part of the speech, then, you would define cholesterol, talk about how it is formed, and share medical evidence about its effects on the body. Even with a largely uninformed audience, you do not want to spend more than half of your allotted time on background information, or you may not have enough time to present your oral arguments.

If you believe your audience has no opinion because it is *neutral,* your strategy is to present the best possible arguments and support them with the best information you can find. If your assessment is correct, then you stand a good chance of success with that strategy because neutral audiences are likely to be looking for information on which they can form an opinion.

If you believe your audience has no opinion because it is *apathetic,* all of your effort can be directed to breaking them out of their apathy. For instance, your audience may know what cholesterol is, how it is formed, and even the medical information on negative effects, but they might not seem to care. With this audience, instead of emphasizing the information, you should emphasize motivation.

Even with a neutral audience you should not expect too much. Major attitude change is more likely to come over a period of time than from a single speech. Because your classroom speaking allows for only one effort, however, you want to make the most of it.

Since the most appropriate speech goals for audiences with no opinion are goals that establish a belief or goals that move the audience to action, you are not likely to need to modify the wording of your goal.

Opposed

An audience that is opposed to your proposal is the most difficult to persuade because they see your proposal as being in their latitude of rejection. The attitudes of audiences that are opposed range from slightly negative to thoroughly hostile. Whether you choose to modify your goal in order to give yourself a greater chance to succeed depends in part on the degree of hostility you believe your audience holds against your goal.

If you believe that your audience is slightly opposed to your proposal, the original wording is still likely to be appropriate. For instance, for the cholesterol topic you could maintain the goal "I want my audience to believe that they should alter their intake of saturated fats to lower their overall cholesterol level." In the speech you can approach them directly with your arguments, hoping that the weight of your argument will swing them to your side. Nevertheless, you want to try to lessen their negative attitude without arousing their hostility. With a negative audience you must be careful to be objective with your material and to make your case clearly so that those who are only mildly negative may be persuaded and those who are very negative will at least understand your position.

If you believe that your audience is hostile toward your goal, you may want to consider a less ambitious goal. For instance, if you believe that your audience is so sick and tired of hearing about cholesterol that nothing you could say is likely to get them to alter their diet, you may want to put the emphasis on the harms of cholesterol. For instance, you might change your goal to read, "I want my audience to believe that new evidence reaffirms the harms of cholesterol to health." In presenting new evidence, you may lay the groundwork for a later speech on lowering the levels of saturated fat. Since it is unlikely that you will be able to swing a hostile audience around in a single speech, you may want to be content with "planting the seeds of persuasion." If you present a modest proposal seeking a slight change in attitude, you may be able to get an audience to at least consider the value of your message. Later, when the idea begins to grow, you can ask for a greater change.

On the other hand, you may decide that even though the audience is hostile, they need to hear what you have to say. If so, you may be able to reach some members of the audience by using one of the indirect organizational approaches, such as the criteria-satisfaction pattern.

In your speech plan, then, you will write a paragraph on how you plan to adapt to your audience's attitude, whether the audience is in favor of, neutral about, or opposed to your speech goal. In addition, you will indicate the kind of organizational pattern you can use, and you will defend that choice on the basis of how it will help you achieve your goal in light of the audience's attitude.

Strategies for Affecting Audience Perception of Your Credibility

From information that you have gained from your audience analysis, you can determine whether the majority of the members of your audience perceive you as a credible source. The less positive the audience perception of your credibility, the more you need to do.

Much of your initial credibility is going to depend on what the audience knows about you ahead of time. Some speakers enter the speaking situation with high credibility based on audience recognition and past knowledge. For instance, when an organization brings in Lee Iacocca to talk about competition with foreign automobile manufacturers, Iacocca begins with (1) high recognition and (2) approval of his efforts. On the other hand, when a relatively unknown person is scheduled to speak, that person's credibility will result from comments made by the introducer and the speaker's behavior during the speech itself.

Since the speech that is given to introduce you to your audience can help build your credibility, you should work with the person introducing you to give enough information to lay a foundation for building credibility. Make sure that the introducer has accurate information, but more important, make sure you have suggested the kinds of material he or she should use. Often people let you create your own introduction, which they then present. If the introducer offers to let you prepare a statement, take advantage of the opportunity. In either case be careful of introductions that go overboard in praise. You want to include information that establishes your credibility without giving the sense of unjustified praise.

Whether your initial recognition and audience approval are high or not, the audience's perceptions of you may rise or fall based on what you do in the speech. Let's consider the kinds of things you need to do to build the audience's perception of your credibility.

Building Expertise

The first step in building a perception of your expertise is to enter the speech situation as well prepared as possible. Audiences have an almost instinctive knowledge of when a speaker is trying to "wing it." If you are not really prepared, you are likely to stumble over facts and figures and leave a poor impression. You want to demonstrate your depth of knowledge on the topic by presenting high-quality information. For instance, in your speech on waste disposal, if you can create a vivid picture of problems created by the shortage of landfills through well-constructed and carefully documented examples, illustrations, and statistics, your audience can begin to appreciate your knowledge and expertise.

Much of the perception of your expertise is likely to result from the audience's sense of your direct experience with your topic. For instance, if you are planning to give a speech in support of Nancy Dawson's candidacy for city council, your audience will perceive you as a more credible source if you know Nancy Dawson personally or if you have worked with her on major civic projects so you can speak about her character firsthand. Likewise, if you are giving a speech in favor of abolishing the use of SAT scores to determine eligibility for college, your audience will perceive you as a more credible source if you have been a member of a blue ribbon committee or task force studying the SAT.

What if you have had no direct experience with the issue? Then you have to go to more general qualities of self that build your credibility. For instance, do you have a reputation for thoughtfulness? Care in making decisions? Leadership? Public service? In short, what do you have going for you that might relate to your ability to give good advice on this proposal?

Building Trustworthiness

If your audience is not aware of your trustworthiness, then you have to show positive character traits in the speech. The following ways of handling your information are likely to build a positive perception of your trustworthiness.

1. *Tell the truth.* Of all the ways to establish trustworthiness, this may be the most important. If people believe you are lying to them, they will reject you and your ideas. If they think you are telling the truth but later learn that you have lied, they will look for ways to get back at you. If you are not sure whether information is true, don't use it until you have verified it. Ignorance is seldom accepted as an excuse. Credible speakers do not twist facts. When facts are well documented, good speakers make the most of them; when facts are weak, they acknowledge the problem. Many times an honest "I really don't know, but I'll find out" is far more effective than trying to deflect a comment or use irrelevant information to make points.

2. *Keep your information in perspective.* Many speakers get so excited about their information that they exaggerate its importance. Although some people seem willing to accept a little exaggeration as a normal product of human nature,

when the exaggeration is defined as "distortion," most people consider it the same as lying. Because the line between some exaggeration and gross exaggeration or distortion is often difficult to determine, most people see any exaggeration as unethical.

3. *Recognize the value of information that conflicts with your position.* Recognizing conflicting information is particularly important for developing trustworthiness. Very few issues are clearly right or wrong, good or bad. As a result, there is likely to be persuasive information on both sides of an issue. When there is information on the other side that appears to be very strong, instead of suppressing it, bring it out yourself and then tell why that information doesn't invalidate your case. Audiences are inclined to respect people who acknowledge negative information and deal with it rationally. Moreover, research shows that this so-called two-sided presentation of information is likely to be more persuasive.[1]

4. *Resist personal attacks against those who oppose your ideas.* There seems to be an almost universal agreement that name-calling is detrimental to your trustworthiness. Even though many people name-call in their interpersonal communication, they regard name-calling by public speakers as unethical.

Increasing Audience Perception of Your Attractiveness

Perceptions of your physical attractiveness can be affected by the way you look and behave. To start, you can dress, groom, and carry yourself in an attractive manner. The old compliment "You clean up really good," is one to remember. Recall how wonderful everyone looks at a formal occasion in their tuxedoes and gowns. Why? Because they have taken extra effort to look nice. You'll be surprised how appropriate professional dress and demeanor will increase your attractiveness to your audience.

In addition, you can behave in a friendly manner. Friendliness is an important component of attractiveness. Goodwill and pleasantness develop a quality of warmth that increases an audience's comfort with the speaker and his or her ideas. Critics were often baffled by President Ronald Reagan's ability to stave off attacks on his ideas and supporting material almost solely by the power of his personality. Even reporters who were dead set against his political vision for the nation usually were forced to confess that personally they liked President Reagan. In fact, there were times when even critics were won over by the force of his personality. Why? Because Ronald Reagan is a very pleasant person. He truly enjoys being with and talking with people. He listens, he smiles, he responds appropriately.

In your speech plan, then, you will write a paragraph on how you plan to build the audience's perception of your credibility. In addition to any other means, you will show how you plan to increase the audience's perception of your expertise, trustworthiness, and attractiveness, including means of showing your friendliness.

Strategies for Increasing Audience Motivation

Whether your speech is designed to affect an audience's belief or to move them to action, the audience's response is likely to depend on your motivational efforts. In this section we look at what you can do to shape and develop oral arguments to trigger emotional reactions. The following is a discussion of several motivational strategies that you may use to help audiences identify with your material.

Create Common Ground. In a persuasive speech you are trying to establish the feeling that both you, the speaker, and the audience are operating from the same value system and sharing the same experiences. In short, you are in this together. The response you seek from the audience is, "We agree, or have so much in common, on so many points that we can reach agreement on a single point of difference." In trying to get support for their latest programs, politicians often try to show that they have the same background, the same set of values, beliefs, and attitudes, the same overall way of looking at things as the audience, so that a point of difference does not represent a difference in philosophy.

Provide Incentives. The analysis of motivation in Chapter 1 showed that an audience is likely to be motivated when it perceives incentives as strong enough to create action. A good illustration of the power of incentives can be seen in the auto makers' use of sales prices and rebates to boost car sales. The greater the reduced price or the rebate, the greater the effect on car sales, if other buying criteria are positive. For instance, a product that is of high quality will sell better with reduced prices or rebates than a product of lower quality. Your emphasis on incentives is likely to motivate only after you have impressed your audience with the quality of the product.

Moreover, people are more likely to act when they see that the suggested incentives present a favorable cost-reward ratio. John Thibaut and Harold Kelley explain social interactions in terms of rewards received and costs incurred by each member of an interaction.[2] Rewards are such incentives as economic gain, good feelings, prestige, or any other positive outcome; costs are units of expenditure such as time, energy, money, or any negative outcome of an interaction.

Consider an example of how people seek situations in which incentives exceed costs. Suppose you are asking your audience to volunteer an hour a week to help adults learn to read. The time you are asking them to give is a negative outcome—a cost; however, volunteering time can be shown to be rewarding.

Members of the audience may feel civic-minded, responsible, or helpful as a result of volunteering time for such a worthy cause. If you can show that those rewards or incentives outweigh the cost, then you increase the likelihood of the audience's volunteering.

Strategies growing from incentive theory are easy for most people to understand because the theory is so easily supported by commonsense observations. Suppose that you are, in fact, trying to motivate the audience to volunteer an hour a week to help adults learn how to read. How do you proceed? You could ask each person to volunteer for 15 minutes a week. Since the cost is very low, you are unlikely to meet much resistance, but then you face the question of whether it is worth spending the additional time to go somewhere to work for 15 minutes. What if you decide to ask people to donate an hour a day? Since an hour a day is likely to represent a major commitment, the audience must be shown that one hour a day is not that much time (a difficult point to make), or they must be shown that the reward for so much service is worth the time.

In general, people look at calls for action on the basis of a cost-reward ratio—the higher the cost, the greater the reward. Thus, the higher the perceived cost, the harder you have to work to achieve your goal. In summary, you must achieve one of the following: (1) show that the costs in time, energy, or money investment are small; or (2) show that the rewards (incentives) in good feelings, prestige, or economic gain are high. In your speech, then, you are looking at ways to minimize cost and maximize gain.

Adapt to Audience Values. Earlier in this book we defined values and considered values that are important to most Americans. How can you appeal to values to motivate? You can stress how your proposal complements an audience's values. For instance, in a speech on restricting the number of hours that children watch television, you could appeal to people's sense of responsibility. Since Americans value behaving responsibly, you could emphasize that restricting children's television viewing is responsible behavior. Then the audience is more likely to support your proposal.

According to expectancy-value theory, a goal or incentive may have a very high *value* for a person, but if the person has a low *expectancy* of gaining that goal, the person's efforts to attain the goal will be weak. As a result, in your speech you want to stress both the value of the behavior and the expectancy of attaining it. For instance, suppose you are giving a speech to youths in which you are trying to motivate them to strive for good grades in school. Since good grades may be a *valued* goal of students, such a speech may appear to have strong incentive. But if the youths have low expectancies of their abilities to get good grades, they will not be motivated by your appeal. If, in addition to appealing to a desire for good grades, you can also show them realistic ways of increasing their expectancies (that is, if you give them pointers about how to improve their study skills so that they can have higher realistic expectancies for achieving good grades), they are likely to be more highly motivated by your appeal.

Adapt to Audience Needs. In Chapter 1 we considered McClelland's analysis of needs for achievement, affiliation, and power and Maslow's hierarchy of physiological, safety, belongingness and love, esteem, and self-actualization needs. What are some specific needs that audiences experience and that you can meet with your speech? You are likely to be able to identify many different needs. The following are four of the kinds of needs that you can appeal to in your speeches.

- **Wealth.** You can appeal to an audience's perceived need for wealth, the acquisition of money and material goods. (Wealth may be considered as an *achievement* motive or an *esteem* need.) For instance, those who have little money can perhaps be motivated to buy a Ford Escort because it gets such good gas mileage and is so economical to operate. Those who have a great deal of money can perhaps be motivated to buy a Rolls Royce or a Cadillac because those cars are prestigious.
- **Authority.** You can appeal to an audience's perceived need for authority. (Authority may be classified as a *power* motive or an *esteem* need.) For many people, personal worth is dependent on their power over their own destiny, the exercise of power over others, and the recognition and prestige that come from such power.
- **Conformity.** You can appeal to an audience's perceived need for conformity. (Conformity may be classified as an *affiliation* motive or a *belongingness* need.) People often behave in a given way because a friend, a neighbor, an acquaintance, or a person in the same age bracket behaves that way. Although some people are more likely to do something if they can be the first one to do it or if it makes them appear distinctive, most people feel more secure when they are acting in ways that conform with others of their kind. The old saying that there is strength in numbers certainly applies to conformity.
- **Pleasure.** You can appeal to an audience's perceived need for pleasure. (Pleasure may be classified as an *achievement* motive or an *esteem* need.) When you are given a choice of actions, you often pick the one that gives you the greatest pleasure, enjoyment, or happiness. Pleasure may also operate as a *self-actualizing* need.

Rework Language to Appeal to the Emotions. The ultimate goal of motivation is to arouse audience emotions. An *emotion* is subjectively experienced as a strong feeling and involves physiological changes that prepare the body for action. Many emotions are triggered by physical happenings. For instance, when a dog jumps from behind a tree it frightens us. Emotions are also triggered by words. When a friend says, "Go to the play. Don't worry about me; I'll be all right alone," we may feel guilt. In this section we are interested in the conscious effort of a speaker to phrase ideas in ways that appeal to the emotions of the listeners.

Suppose you are to give a speech calling for more humane treatment of the elderly in our society. You want to make the point that older people often feel alienated from the society that they worked so many years to support and develop. In so doing, you can present facts and figures to show how many older citizens are not employed, how many are relegated to nursing homes, and how many skills and talents are lost. These are all good points. If, in addition, you can cause your listeners to feel sad, angry, or guilty about that treatment, you add an affective dimension to the material. The role of emotional appeal is to compel listeners to feel as well as to think about what is being said. Let's consider how to create wording that has emotional impact.

First, clearly identify the emotions you want your listeners to experience. What emotion or emotions do you want your audience to experience as a result of your speech? If you are giving a speech designed to get the audience's support for more humane treatment of the elderly, you may want your listeners to feel sadness, anger, grief, caring, or perhaps guilt. If you are giving a speech designed to get the audience to attend your school's production of a musical, you may want your listeners to feel joy, excitement, or enthusiasm. If you're not sure what it is that you want your audience to feel, any speech effectiveness is likely to be accidental.

Second, identify the information you have that is likely to stimulate those emotions in your listeners. Suppose you have determined that you want your listeners to feel sad about the lack of positive goals or aspirations of the elderly. What information do you have that will show the lack of goals or aspirations? Perhaps you have data from interviews with elderly in which their only talk of the future is the inevitability of death. Perhaps you have accounts of social workers saying that many elderly live totally in the past—that they are reluctant to talk or even think about the future. Or perhaps you have information to show that many nursing homes do very little to give their clients anything to look forward to. These are all examples of the kinds of information that are likely to cause a listener to feel sad.

Third, in practice sessions, try to replace vague, flat sentences that carry no emotional impact with specific, vivid descriptions and explanations. Your first practice sessions are unlikely to use your most specific and vivid language. As you get comfortable with the organization of the speech, you can begin revising the wording. As the following comparison shows, a situation doesn't have to be a deeply emotional one to develop emotional appeal through specific, vivid language.

In an early practice session you might make the following point about the lack of goals and aspirations for the elderly:

> What struck me most about many of the elderly living in nursing homes is their lack of goals. They occupy their time mostly watching television, but they don't pay much attention to it. It's as if they're just passing time.

This explains the point, but there is little in it that would cause a person to feel sad about the lack of goals. Now let's see how you could make the same point but increase its emotional impact.

> What struck me most about many of the elderly living in nursing homes is the emptiness of their lives. They spend much of each day huddled in front of a television set. But they show virtually no involvement, seldom any change in expression, as if what they see is largely unimportant. Their life is largely past; they look forward to nothing. Each day is but a repeat of the past—another hollow experience—that leads inevitably to death.

With just a few changes, mostly the inclusion of phrases that help to create the image of emptiness, you have a much more powerful statement.

As you practice your speech, you should place special emphasis on the wording of your main points. If a speech is well designed, the listeners are most likely to remember the main points, for these are the ideas that are expected to provide the primary reasons for the audience to believe or act as you wish. If listeners do not also feel the power of those main points, you are losing much of their value. Suppose that in a speech in which you want the audience to believe that television commercials are sending negative messages about women's roles, you make the following point:

> Television commercials still portray women primarily as housewives whose major thoughts are restricted to domestic issues.

Although this is a clear statement that may well be remembered, it has very little emotional power. With just a slight revision you could make the point as follows:

> Television commercials still portray women primarily as housewives whose major thoughts are restricted to the comparative cleanliness of their wash and their floors.

This phrasing has a greater chance of stimulating a sense of outrage because the vague phrase "domestic issues" has been replaced by a more vivid image. With a little more thought you might be able to ridicule the silliness of the premises of such commercials and heighten the sense of outrage:

> Tell me, what is a woman's role as seen through the eyes of a television commercial? Primarily as a housewife—a housewife with two deep all-consuming prayers: "Oh, that my clothes will come out white!" and "Oh, that my floors will be spotless!"

Each of the statements makes essentially the same point, but the third example has more staying power because it has more emotional clout.

Writing the Speech Plan

Although you may be able to achieve some success in adapting to your audience without conscious strategic planning, most speakers need to get their strategies down on paper. The speech plan is a written document that includes your strategies for adapting your speech to the audience. The plan should include short statements on each of the subjects of audience interest, knowledge, attitude, perception of credibility, and motivation.

The following sample plan indicates both what should be included and the kinds of statements that are appropriate.

A SAMPLE SPEECH PLAN

1. *Speech goal.* (Write your speech goal in full.) City governments should institute recycling programs to help deal with the problem of waste disposal. (This is a goal designed to establish a belief.)

2. *Audience profile.* (Indicate the key aspects of audience analysis upon which your speech plan is based.) In analyzing my audience, I believe the following are the most significant factors: age (mostly 18 to 20), education (college sophomores and juniors), and group affiliation (combination of business students and communication majors).

3. *Audience interest.* (Include strategies for building and maintaining audience interest.) Since garbage disposal affects everyone, my strategy will be to dramatize the immediacy of the problem through attention-getting examples and statistics. I also hope to build interest through the power of my delivery. I plan to keep my energy level high throughout the speech.

4. *Audience knowledge.* (Include strategies for adapting to audience information levels.) Since I predict that the audience is aware in general of the garbage problem, I have at least some knowledge as a starting point. Still, I believe they are relatively uninformed about the technical aspects of landfills, incineration, and recycling. As a result, I see part of my responsibility as "educating" the audience about the extent of the problem and the real value that can be gained from recycling.

5. *Audience attitude.* (Include strategies for adapting to predicted audience attitude.) Since I believe a majority of my audience is likely to be either uninformed or apathetic, I believe I can move directly to my arguments in favor of recycling.

6. *Speaker credibility.* (Include strategies for building your credibility.) I believe that the good evidence I have in support of my arguments will show my expertise. I hope that from the way I present the information my audience will

see me as honest and sincere about the topic. Since I have been active in personal recycling ventures for two years, I can use my experiences to build my credibility. Moreover, since I strongly believe that recycling is a necessity, I hope that my intentions will be perceived as in the interests of all people. I also hope that my caring attitude and friendly approach will give a positive impression of my personality.

7. *Motivational elements.* (Indicate what you will do to increase your audience's motivation.) Since my audience is likely to be apathetic, I am going to have to do a great deal to motivate them. First, I am going to appeal to safety needs. Since waste buildup can lead to environmental problems, I am going to stress that point. Second, I am going to appeal to belongingness needs. Since we are all members of this community, we should be interested in plans that will improve the environment of the city. Moreover, I believe my enthusiastic delivery will be a further motivating factor.

8. *Organizational plan.* (Justify the organizational plan that you have chosen to adapt to audience attitude and needs.) Since I predict that this audience's attitude is neutral, I believe I can further my cause with a straightforward problem-solution organization. In the problem part of my speech, an objective analysis of the size and seriousness of the problem will lay the groundwork for audience receptivity to a reasonable solution. In discussing the solution I will try to keep recycling in perspective; that is, I will point out that recycling will be a good start in solving the problem but will not solve it entirely.

Summary

A speech plan is a strategy for adapting your speech to a specific audience.

To build audience interest in your speech, you need to emphasize the relevance of your material by showing its timeliness, proximity, and personal effect.

If your audience doesn't have the necessary information to understand your arguments, you need to present sufficient background information without using so much time that you are unable to develop your arguments.

The way you present your information depends in part on whether you perceive your audience to be in favor of your proposal, neutral to it, or opposed to your proposal. If the audience is in favor, you want to put emphasis on the solution to the problem. If your audience is neutral, you want to emphasize good arguments and evidence and motivation. If your audience is opposed, you want to plant the seeds of persuasion.

You build and maintain your credibility by demonstrating your knowledge and expertise, convincing the audience you are trustworthy, demonstrating good intentions, showing a dynamic personality, and behaving ethically.

The major product is your speech plan, in which you (1) write your speech goal, (2) identify the significant features of the audience analysis upon which your speech strategies are based, (3) indicate strategies for building audience interest, (4) indicate strategies for adapting to audience information levels, (5) indicate strategies for adapting to your audience attitude whether they are in favor of, neutral about, or opposed to your goal, (6) indicate strategies for building your audience's perception of your credibility, (7) indicate strategies for motivating your audience, and (8) justify your choice of organizational pattern.

Skill Development Exercises

1. From a recent issue of *Vital Speeches* select the three speeches that are *most* persuasive to you. From each speech find examples of (a) building audience interest in the topic and (b) adapting to audience knowledge.
2. From the content of each speech, would you say that the speakers determined that the audience was in support of, neutral to, or opposed to the goals?
   a. Cite evidence for your opinions.
   b. How, if at all, did the speakers adapt to the supposed attitudes?
3. What, if anything, do the speakers do to build their credibility? Which speaker is most effective? Least effective? Why?
4. Which, if any, of the five methods listed in the text do the speakers use to motivate their audience? Which is the most effective? Why?

Speech Preparation Exercises

Write your speech plan for the first persuasive speaking assignment.

1. Write your speech goal.
2. Indicate the features of your audience analysis that are most significant in drawing conclusions about the audience.
3. Indicate what you plan to do to build audience interest. Include methods of showing timeliness, proximity, and personal effect.
4. Indicate what you plan to do to adapt to the knowledge level of your audience, including what background information you will have to include to orient them.
5. In light of the audience's attitude (in favor, neutral, or opposed), what do you plan to do to adapt to that attitude?
6. Indicate what you plan to do to build your credibility in the speech.

7. Indicate what you plan to do to motivate your audience.
8. What organization do you believe is most appropriate for your speech in light of that attitude?

Study Questions

For each of the following, be prepared to give examples in support of your answers.

1. Suppose you are planning a speech for three audiences, one that is supportive of your goal, one that is uninformed, and one that is hostile. Contrast your overall approaches to these audiences.
2. If your audience knows little about you, explain what you should do in the speech to increase the audience's perception of your credibility.
3. What kinds of things are likely to provide incentives to an audience?
4. What is the goal of a speech plan?

Notes

[1]Mary John Smith, *Persuasion and Human Action* (Belmont, CA: Wadsworth Publishing Co., 1982), pp. 229–230.
[2]John W. Thibaut and Harold H. Kelley, *The Social Psychology of Groups* (New York: Wiley, 1959).

Chapter **8**

Implementing Your Speech Plan: Developing a Persuasive Speaking Style

No matter how strong your plan, your speech will fall on deaf ears if your ideas and feelings don't "get through" to the audience. Much of the burden of implementation falls on your speaking style. Your *style* is your personal use of language combined with your delivery. In this chapter we look at the elements of an effective language style; in the next chapter we will look at the elements of effective delivery.

People are intrigued with those who "have a way with words"; the language master has considerable advantage over those with poorer language skills. You can maximize the power of your presentation through language that is personal, clear, vivid, and emphatic.

Personalizing Your Language

Kenneth Burke, a twentieth-century rhetorical scholar, said, "You persuade a [person] only insofar as you can talk his language by . . . *identifying* your way with his."[1] You begin the identification process by personalizing your language through your use of pronouns, questions, and common experiences.

Using Personal Pronouns. You can begin personalizing your language by always speaking in terms of "you," "us," "we," and "our." To make the point that working women should give up the thought that they can change people who stereotype and dislike them, suppose you said, "The more people try to be accepted by people who don't like them, the more acceptance will elude them—people just can't control what others think." See how much more powerfully Carol Crosthwaite was able to give this advice when she said, "The harder you try to be accepted by these people, the more their acceptance will elude you. You cannot control what they think. Don't waste your time: Focus instead on what you *can* control."[2] Notice that although the only real difference in the two versions is the use of "you," this change alone contributes significantly to personalizing the message.

Asking Rhetorical Questions. Another way of personalizing your language is through the use of *rhetorical questions,* questions that do not expect a direct audience response. Suppose that in your speech analyzing the 1988 presidential campaign, you planned to say, "In the 1988 presidential contest, Michael Dukakis, who appeared to have a clear lead over George Bush in the summer polls, didn't take advantage of that lead in the final stages of the campaign." Look at how much more intriguing the sentence becomes when it is revised to include a question: "When you think of the 1988 presidential contest, you may have asked yourself, 'Why didn't Michael Dukakis, who appeared to have a clear lead over George Bush in the summer polls, take advantage of his lead in the final stages of the campaign?'" Rhetorical questions personalize by stimulating audience participation; once the audience starts participating, it becomes more involved in the content.

You may think that you can be even more effective by asking direct audience questions that seek a verbal response. But because direct audience questions may disrupt your flow of thought (and sometimes bring unexpected answers), the rhetorical question that requires only a mental response is usually safer. Rhetorical questions encourage the same degree of involvement, but they are easier to handle. Rhetorical questions may be used in any part of your speech.

Sharing Common Experiences. A third and especially creative means of establishing a bond between you and your audience is to talk about commonly held experiences in your speeches. Suppose you are talking to a community action group about the satisfaction derived from canvassing voters. You might say, "Remember the hours you put in going from door to door to pass along the message about the problems with the infrastructure? Remember wondering whether the information was really getting through? And do you remember how good it felt to know that the time you put in really paid off?" Recounting common experiences helps to build a bond between you and the audience. Notice also how the common experience is communicated through rhetorical questions and personal pronouns. When members of an audience identify with you as a speaker, they pay more attention to what you have to say.

The following excerpt from a speech by May Bender to the Conference of the Gerontology Institute, in which she makes the point that manufacturers have not considered the convenience of older people in their product design, shows creativity in personalizing experiences:

> When jars and lids start slipping from your hands; when door knobs and drawer handles reach out and catch your clothing to unbalance you; when chairs and stools slip away from you; when you can't reach up high enough to get to your dishes, or packages from an upper shelf; or conversely, when you feel a contraction in your back or a constriction in your legs as you reach under the sink or into too low cabinets; when juice and milk bottles get too heavy . . . to say nothing of detergent bottles and other packs. . . . That's when you realize you've passed the age of total agility. It also makes you realize that too many manufacturers of products, packages, furniture, cabinets and simple ordinary conveniences . . . are *not* so convenience-minded after all.[3]

As you practice wording your arguments, include personal pronouns, rhetorical questions, and common experiences.

Speaking Clearly

A second way of adding power to your speech is to speak clearly. Clarity of language involves speaking precisely, specifically, and without unnecessary clutter.

Speaking precisely means selecting words that create the most accurate depiction of your meaning. Precision begins with being very careful in your use of factual details. Suppose you want your audience to be aware of the number of doctors who have been sued. Instead of saying, "The American Academy of Obstetrics and Gynecology has had a very high percentage of its members sued," notice how much clearer the image becomes if you say, "The American Academy of Obstetrics and Gynecology has had 73 percent of its members sued."[4] In this context "very high" is not precise. The range of what people might see as "very high" is too wide. If you can't be precise because you don't have the information, then try to get the information.

Too often, especially in extemporaneous, or off-the-cuff impromptu comments, speakers tend to get sloppy. They use a word that isn't quite right, hoping that listeners will understand the point anyway. Suppose a speaker says, "The problem lies in marketing." Now "marketing" is a very precise word, but it is the wrong one if the problem is really in advertising.

Precision is especially important when you are trying to communicate a shade of meaning. Suppose you want to make a point about the department director's goal on behalf of a staff member. Notice the change in the perception of the effort if instead of saying, "He's going for a total *acquittal,*" you choose the word "vindication," "justification," or "whitewashing."

Speaking specifically means helping the listener picture a single image. People who don't discipline themselves to think sharply fill their speeches with words that are too general or too abstract to limit choices. For instance, saying "The senator brought several things with him" begins a picture, but it remains vague and fuzzy. Notice how much sharper the picture becomes when the speaker says, "The senator brought an outline of his proposal and the documentation for the figures he was planning to present."

When you select general or abstract words to communicate ideas, you invite confusion. When audiences are confused, they are less likely to be affected by your arguments.

Let's consider another example that contrasts the force of general and specific language. Suppose you wish to make a point about the shortage of teachers in math and science. You could say:

> Here's the problem. We've got a scarcity of teachers in a lot of the sciences—largely because there are more people leaving the profession than starting.

Contrast this imprecise, general statement with the wording of Lauro Cavazos, U.S. Secretary of Education:

> Yet here is a dilemma. Qualified individuals teaching math and science are becoming scarce. Most high school principals say they have a tough time filling teaching slots in physics, chemistry, computer science, and mathematics. In at least one recent year, for every new science or math teacher entering the classroom, 12 left.[5]

How is this statement better? Cavazos begins with the emphasis on the scarcity of "qualified individuals" in "math and science." Then he specifies shortages in "physics, chemistry, computer science, and mathematics." Finally, he makes the scarcity more specific by saying that in a recent year "for every new science or math teacher entering the classroom, 12 left."

Whereas there may be some excuse to lapse into vague, general, and imprecise words in spontaneous conversation, there is no excuse for doing the same in a speech for which you have ample opportunity to consider your wording. For instance, in a first practice session on a speech about the misuse of information, you might say:

> *Newsweek* had the goods to show that Barnes didn't use his information the way he should have.

This sentence gives us very little specific information. Let's be specific—what were his mistakes? In a second practice you might say:

> *Newsweek* gave evidence to show that Barnes had frequently leaked key information to the press and that he had failed to support his superiors when he had information that would do so.

Now we not only know that Barnes made mistakes, but we also know exactly what those mistakes were. This gives the listener a sharper picture as well as the data upon which to judge whether he used information well or not.

You can make ideas more specific by using examples, comparisons, and comparative statistics. Notice how Lauro Cavazos continues to build his argument that "students in this country are not learning much about science and math" through specific examples and comparisons:

> Compare our high school students' achievement to that of their age-mates in other countries. In mathematics, our students consistently come out near the bottom of the heap. The *top* 5 percent of our high school students know less about math than the *average* high school student in Japan.
>
> In science, again, our best high school students—students bound for college—rank near the bottom of a list of 13 countries in chemistry and in physics. In biology, our students finish dead last.[6]

In the following example, May Bender uses comparative statistics to specify her point that designers and developers must know that the population is getting older:

> Surely, they are reading the same demographics which I'm reading. Surely, their conjectures must be the same as mine. They must know that, while "only 1 out of 25 Americans (3 million) were over 65 at the turn of the century," to quote the *Christian Science Monitor,* the nation by 1983 had lost its youthful image as over-65-ers exceeded the teenage population. By 1985, 28.5 million, 1 out of every 8, had crossed the 65-year line. And for year 2020, the Census Bureau projects an over-65 population of approximately 51 million, or about 1 out of every 6 Americans.[7]

Speaking without unnecessary clutter is another aspect of clarity. One of the greatest enemies of building power in speech is the profusion of such verbal clutter as extraneous words, unnecessary repetition of words, repetitious modifiers, and empty adjectives. Not only does clutter crowd out meaning, it also drives listeners up the wall. Although we tolerate clutter in conversation, we are much less likely to accept it in public speeches.

Clutter is particularly noticeable in early stages of rehearsal when speakers grapple with ways to make their points. Suppose a person wants to begin a speech on earthquakes with a reference to the 1989 quake that rocked San Francisco. Her first practice of a speech might be worded like this:

> It was a night to be remembered, but, you know, not for the reasons that most people would be thinking about remembering that night. Instead of remembering it as the night of the third game of the World Series in San Francisco, they would remember it as the night when San Francisco was hit with a really big, I mean huge, earthquake that took *lots* of lives and cost *lots* of money.

This example shows how clutter not only interferes with clarity but also wastes precious speaking time, time needed to develop more important points in the speech. The following example eliminates much of the clutter by replacing vague and general expressions with precise, specific ones:

> October 17, 1989, was a night to be remembered—not for the highly anticipated third game of the World Series, but for a 15-second earthquake that took at least 55 Bay Area lives and caused more than $7 billion in property damage.

As you practice your speeches, you can limit or even eliminate clutter by following these suggestions:

1. Eliminate repetitions that do not add emphasis.
   Wordy: He found that the bill that he supported is not one that he should have supported.
   Better: He found that he should not have supported that bill.
2. Eliminate empty words and phrases—especially meaningless modifiers—that add nothing to the meaning.
   Wordy: Sarah became the leader she is through very, very hard work and a lot of attention to detail.
   Better: Sarah became an accomplished leader through hard work and attention to detail.
3. Boil down long sentences into shorter, harder-hitting sentences.
   Wordy: A few of the people who had become very angry rose to take the opportunity of refuting the arguments set forth by Councilman Roddy.
   Better: A few angry people rose to refute Councilman Roddy's arguments.
4. Combine sentences or simplify phrases and clauses that include the same ideas.
   Wordy: The speeches prepared by Martin Luther King for the period of the 1960s are different from those speeches prepared by other civil rights speakers of the period.
   Better: Martin Luther King's speeches are different from speeches by other civil rights speakers of the 1960s.

How do you practice eliminating clutter? Tape a one- or two-minute segment in which you narrate an event that you witnessed. Perhaps you could talk about a portion of a professor's lecture, or a segment of a game that you saw, or the plot of a situation comedy. Then transcribe your talk and edit it following the guidelines for eliminating repetitions, eliminating empty phrases—those that add nothing to the meaning, boiling down long sentences into shorter, harder-hitting sentences, and combining sentences or simplifying phrases and clauses. Then record another segment describing the same event, but try to concentrate on eliminating the kinds of problems you found in the first exercise.

During your first practice sessions, your speaking may not appear to be natural. You may be concentrating so heavily on speaking without clutter that your meaning may suffer. But the more you practice, the more easily you will find yourself reducing clutter.

Improvement in speeches should come naturally as a result of improvement in practice. Just as an athlete works on skills in practice but concentrates on the game in competition, so you should stress words in practice but concentrate on your ideas and on the audience when you are giving a speech. Nevertheless, if practice is successful, you will find yourself able to monitor even public speaking without conscious effort.

Portraying Ideas Vividly

Perhaps the most important way of adding power to your language style is through a vivid portrayal of ideas. The two major benefits of speaking vividly are that you increase the audience's retention and you trigger an emotional reaction. In your own experience you have vivid memories of happenings, events, experiences, or accidents that had a highly emotional impact. Perhaps you remember falling from a ladder or your first kiss. Effective speakers can create this kind of impact through vivid anecdotes, illustrations, and examples. The more vivid you make your development, the more powerful the emotional impact will be. Too much repetition can become boring, but audiences seldom tire of those kinds of development that have emotional impact.

Vivid means full of life, vigorous, bright, and intense. If your language is vivid, your audience can picture your meanings in striking detail. Consider the following two sentences:

> Don't feel a need to talk forcefully, just make sure that you have the military might to back up your words.
> Speak softly, but carry a big stick!

The first sentence is clear; the second is vivid. Vividness gives language staying power, makes it memorable.

Vivid speech is the result of creative thought. If you have a striking mental picture, you are more likely to communicate a vivid picture to your audience.

One way of creating vividness is to use specific words that form sharp mental pictures. In his speech on integrity, notice how Ronald Roskens, president of the University of Nebraska, vivifies his point that people have been apathetic in their reaction to excesses that are detrimental to society:

> Excess, the traveling companion of moral malaise, has been tolerated, excused, ignored and otherwise buried for some time in our national life. The flotsam and jetsam of "It's OK, it doesn't matter" tends to collect layer upon layer until at last it bubbles to the surface at some inconvenient time, all toxic and sulphurous.[8]

In addition to emphasizing "tolerated" with the synonyms "excused" and "ignored," the words "bubbles to the surface," "toxic," and "sulphurous" portray an image that is hard to ignore.

If you can't seem to develop a wording that is just right, you may find a vivid quotation to use. In his speech, "Lawyers and Lawyering," Richard Lamm lets his quotation vivify his point that the legal system is the cause of great costs to American society:

> Litigation is having a traumatic effect on American society. Lawrence H. Silberman, formerly a deputy attorney general of the United States, said, "The legal process, because of its unbridled growth, as become a cancer which threatens the vitality of our form of capitalism in democracy."[9]

Lamm's word choices of "unbridled growth," "cancer," and "threatens the vitality" vividly make the point that "litigation is having a *traumatic* effect."

A third way you can make your ideas more vivid is through imagery. Imagery occurs through precise of word choice, specific/concrete language, and figurative language. What is basic to all figures of speech is imaginative comparison, the likening of two dissimilar things. For instance, in the sentence, "The stock market is like a turbulent sea with sharp ups and downs coming with no visible warning," the basic comparison is between the stock market and a turbulent sea, two entities that are unlike each other in most ways.

In his analysis of language, Walter Nash identifies more than 20 figures of syntax and semantics.[10] The figures that you are most likely to make use of in your speeches are simile and metaphor.

Simile. Perhaps the easiest form of comparison to create is the simile, a direct comparison of dissimilar things recognized by the use of "like" or "as." Suppose you want to express the following thought, "Telling a lie about a person can really hurt that person's reputation." Notice how much more vivid the image is when the idea is expressed in a simile: "The telling of a lie wounds one like the sear of a bullet."[11] How do you form similes? Take the subject and ask yourself, What is it like? For instance, suppose you are upset that newspaper reporters are attacking politicians rather than keeping an eye on what they were doing. You could ask yourself, Under these circumstances, what is the press like? Then you might think of this:

> The press was acting, many times, like mad dogs rather than watch dogs.[12]

Let's consider a few additional examples of vivid similes.

> Canada and the United States are major trading partners. We are tied together like Siamese twins at the 49th parallel.[13]

> Most of you have watched the gyrations of major world stock markets for the past three weeks. They followed each other up and down like squirrels playing in the park.[14]

> The constitution was like a skeleton; it had to be turned into a living being or document.[15]

These final two similes are a little more complex, but perhaps even more powerful:

> Tooth decay, which stretches back to prehistoric times, cutting across human history like a painful scar, doesn't even exist in a third of American children today.[16]

> Watching public school teachers send their children to private schools is "like sitting in a restaurant and watching the chef go next door to eat."[17]

Although similes are easy to think of, be careful of relying on cliches (It's as big as the outdoors; He's quick as a fox), figurative expressions that have been so overused that they have lost much of their power.

Metaphor. The second most common type of figurative language is the metaphor. Although metaphors are much like similes, they have one important difference. Instead of building a direct comparison with "like" or "as," they build an identification: instead of saying that an object is *like* another, you say it *is* the other. How do you construct a metaphor? Begin with a word and then brainstorm various images that come into your mind. For instance, start with the question, What is *human creativity*? You might then brainstorm some of the following: "creativity is a light bulb that suddenly turns on" or "creativity is an idea that is turbocharged." Perhaps as you brainstorm you will develop an image as fresh as the following: "Human creativity is a spark struck from the fiery creativity of God himself."[18]

The following are additional examples of metaphor:

> I have come to tell you today that I have found another "underground railroad" in America. This time it's helping inner-city youth all across this country escape the slavery imposed on them by traditional mass education in our inner cities. It

is helping them escape these modern plantations of desolation so they can later return and build stronger communities.[19]

In effect the Baker plan has created a three-ring circus involving the private banks, the MDB's, and the debtor governments, but there has been no ringmaster to weave these separate shows together into an effective whole.[20]

We are sailing into a whole new and much more volatile world of public policy. Specifically I believe we are heading for shoals. I believe we can navigate around them, I believe we can change course: but unless we change course in some important areas we shall crash into the future.[21]

Emphasizing Ideas

Ideas are more likely to affect belief and motivate action when they are emphasized. Although what your audience will remember is not entirely in your control, you can attempt to guide audience retention through careful use of repetition and transition.

If you leave it up to listeners to decide which words and ideas are most important, they may select the wrong ones. You are the speaker; you should know what you want to emphasize. How can you do it? Although you can emphasize with your voice and body, in this section we want to consider how you can emphasize with wording by means of proportion, repetition, and transitions.

Emphasizing Through Proportion

Proportion means spending more time on one point than on another. If a speaker devotes five minutes to the president's role as head of the executive branch and only two minutes each to the president's roles as head of the party and commander in chief of the armed forces, the audience will assume that the role as head of the executive branch is the most important.

To help the audience perceive the importance of a point, you can add examples or an illustration to build its strength. If the point really is important, you should have enough material to use to build it.

Although proportioning is effective by itself, it may be too subtle for some audiences. Consequently, you should also consider emphasizing crucial ideas through repetition and transitions.

Emphasizing Through Repetition

Deliberate—as opposed to wordy—repetition is one of the easiest ways to emphasize an idea. If you say, "There are 500 steps—that's 500," a listener will probably perceive the repetition as an indication that the point should be remembered. Repetition is widely used because it is relatively easy to practice and quite effective.

If you want the audience to remember your exact word, then you can repeat it once or twice: "The number is 572638—that's 5, 7, 2, 6, 3, 8" or "A ring-shaped coral island almost or completely surrounding a lagoon is called an atoll—the word is atoll."

If you want the audience to remember an idea but not necessarily the specific language, you may restate it rather than repeat it. Whereas repetition is the exact use of the same words, restatement means echoing the same idea but in different words. For instance, "The population is 975,439—that's roughly 1 million people" or "The test will be composed of about four essay questions; that is, all the questions on the test will be the kind that require you to discuss material in some detail."

Emphasizing Through Transitions

An even more imaginative way of emphasizing is through transitions. *Transitions* are the words, phrases, and sentences that show idea relationships. Transitions summarize, clarify, forecast, and in almost every instance emphasize. The value of a transition is that it calls special attention to particular words and ideas. You can use transitions to accent shifts in meaning, degree of emphasis, and movement from one idea to another.

Internal Transitions. Internal transitions are words and phrases that link parts of a sentence in ways that help people to see the relationships among the parts. In the following sets of sentences, notice how the relationships between ideas are clarified and emphasized through the use of internal transition words in the second phrasings.

> Miami gets a lot of rain. Phoenix does not.
> Miami gets a lot of rain, *but* Phoenix does not. (or) *Although* Miami gets a lot of rain, Phoenix does not.
> You should donate money to United Way. It will make you feel better.
> You should donate money to United Way *because* it will make you feel better.
> Buckeye Savings is in good financial shape. Buckeye pays high interest.
> Buckeye Savings is in good financial shape; *moreover,* it pays high interest.

Our language contains many words that show idea relationships. Although the following list is not complete, it contains many of the common transition words and phrases that are appropriate in a speech. You can use words like "also," "likewise," "in addition to," and "moreover" to add material; words like "therefore," "and so," "finally," and "on the whole" to add up consequences, to summarize, or to show results; words like "but," "however," "yet," "on the other hand," and "although" to indicate changes in direction, concessions, or a return to a previous position; words like "because" and "for" to indicate reasons; words like "then," "since," and "as" to show causal or time relationships; and words like "in fact," "in other words," and "that is to say" to explain, exemplify, or limit.

External Transitions. External transitions are complete sentences that are placed between major sections of a speech to call attention to shifts in meaning, degree of emphasis, and movement from one idea to another. External transitions tell the audience exactly how it should respond.

First, external transitions act like a tour guide leading the audience through the speech. You use them because you do not want to take a chance that the audience might miss something. Speakers make use of the following kinds of statements:

(At the start of the body of the speech) This speech will have three major parts.

(After a main heading in a speech in which you are showing how to refinish antique furniture) Now that we see what the ingredients are, let's move on to the second step: stripping the surface.

Second, external transitions can announce the importance of a particular word or idea. You know which ideas are most important, most difficult to understand, or most significant. If you level with the audience and state that information, the audience will know how to react. For instance, you might say any of the following:

Now I come to the most important idea in the speech.
If you don't remember anything else from this presentation, make sure you re-
    member this.
But maybe I should say this again because it is so important.
Pay particular attention to this idea.

These examples represent only a few of the possible expressions that interrupt the flow of ideas and interject keys, clues, and directions to stimulate audience memory or understanding.

Avoiding Inappropriate Language

Under strain, or in your eagerness to make a point, you may sometimes say things you do not really mean or express feelings in language that is unlikely to be accepted by your listeners. If you do that, you may lose all that you have gained.

Effect of Inappropriate Language

You have heard children shout, "Sticks and stones may break my bones, but words will never hurt me." I think this rhyme is so popular among children because they know it is a lie, but they do not know what else to do. Whether we are willing to admit it or not, words do hurt—sometimes permanently. Think of the great personal damage done to individuals throughout history as a result of being called "hillbilly," "nigger," "wop," "yid." Think of the fights started by one person calling another's sister or girlfriend a "whore." Of course, we all know that it is not the words alone that are so powerful; it is the context of the words—the situation, the feelings about the participants, the time, the place, the tone of voice. You may recall circumstances in which a friend called you a name or used a four-letter word to describe you and you did not even flinch; you may also recall other circumstances in which someone called you something far less offensive and you became enraged.

The message to remember is that we must always be aware that language may have accidental repercussions. When we do not understand the frame of reference of the audience, we may state our ideas in language that distorts the intended communication. Many times a single inappropriate sentence may be enough to ruin an entire speech. For instance, if you say, "And we all know the problem originates downtown," you may be referring to the city government. However, if the audience is composed of people who see downtown not as the seat of government but as the residential area of an ethnic or social group, the sentence may have an entirely different meaning to them. Being specific helps you avoid such problems; recognizing that some words communicate far more than their dictionary meanings helps even more.

I must also caution against using words like "genocide" for their shock value. Such language often backfires on the user. Arousing anger and hostility toward an issue often results in anger and hostility toward the speaker.

Avoiding inappropriate language requires sensitivity to an audience's feelings. Some of the mistakes we make result from using expressions that are perceived as sexist or racist. Although the speaker may be totally unaware of being offensive, the audience may take legitimate offense.

Sexist, Racist, and Other Unfair Language

Sexist, racist, and other unfair language is any language that is perceived as belittling any person or group of people by virtue of their sex, race, age, handicap, or other characteristic. Three of the most prevalent linguistic uses that result in unfair perceptions are nonequal language, nonparallel language, and stereotyping.

Nonequal Language

Nonequal language is exclusionary; that is, it involves eliminating a sex or race, grammatically or connotatively. Let's consider some examples.

Generic "He." Traditional English grammar calls for the use of the masculine pronoun "he" to stand for the entire class of humans regardless of sex. So standard English calls for such usage as "When a person shops, he should have a clear idea of what he wants to buy." Even though these constructions are grammatically correct, since they contain an inherent bias, they are by definition sexist.

Guideline: Do not construct sentences that use male pronouns when no sexual reference is intended. You can often avoid the dilemma by using plurals. For instance, instead of saying "Since a doctor has high status, his views may be believed regardless of topic," you could say, "Since doctors have high status, their views may be believed regardless of topic." The change may seem small, but it may be the difference between persuading or failing to persuade an audience.

Generic "Man." A second example of exclusion results from the reliance on the use of the generic "man." Many words that are inherently sexist have become a common part of our language. Look at the term "man-made." What this means is that a product was produced by human beings rather than by machines, but what it says to many people is that a masculine human being was involved. Using such terms in speaking about human beings in general is bad enough; using them to describe actions done by women (as in the sentence, "Sally is particularly proud of her pies because they are totally man-made) becomes ludicrous.

Guideline: Avoid using words that have built-in sexism, such as "policeman," "postman," "chairman," "man-made," and "mankind." For most expressions of this kind you can use or create suitable alternatives. For instance, for the first three examples you can use "police officer," "mail carrier," and "chairperson." For "man-made" and "mankind" you can change the constructions. For "All of mankind benefits," you might say, "All the people in the world benefit." For "The products are man-made," you might say "The products are made entirely by hand" (or by people or by human beings).

Nonparallel Language

Nonparallel language is also belittling. Two common forms of nonparallelism are marking and destructive word pairings.

Marking. *Marking* means adding sex, race, age, or other designations unnecessarily to a general word. For instance, "doctors" is a word that represents all people with medical degrees. To describe Jones as a doctor is to treat Jones linguistically as a member of the class of doctors. You might say, "Jones, a doctor, contributed a great deal to the campaign." If, however, you said, "Jones, a female doctor" (or a black doctor, or an aging doctor, or a handicapped doctor), you would be marking. By marking, you are trivializing the person's role by laying emphasis on an irrelevant characteristic of the person. If you say, "Jones is a really good female doctor" (or black doctor, or old doctor, or handicapped doctor), you may be intending to praise Jones. In reality, your audience can interpret the sentence as meaning that Jones is a good doctor for a female (or a black, an old person, or a handicapped person), but not necessarily good compared to a male.

Guideline: Avoid markers by treating all groups alike. If it is appropriate to identify the person by sex, race, age, and so on, do so, but leave such markers out of your labeling when they are irrelevant. One test of whether a characteristic is relevant and appropriate is to ask whether you would mention the person's sex, race, or age (etc.) regardless of what sex, race, or age the person happens to be. It is relevant to specify "female doctor," for example, only if in that context it would be equally relevant to specify "male doctor." If you need to label a person as a doctor, teacher, athlete, or politician, do so, but leave sex, race, and other markers out of your labeling.

Unnecessary Association. Another form of nonparallelism is to emphasize someone's association with another person when you are not talking about that other person. Very often you hear a speaker say, "Gladys Thompson, whose husband is CEO of Procter & Gamble, is the chairperson for this year's United Way campaign." You might say that the association of Gladys Thompson with her husband is one of her credentials. But using the association seems to imply that Gladys Thompson is important not in herself but because of her relationship with her husband. The following is a more flagrant example of unnecessary association: "Dorothy Jones, the award-winning principal at Central High School and wife of Bill Jones, a local contractor, is chairperson for this year's United Way campaign." Here Bill Jones's occupation and relationship to Dorothy Jones are clearly irrelevant.

In either case the pairing takes away from the person who is supposed to be the focus. For instance, I recall reading such statements as "Robin Smith, wife of dancer Fred Astaire, was one of the leading jockeys at Belmont Park this year." Fred Astaire was certainly a famous person, but what did he have to do with Robin Smith's riding success? Again, the test of parallel treatment is whether you would do the same thing for all people. How often do you see statements such as "Fred Astaire, husband of Robin Smith, a leading jockey, is starring in a new made-for-television movie"?

Guideline: Avoid associating a person irrelevantly with his or her partner. If the person has done or said something noteworthy, it should stand alone.

Stereotyping

Stereotyping consists of assigning characteristics to a person solely on the basis of class or category. Stereotyping represents a shortcut in thinking. By developing an attitude or belief about an entire group and then applying that attitude to every member of the group, a person no longer has to consider the potential for individual differences—the stereotypic view applies to all persons in the group. It provides some people with a certain comfort to talk about social issues in a way that states or implies that blacks are lazy, Italians are naturally hot-headed, old people are cantankerous, and white Americans are racist.

Guideline: Avoid making statements that treat groups of people as if they can be identified by the same characteristics. If you must make value judgments about people, make them about a specific individual, and make the statement without reference to any group of people to which the person may be associated.

Very few people manage to avoid all unfair language. By monitoring your usage, however, you can guard against frustrating your communication by assuming that others will react to your language the same way you do, and you can guard against saying or doing things that offend others and perpetuate outdated sex roles, racial stereotypes, and other unfair language.

Summary

Your style is your personal use of language combined with your delivery. You can maximize the power of your style by using language that is personal, clear, vivid, and emphatic.

Your overall language goal is to develop a personal oral style that captures your uniqueness. You personalize your language by using personal pronouns, audience questions, and allusions to shared experiences.

Ideas are clarified through precise, specific language that is devoid of clutter. Precise words are those that accurately depict your meaning. Specific words are those that call up a single image. You can eliminate clutter by eliminating repetitions that do not add emphasis, avoiding empty phrases, boiling down long sentences into shorter, harder-hitting sentences, and combining sentences and phrases that express like ideas.

Vividness means full of life, vigorous, bright, and intense. One way of increasing vividness is to use specific words that form sharp mental pictures.

Another way is to use vivid quotations. The third way is to create verbal images using figurative language, especially similes and metaphors.

Emphasis means giving certain words and ideas more importance than others. One way of emphasizing is through proportion, spending more time on one point than another. A second way is through repetition. A third way is through transitions, words and phrases that show relationships between ideas.

Inappropriate language can be minimized by avoiding such exclusionary usages as generic "he" and "man," by eliminating such nonparallel usages as marking and unnecessary association, and by avoiding stereotyping.

Skill Development Exercises

1. From a recent issue of *Vital Speeches* select the three speeches that are *most* persuasive to you. From each speech find examples of personalizing and precise and/or specific, vivid, and emphatic language.
2. Write a short factual paragraph about an event, place, or person. Then, using the same facts, first write a paragraph that discusses the person, place, or event from a positive perspective and then write a paragraph from a negative perspective. Don't change the basic facts, only the means of expressing them. For instance, based on the same information, Tom may be described as a sharp-tongued political satirist or as a mean-spirited backstabber.
3. Select an instructor whose language style you consider to be above average and one whose language style you consider to be below average. As you listen, make notes on their word choice, clarity, vividness, and means of verbal emphasis. Contrast them; be specific.
4. Consult a book like Roget's *Thesaurus* and compile a list of words that have meanings similar to each word given here:
   concealed
   cunning
   exciting
   mistake
   stated

Speech Preparation Exercises

1. During a speech practice period, record the development of one point of the speech you are planning to give.
   a.   Identify places where you use language well.

b.   Select three sentences that were bland, imprecise, wordy, or otherwise mediocre. Edit them.
2.   Re-record the same portion. How much were you able to improve?

Study Questions

For each of the following, be prepared to give examples in support of your
answers.

1.   How do rhetorical questions differ from direct questions?
2.   What are the qualities and characteristics that are likely to personalize
your language?
3.   Contrast simile and metaphor. In what ways are they alike? How do they
differ?
4.   Of the ways that you can use language to emphasize, which is likely to be
the most successful? Explain.
5.   Why is "marking" considered to be an inappropriate use of language?
6.   Can language alone influence an audience's perception of ideas, people,
and places?

Notes

[1]Kenneth Burke, A *Rhetoric of Motives* (New York: Prentice-Hall, Inc., 1950), p. 55.
[2]Carol Crosthwaite, "Working in a Man's World: Are Women Making Progress?" *Vital Speeches*, January 1, 1986, p. 179.
[3]May Bender, "Packaging for the Older Consumer," *Vital Speeches*, June 1, 1987, p. 490.
[4]Richard D. Lamm, "Lawyers and Lawyering," *Vital Speeches*, January 15, 1989, p. 208.
[5]Lauro E. Cavazos, "The Huge Problem in American Schools," *Vital Speeches*, February 1, 1989, p. 237.
[6]Ibid., p. 236.
[7]Bender, p. 491.
[8]Ronald W. Roskens, "Integrity," *Vital Speeches*, June 1, 1989, p. 511.
[9]Lamm, p. 207.
[10]Walter Nash, *Rhetoric: The Wit of Persuasion* (Cambridge, MA: Basil Blackwell Ltd., 1989), pp. 110–129.
[11]Benjamin Alexander, "Before You Lambast This Generation," *Vital Speeches*, November 15, 1987, p. 71.
[12]Earl R. Hutchinson, Sr., "To Kill a Messenger," *Vital Speeches*, July 1, 1987, p. 573.
[13]Grant Devine, "Canadian–United States Trade," *Vital Speeches*, November 15, 1987, p. 77.
[14]Ben Craig, "Financial Globalization," *Vital Speeches*, February 1, 1988, p. 232.
[15]Diane Pikcunas, "The United States Constitution," *Vital Speeches*, February 1, 1988.
[16]James Saddoris, "Your Professional Organization: A Tool for the Future," *Vital Speeches*, October 1, 1987, p. 768.

[17]David T. Kearns, "Economics and the Student," *Vital Speeches*, July 1, 1986, p. 566.
[18]William E. Simon, "Liberty to All," *Vital Speeches*, October 15, 1987, p. 8.
[19]Joan Davis Ratteray, "Escape to Freedom," *Vital Speeches*, June 1, 1987, p. 497.
[20]John J. La Falce, "The Third World Debt Crisis," *Vital Speeches*, January 1, 1987, p. 163.
[21]Richard D. Lamm, "The Ten Commandments of an Aging Society," *Vital Speeches*, December 15, 1987, p. 134.

Chapter **9**

Implementing Your Speech Plan: Developing a Persuasive Delivery

The second component of a speech style is delivery. *Delivery* refers to the use of voice and bodily action in presenting the speech. In his major work, *De Orator,* Cicero said, "Delivery, I assert, is the dominant factor in oratory."[1] Although the best use of voice and bodily action will not save a bad speech, if all other aspects of the speech are of high quality, it is through the delivery that audiences receive the maximum value of the speech.

Curiously, many speakers hold an "I am what I am" attitude about speaking. This suggests that the "persona" they present to their audience is largely out of their control. This naive view dooms speakers to failure. Although few speakers take advantage of the potential power of delivery, the elements of developing a positive delivery style are not that difficult to learn. Effective persuaders are likely to speak enthusiastically, maintain audience contact, vocalize expressively, articulate clearly, gesture meaningfully, and practice diligently.

Speak Enthusiastically

First, and perhaps most important, you need to practice until you can speak enthusiastically. *Enthusiasm* is a state of mind, a feeling of excitement you have about the value of your message that is reflected in the sound of your voice. Enthusiasm may be the single most important element of an effective delivery style, for the persuasive speaker who is enthusiastic is likely to generate that same enthusiasm in the audience.[2]

If you don't seem to show much enthusiasm in your delivery, ask yourself the following questions: (1) Are you really committed to your speech goal? Whereas an outgoing person might be able to generate enthusiasm for an uninspiring topic, the reserved person probably cannot. If your goal doesn't excite you, change it. (2) Are you psychologically involved in the material? Focus on *why* you care about the topic. Mental activity leads to physical activity. If you can rekindle your initial excitement for wanting to accomplish your goal, your voice is likely to show your enthusiasm. (3) Will believing or acting as you suggest really benefit the audience? If you are convinced that it is in the audience's best interests to listen, that thought may raise your level of enthusiasm.

Maintain Eye Contact

A second powerful element is surprisingly simple—maintain eye contact with the audience at all times. *Eye contact* involves looking at various groups of people in all parts of your audience throughout your speech. So long as you are looking at people (at times at those in front of you, at times at those in the left-hand rear of the room, at times at those in the right center of the room, etc.) and not at your notes or at the ceiling, the floor, or out the window, *everyone* in the audience will perceive you as having good eye contact. Don't let your eyes linger too long on those immediately in front of you. The people at the ends of the aisles and those in the back of the room are every bit as important as those in front.

Maintaining eye contact is important for several reasons. First, eye contact helps you hold audience attention. You establish a bond of communication with your audience. Your eye contact says to your audience, "This message is for you." When members of your audience perceive that they are part of the communication process, they become involved—they look back at you. When an audience's visual attention is directed toward you, their mental attention is likely to follow.

Second, eye contact increases the audience's confidence in you. Just as you are likely to be skeptical of people who do not look you in the eye when they are conversing with you, so too are audiences skeptical of speakers who do not look at them. Eye contact is perceived as a sign of sincerity.

Perhaps most important, by maintaining eye contact you gain insight into the audience's reaction to what you are saying. Since communication is two-way, your audience is responding to you at the same time you are speaking to them. In conversation, the audience's response is likely to be both verbal and nonverbal; in public speaking, the response is more likely to be shown by nonverbal cues alone. Audiences that are paying attention are likely to be looking at you with varying amounts of intensity. Audiences that are not paying attention are likely to be yawning, looking out the window, and slouching in their chairs. By monitoring the audience's behavior, you can determine what adjustments, additions, and deletions you need to make in your plans. The greater your speaking skill, the more and better use you can make of the information you are getting from your audience through your eye contact.

Vocalize Expressively

The third source of power, vocal expressiveness, is equally important but a little more difficult to accomplish. Although enthusiasm and eye contact hold audience attention and build your credibility, it is your vocal expressiveness that affects the meanings your audience gets from your speech. Your voice is a product of four components: pitch (the notes of the scale that you use with your voice), volume (loudness), rate (speed), and quality (the tone or sound of your voice). The effective persuader understands that individually these have only a marginal effect on audience understanding. For instance, a speaker who speaks 130 words per minute is not necessarily any more understandable than a speaker who speaks 190 words per minute. Meaning is affected not by the individual components of voice but by how they are used together. For instance, the sentence "The president must use his power to affect Congress" has different meanings depending on whether the word "president," "use," "power," or "Congress" is emphasized. Emphasis is determined by variations in pitch, volume, rate, quality, or some combination of these.

Effective speakers make sure they get the most out of every sentence they deliver. To make the most of your delivery you must be sure that your voice is achieving what it should. Powerful words lose most of their force if they are not delivered expressively. For instance, in the passage, "It's for the benefit of the *people* they say? *We* are the people—*we* are the ones to decide who's *benefiting.*" If the italicized words are not well emphasized, the ideas lose their meaning.

Before you make any judgments about your delivery, you need to analyze your vocal methods. You can do the analysis yourself by listening to a tape recording of a portion of a practice session or you can use a partner to help you determine your relative effectiveness.

Your analysis should have two goals: to determine (1) whether your voice is expressive and (2) whether your expression is well used to maximize audience understanding. If you tape your speech, listen carefully and make notes. If you choose to use a partner, ask the person to tell you which words are higher/lower in pitch, louder/softer, or faster/slower. When you can speak in such a way that the person recognizes which words you were emphasizing, you will be using vocal expressiveness effectively.

Our voices may work against an audience's attention. For instance, people do not enjoy listening to a voice that is perceived as being too high in pitch, too fast or too slow, too loud or too soft. And people do not enjoy listening when a voice has unpleasant qualities: harshness, nasality, or hoarseness, for example. These have the same effect as trying to read words on a page that are blurred, too small, or crammed together.

Although it is possible that your voice may be perceived as too high or low on the scale, too loud or too soft, too fast or too slow, or unpleasant, it is far more likely that the audience perceives your voice as monotonous or peppered with interferences.

Speaking in a Monotone

A *monotone* is the perception that pitch, volume, and rate are all on virtually the same level throughout the speech. I say the "perception" for in reality very few people speak in a true monotone. Even when some slight variations of voice are present, however, audiences may still perceive the speech as monotonous.

A variation of the true monotone is the use of a monotonous pattern, a melody pattern in which vocal variation is the same for every sentence regardless of meaning. This pattern is nearly as detrimental as a true monotone. For example, you might end every sentence with an upward pitch or go up in pitch in the middle and down at the end of every phrase. Changes in pitch, volume, and rate do not help communicate meaning unless they are appropriate to that intended meaning. To cure a monotonous pattern, you have to learn to correlate changes in voice with meaning.

People perceive monotonous speech as "hard" to listen to. Although there is no reason a person cannot listen to monotonous speech, most people *choose* not to. Monotonous speech *bores* us. When we become bored, our attention is likely to go elsewhere. Thus, when a person says, "Senator Jones has not lived up to his promises to the poor," the audience must perceive an emphasis on "has not" or the sentence lacks sufficient force to make the point. Stop for a minute and say the sentence aloud: "Senator Jones has not lived up to his promises to the poor." What happened? To maximize the power of the sentence, the words "has not" should be louder, with "not" on a higher note of the scale than the other words. Likewise, the word "poor" should be somewhat louder and slightly higher in pitch.

If you did not notice those differences, then you need to practice to create them.

Vocal Interferences

A second problem of voice is the peppering of speech with such vocal interferences as "uh," "er," "well," and "OK," as well as those nearly universal interrupters of thought, "you know" and "like."

The "you know" habit may begin as people seek to find out whether what they are saying is already known by others. For some, "you know" may be a source of identification; some people seek to show that they and those to whom they are talking have common knowledge as a binding element. For most people, however, the flooding of sentences with "you know" is just a bad habit, resulting in such abominations as: "You know, Maxwell is, you know, a good, you know, lecturer."

Similarly, the use of "like" may start from making comparisons such as "He's hot; he looks like Tom Cruise." Soon the comparisons become shortened as in "He's, like, really hot!" Finally, the use of "like" becomes pure filler: "Like, he's really cool, like, I can't really explain it, but I'll tell you he's, like, wow!"

Curiously, no matter how irritating the use of "you know" or "like" may be, listeners are unlikely to acknowledge their irritation. Seldom, if ever, do people say openly to others, "Your use of 'you know' or 'like' at every break in thought is really very annoying to me." If it seems appropriate, you might start pointing out this irritant in others' speech; most important, you should request others to tell you whether you are an offender.

In the normal give and take of conversation, even the most fluent speakers may throw in an occasional "uh" or "you know"; few people can completely avoid their use. Interferences become a problem when they are perceived by others as excessive, when they begin to call attention to themselves and prevent a person from concentrating on meaning. These interferences become especially detrimental to public-speaking effectiveness. With some practice you can limit their occurrence in your speech. Remember, although people may not be willing to tell you, they are likely to be distracted or irritated by your interferences. So what do you do? Try these suggestions:

1. Train yourself to hear your interferences. Even people with a major problem seem unaware of the interferences they use. You can train your ears by

tape-recording yourself talking for several minutes about any subject—the game you saw yesterday, the course you plan to take next term, or anything else that comes to mind. Before you play it back, estimate the number of times you used interferences. Then compare the actual number with your estimate. As your ears become trained, your estimates will be closer to the actual number.

Another way to train yourself is to have a close friend listen to you and raise a hand every time you say "like" or "you know." You may find the experience traumatic or nerve-racking, but your ear will soon start to pick up the interferences as fast as the listener does.

2. Practice to see how long you can go without using a vocal interference. If you can learn to practice without vocal clutter, you will do better in your speeches. Set up practice periods two or three times a week. Start out by trying to talk for 15 seconds. Continue to increase the time until you can talk for two minutes without using an interference. Meaning may suffer; you may spend a disproportionate amount of time avoiding interferences. Still, it is good practice.

During practice sessions, your speaking may not seem natural. You will concentrate so heavily on speaking without interferences that meaning may suffer. Eventually, however, you will speak more naturally and listen for and eliminate interferences. As your speaking becomes less cluttered, create practice situations that may ordinarily lead to increases in clutter. If you lapse into vocal interferences when you are under pressure, mentally re-create situations where you are required to speak under pressure. Likewise, if interferences occur when you are speaking to people in authority, create practice situations where you are speaking to your parents, college professors, city officials, and so forth.

3. Mentally note your use of vocal interferences in your speeches. You will be making real headway when you can reduce clutter in actual speaking situations, but don't worry about trying too hard in speeches. Improvement in speeches should come naturally as a result of improvement in practice. If practice is successful, you will find yourself able to monitor even public speaking *without* conscious effort.

Articulate and Pronounce Words Correctly

Effective speakers articulate and pronounce words correctly. *Articulation* is the shaping of speech sounds into recognizable oral symbols that go together to produce a word; *pronunciation* is the form and accent of various syllables of words. Sloppy articulation and mispronunciation can have negative effects on an audience's response to your speech.

Although there are people with real articulation or pronunciation problems, most speakers suffer from sloppiness. They either slur sounds (run sounds and words together) or leave off word endings. Some running together of sounds is normal. For instance, everyone says "tha table" for "that table." It is just too difficult to make two *t* sounds in a row. But many of us slur sounds and drop word endings excessively with such utterances as "Wutcha doon?"

If you believe that you slur sounds or drop endings so much that audiences have a difficult time understanding you, you can improve considerably by taking 10 to 15 minutes three days a week to read passages aloud, trying to *overaccentuate* each of the sounds. For instance, with the sentence "Has she dropped her option, or is she going to begin construction?" you will want to make sure you articulate the *t* sound at the end of "dropped," the *ing* sound at the end of "going," and the *c* sound in the middle of "construction."

Use Bodily Action Effectively

Effective speakers use bodily action to enhance meaning. Bodily actions should have the same value to you in communicating meaning in a speech as they do in normal conversation. Unfortunately when people get in front of an audience they tend to freeze up—that is, they limit their normal nonverbal behavior—and occasionally show nervous mannerisms that are not so noticeable in their daily speaking. If you are thinking actively about what you are saying, your bodily action is likely to be appropriate. If your bodily action is too stilted or too animated (very unlikely), your professor can give you some pointers. We all have minor problems. You should not be concerned unless your bodily action calls attention to itself.

The variables of bodily action are facial expression, gestures, posture, and movement that affects meaning.

Facial expression refers to the movement of the eyes and mouth. The eyes and mouth communicate far more than you might realize. You need only recall the icy stare, the warm smile, or the hostile scowl that you received from someone to understand the statement that the eyes (and the mouth as well) are the mirror of the mind. Your facial expression should be appropriate to what you are saying. Audiences respond negatively to deadpan expressions and perpetual grins or scowls; they respond positively to honest and sincere expressions that reflect your thoughts and feelings. Think actively about what you are saying, and your face will probably respond accordingly.

Gestures are the movements of hands, arms, and fingers. Gestures are usually descriptive or emphatic. When speakers say, "about this high" or "nearly this round," we expect to see a gesture accompany the verbal description. Likewise, when speakers say, "We want you" or "Now is the time to act," we look for a pointing finger, pounding fist, or some other gesture that reinforces the point. If you gesture in conversation, you will usually gesture in speech. If you do not gesture in conversation, it is probably best not to force yourself to gesture in a speech. Try to leave your hands free at all times to help you "do what comes naturally." If you clasp them behind you, grip the sides of the speaker's stand, or put your hands into your pockets, you will not be able to gesture even if you want to.

If you wonder what to do with your hands at the start of the speech so they do not seem conspicuous, you may either rest them on the speaker's stand partially clenched or hold them relaxed at your sides—perhaps with one arm slightly bent at the elbow. Once you begin the speech, forget about your hands; they will be free for appropriate gestures. If, however, you discover that you have folded your arms in front of you or clasped them behind you, put them back in one of the two original positions. After you have spoken a few times, your professor will suggest whether you need to be more expressive or somewhat restrained with your hands and arms.

Posture refers to the position or bearing of the body. Good posture, upright stance and squared shoulders, communicates a sense of poise to an audience. Speakers who slouch give an unfavorable impression of themselves, including the impression of lack of confidence and an uncaring attitude.

Movement refers to motion of the entire body. Some speakers stand perfectly still throughout an entire speech. Others are constantly on the move. In general, it is probably better to remain in one place unless you have some reason for moving. However, a little movement adds action to the speech, so it may help you hold attention. Ideally, movement should help focus on transition, emphasize an idea, or call attention to a particular aspect of the speech. Avoid such unmotivated movement as bobbing and weaving, shifting from foot to foot, and pacing from one side of the room to the other. At the beginning of your speech, stand up straight and on both feet. If during the course of the speech you find yourself in some peculiar posture, return to the upright position standing on both feet.

Are you concerned with problems that you discover in your bodily actions? It is helpful to keep in mind that if you find some problems, you are not alone. Hardly anyone has such good delivery that interest factors, meaning factors, and affect factors come automatically. Most people need a great deal of work on one or more aspects of their delivery in order to maximize interest, meaning, and affect factors.

With any bodily action, avoid mannerisms that distract the audience, like taking off or putting on glasses, smacking the tongue, licking the lips, or scratching the nose, hand, or arm. As a general rule, anything that calls attention to itself is bad, and anything that helps reinforce your ideas is good.

During practice sessions you may try various methods to monitor or alter your bodily action. Videotape is an excellent means of monitoring your action.

You may want to practice in front of a mirror to see how you look to others when you speak. (Although some speakers swear by this method, others find it a traumatic experience.) Perhaps the best method is to get a willing listener to critique your bodily action and help you improve. Once you have identified the behavior you want to change, you can tell your helper what to look for. For instance, you might say, "Raise your hand every time I begin to rock back and forth." By getting specific feedback when the behavior occurs, you can make immediate adjustments.

Practice Diligently

Can delivery be improved? Yes. During the 1988 nomination campaigns both George Bush and Michael Dukakis were regarded as mediocre public speakers. Yet, at their party's conventions, both were praised for giving "the best speeches of their lives." Both of them used advisers to help them and both worked very hard, especially on delivery. Unfortunately, neither of them matched those performances in most of the speeches they delivered along the campaign trail during the the final months of the campaign.

The fact is that everyone can improve if they wish to. But as with anything else in life, change is not easy. You have to be motivated to change, you have to know what to work on, and you have to work at it to change.

Learn the Extemporaneous Method

How you proceed with your practice sessions depends on your method of delivery. Although the "persuasive speeches" you give in conversational settings are likely to be *impromptu,* composed on the spur of the moment without specific preparation, most formal persuasive speeches are delivered from manuscript, memorized, or, the method I recommend for most of your speeches, extemporaneous.

Manuscript speeches are written out in full and then read aloud. Reading from a manuscript is a common form of delivery by speakers who don't prepare their own speeches. For instance, presidents and other heads of state often have a team of speech writers helping them with their speeches. On some occasions they may receive their speeches only moments before they are expected to read them. The advantage of a manuscript is that wording can be carefully planned with nothing left to chance. For some particularly sensitive speech situations, the change of even a few words could have serious consequences. Although a speaker who has a well-written manuscript and who has practiced the speech carefully may give an excellent speech, speeches that are delivered from manuscript are often not well done. Despite the sense of security that a manuscript gives, few speakers deliver their speeches well enough to sound enthusiastic or to maintain good eye contact. Moreover, most speakers rely on their manuscript so heavily that they are not able to adapt to their audience. So, as a general rule, if you are preparing your own speech, don't speak from manuscript.

Since many speakers feel uncomfortable preparing their own speeches, though, especially for formal or sensitive occasions, I will discuss writing speeches for others and good manuscript delivery in Module E in Part 3.

A *memorized* speech is merely a manuscript committed to memory. In addition to the opportunity to polish the wording, memorization allows the speaker to look at the audience while speaking instead of at a manuscript. But because a speech that sounds memorized affects an audience adversely, I don't recommend memorization for most speakers.

An *extemporaneous* speech is prepared and practiced, but the exact wording is determined at the time of utterance. Why should most of your speeches be given extemporaneously? Extemporaneous speaking permits you to control the speech far more than does impromptu speaking, while at the same time allowing far greater spontaneity and adaptation to the audience than the manuscript or memorized speech. Most experienced speakers prefer the extemporaneous method for most of their speeches. Now let's consider how a speech can be carefully prepared without being memorized.

Practice Systematically

Effective speakers learn to include practice sessions as a major part of their speech preparation. Practice gives you a chance to revise, evaluate, mull over, and consider all aspects of the speech, including both the wording and the delivery. I recommend completing your speech plan at least two days before the speech is due so you have enough time for practice.

An effective practice session involves giving the speech, analyzing it, and then giving it again with changes based on the analysis. You will have to learn how many practice sessions you need to cement the key ideas in your mind and to get the oral, conversational, spontaneous quality that is so important to good speaking without getting stale or beginning to memorize.

First Practice
1. *Read through your outline once or twice to get ideas in mind. Then put the outline out of sight.*
2. *Stand up and face your imaginary audience.* Make the practice as similar to the speech situation as possible. If you are practicing in your room, pretend that the chairs, lamps, books, and other objects in your view are

people. You may want to record your practice session. If you do not own a tape recorder, perhaps you can borrow one. Or you may want to ask a friend to listen to one or more of your practices. If you are self-conscious about practicing in front of an audience of friends or relatives, train your ear to really listen to what you say while you are practicing.

3. *Time the speech.* Write down the time that you begin.
4. *Give the speech.* Keep going until you have finished the ideas.
5. *Write down the time you finish.* Compute the length of the speech for this first practice.

Analysis

Look at your outline again. Then begin the analysis. If you practiced in front of a friend, you can ask that person to share in the criticism. But do not ask simply, "Well, what do you think?" Be specific. Did you leave out any key ideas? Did you talk too long on any one point and not long enough on another? Did you clarify each of your points? Did you try to adapt to your anticipated audience? To help you with your analysis, you may wish to refer to the persuasive speech checklist in Figure 9-1.

Second Practice

Go through the entire process again, including the analysis.

After you have completed a session consisting of two practices and two analyses, put the speech away for a while. Although you may need to go through the rehearsal process several times, there is no value in doing all your rehearsal at one time. You may find that a practice session right before you go to bed is very helpful; while you are sleeping, your subconscious can continue to work on the speech. As a result, you are likely to find tremendous improvement in mastery of the speech at the first practice session the next day.

How many times you practice depends on many things, including your experience, familiarity with the subject, and length of the speech. In your practices you should be trying to learn the speech, not memorize it. Learning the speech involves giving it differently during each practice.

Using Notes in the Speech

Should you use notes in practice or during the speech itself? The answer depends on what you mean by notes and how you plan to use them. Appropriate notes are composed of key words or phrases that help trigger your memory. Notes will be most useful to you when they consist of the fewest words possible written in lettering large enough to be seen instantly at a distance. Many speakers condense their written preparatory outline into a brief word or phrase outline.

For a speech in the five- to ten-minute category, one or two 3 x 5 note cards should be enough. When your speech contains a particularly good quotation or a complicated set of statistics, you may want to write them out in detail on separate 3 x 5 cards.

During practice sessions you should use notes the way you plan to use them in the speech. Either set them on the speaker's stand or hold them in one hand and refer to them only when you have to. Speakers often find that the act of making a note card is so effective in helping cement ideas in the mind that

Figure 9-1 *Persuasive Speech Checklist*

SPECIFIC GOAL

_____ 1. Was the specific goal clearly written?
_____ 2. Was the specific goal designed to (circle one): Reinforce a belief? Establish a belief? Change a belief? Move to action?

CONTENT

_____ 3. Did the speaker present clearly stated reasons?
_____ 4. Did the speaker use facts and expert opinions to support these reasons?
_____ 5. Was the speaker effective in establishing his or her credibility on this topic?
_____ 6. Was the speaker ethical in handling material?
_____ 7. Did the speaker use material effectively to motivate the audience?

ORGANIZATION

_____ 8. Did the introduction gain attention and goodwill for the speaker?
_____ 9. Did the speech follow a (circle one): Problem-solution order? Comparative-advantages order? Criteria-satisfaction order? Negative order? Motivated sequence?
_____ 10. Was the order appropriate for the type of goal and assumed attitude of the audience?
_____ 11. Did the conclusion further the persuasive effect of the speech?

LANGUAGE

_____ 12. Was the language (circle goals that were met): Clear? Vivid? Emphatic? Appropriate?
_____ 13. Did the speaker use emotional language to motivate the audience?

DELIVERY

_____ 14. Was the delivery convincing?

Evaluate the speech as (check one): ____ Excellent ____ Good ____ Average ____ Fair ____ Poor
Use the information from your checklist to support your evaluation.

---

during practice, or later during the speech itself, they do not need to use the notes at all.

Summary

Your presentational style is a combination of your language and your delivery. Depending on how you deliver your speech, you can strengthen or weaken, enlarge or diminish, improve or destroy your message. Effective persuaders are likely to speak enthusiastically, maintain audience contact, vocalize expressively, articulate clearly, and gesture meaningfully.

Enthusiasm is a state of mind—it is the feeling of excitement you have about the value of your message. Eye contact involves looking at various groups of people in all parts of your audience throughout your speech. Although enthusiasm and eye contact hold audience attention and build your credibility, it is your vocal expressiveness that affects the meanings your audience gets from your speech.

In addition to these three major qualities, effective speakers articulate and pronounce words correctly and use bodily action effectively. Articulation is the shaping of speech sounds into recognizable oral symbols that go together to produce a word; pronunciation is the form and accent of various syllables of the words. Sloppy articulation and mispronunciation can have negative effects on the audience's responsiveness to your speech. The variables of bodily action are facial expression, gestures, and movement that affect meaning.

You can improve your delivery if you're willing to work, but as with anything else in life, change is not easy. You have to be motivated to change, you have to know what to work on to change, and you have to work at it to change. How you practice depends on whether you will present your speech by manuscript, by memorization, or, the way I prefer, extemporaneously. An effective practice session involves giving the speech, analyzing it, and then giving it again with changes based on the analysis.

Skill Development Exercises

1. From a recent issue of *Vital Speeches* select the three speeches that are *most* persuasive to you. From one of those speeches select a particularly powerful passage.
    a. Think of ways to maximize the power of the passage through effective delivery.
    b. Record the passage.

    c. Analyze your recording. Where did you succeed in maximizing the power? Where did you fail?

    d. Re-record the passage.

2. Select an instructor whose delivery you consider to be above average and one whose delivery you consider to be below average. As you listen, make notes of their vocal expressiveness and bodily action. Contrast them; be specific.

3. Pronounce each of the following words; then look up their pronunciation. Which of them do you tend to mispronounce? Why?

athlete	comparable	grievous	inexplicable
infamous	inquiry	irreparable	larynx
length	mischievous	picture	preferable

4. For one or more of the speeches you hear during a round of persuasive speeches, complete Figure 9-1 and then write a two- to five-paragraph evaluation of the speech.

5. For a persuasive speech you hear outside of class, complete Figure 9-1 and then write a two- to five-paragraph evaluation of the speech.

Speech Preparation Exercises

1. Prepare a six- to ten-minute persuasive speech developing a persuasive speech goal designed to change a belief or to motivate an audience to action. A complete written speech plan, including an outline, is required.

2. Record the development of one point of the speech you prepared.

    a. Identify places where you use particularly good vocal variety and emphasis.

    b. Select three sentences that are not well delivered. Then think of what you need to do to increase the expressiveness.

3. Re-record the same portion. How much were you able to improve?

Study Questions

For each of the following, be prepared to give examples in support of your answers.

1. What can you do to make your speech more vocally expressive?

2. What is the relationship between effective bodily action and vocal expressiveness?

3. Contrast extemporaneous with impromptu speaking. How are they alike? How do they differ?
4. What can a speaker do in practice to develop or ensure spontaneity?
5. How does content differ from delivery?
6. How much movement should speakers use in a speech?
7. Can a speaker use too many gestures? Explain.

SAMPLE SPEECH PLAN AND SPEECH

Year-Around Schools, by Martha Harris[3]

1. *Speech goal.* I want my audience to believe that public elementary and secondary school years should be extended to 12 months.

2. *Audience profile.* As I look at my audience, I believe the most significant factors in reference to this proposition are age (early 20s) and education (soon to be college graduates).

3. *Audience interest.* Since the audience is composed of students who I assume value education, they are likely to be interested in the improvement of education. Early in the speech I plan to present information that will dramatize the shortcomings of our current nine-month system. As a result, I believe the listeners will be interested in hearing about a solution that has worked to improve student learning. In addition, I plan to show relevancy by telling the audience that as prospective parents, they will directly benefit from this proposal.

4. *Audience knowledge.* Since it is likely that the audience will have heard about many of the weaknesses of public education, I'll review them briefly in the speech introduction. Since it is unlikely that the audience will be familiar with the details of year-around schools, I will have to define and clarify the concept.

5. *Audience attitude.* Because I'm battling a traditional orientation of a nine-month school year, I predict that my audience will have a slightly negative attitude toward the belief statement. But as students who understand the value of education or as potential parents who want to provide for their children, I believe that the audience will listen to the proposal. Moreover, the emphasis of my speech will be on the benefits of the year-around program to students. As I present my reasons, I will be contrasting what is happening in nine-month systems with what would happen in year-around systems.

6. *Credibility.* I do not think that my expertise level will be perceived as high at the beginning of the speech. Therefore, I will have to build my credibility through quality of information and strength of argument. By displaying a sincere interest in the future of public education and our children's futures, I will demonstrate my good intentions to listeners.

7. *Motivational elements.* The information presented in the speech shows a strong need for educational reform and one solution to the problem: extending the school year. I can create dissonance in the audience members and make them feel uneasy about the inadequate quality of our public schools. If the audience is uncomfortable, they may be more willing to listen and possibly to support my proposal. But in the main part of the speech I will be appealing to the audience's sense of need for improvement—or in McClelland's words, need for achievement.

8. *Organizational plan.* Because I see the audience as uninformed and slightly negative (based on tradition) and because the material I have shows both the nature of the problem and the advantages of the solution, I believe the problem-solution plan will work best for me. But it will be a modified problem-solution plan. Since the audience will be familiar with the indictments of public education, I will review those briefly in the introduction so that I can put my emphasis on the strength of the proposal itself.

SPEECH OUTLINE

Speech goal: I want my audience to believe that public elementary and secondary school years should be extended to 12 months.

Introduction

   I. We are a nation at risk.
   II. We're all aware of the alarming information that has surfaced in reference to public education.
   - A. National tests show the poor state of education.
     1. The National Association for Assessment of Educational Progress found the history test average was 54 percent.
     2. Students are not learning the skills they need.
   - B. International tests show the poor state of education in the United States.
     1. A study of American, Japanese, and Chinese students found that the lowest average score in a fifth-grade American classroom was only slightly higher than the average score for the best first-grade Japanese and Chinese classrooms.
     2. Among the top 100 in the fifth grade, only one was American.
   III. Since American students are not performing at competent levels, it's time to try a fundamental change.
   - A. This is not some crackpot idea. It has been tested in various places in this country.

    B. A typical year-around program expands the year to four sessions with about two weeks off between each session, making for about a 44-week school year.

Body

  I. The first reason for making a change to year-around education is that students would learn more.

    A. The current nine-month year just doesn't provide enough time to cover the topics that need to be covered.

      1. The nine-month school year is based on an outdated agricultural society.

      2. This pattern found ready acceptance in an agricultural America and it has persisted even though summer is less of a harvest time than a vacation period.

      3. Perhaps the classic examples of what happens with a nine-month year can be seen by looking at history courses.

      4. Part of the problem with the nine-month year is that teachers typically spend much of their time reviewing from the year before.

    B. With a year-around school program, all this would be changed.

      1. The educational results of the lengthened school year are dramatic.

        a. After 3.7 months in an extended program at Commack Elementary School, the reading comprehension increased an average of 6.5 months.

        b. The slow-learner group even gained over the control group.

      2. Teachers don't have to spend so much time reviewing.

  II. A second major reason for making such a change is that it would increase students' motivation to stay in school.

    A. Year-around school virtually eliminated the dropout problem in one high school.

    B. This motivation is seen not only in the dropout rate but also in daily attendance.

      1. It has been reported that attendance has improved dramatically in the 65 year-around schools in Los Angeles.

      2. If students had difficulty with a course in a term, since most schools are on a six-term system throughout the year, they could come back in the second term and retake that class.

 III. A third reason is that teachers would be more highly motivated.

    A. More frequent breaks help prevent teacher burnout.

    B. Teachers salaries would be increased.

Conclusion

I. I am not saying that adopting a year-around program is going to cure all the ills in our educational system, but it is going to give us a foundation to build from.

II. Why don't we move to the full year? It's educationally sound—it will increase motivation.

III. We all know it is bucking tradition, but I think it is an idea whose time has come.

Sources

Cook, Beverly. "Does Year-Round Schooling Work?" *American Teacher*, April/May 1988, p. 4.
Cruz, John. "Year Round Education: One District's Experience." *Thrust*, Nov./Dec. 1988, pp. 35–37.
Dirr, Kenneth. Interview, Nov. 8, 1989.
"Doomsday School Days." *America*, Sept. 20, 1986, p. 109.
Gitlin, Lisa. "Does Year-Round School Really Make Sense?" *Education Digest*, Nov. 1988, pp. 16–19.
Gitlin, Lisa. "Year-Round School." *Instructor*, August 1988, pp. 16–19.
Henson, Kenneth. "Reforming America's Public Schools." *USA Today Magazine*, March 1986, pp. 75–77.
Jones, Peter. "Can Americans Learn From Foreign Schools?" *Scholastic Update*, Nov. 6, 1987, pp. 16–17.
Lacayo, Richard. "A Pass, with Room for Improvement." *Time*, Sept. 15, 1986, p. 77.
Marshall, Elliot. "School Reformers Aim for Creativity." *Science*, Sept. 18, 1986, pp. 267–270.
Schoenfeld, C., and N. Schmitz. *Year-Round Community Schools: A Framework for Administrative Leadership*. 1973.
White, William. "Year-Round High Schools: Benefits to Students, Parents and Teachers," *NASSP Bulletin*, Jan. 1988, pp. 103–106.

Read the following speech aloud. Then analyze it on the basis of organization, reasoning and evidence, motivation, and speaker credibility. After you have read and analyzed the speech, refer to the analysis on the right.

Speech

We are a nation at risk. You've all heard the indictment: the educational system is not producing educated students. Let me recall evidence we've all been reading. According to *Scholastic Update*, the National Association for Assessment of Educational Progress gave a history test to 7817 17-year-olds. The average score on this test was 54 percent. According to another study reported in the *U. S. News & World Report*, less than half of the high school seniors surveyed could identify Julius

Analysis

Notice how the speaker opens by appealing to common ground; we're all in agreement that a problem exists. Nevertheless, she supplies material to reinforce that perception. The

Caesar. And less than one in three knew what century—
that's what century—the Civil War took place in. On a
comparative level with other countries, we're subpar. A
study that compared math scores of American, Japanese,
and Chinese first- and fifth-graders showed that the
lowest average for a fifth-grade American class was only
slightly higher than the lowest average for the Chinese
first-grade class. Moreover, among the top 100 fifth-
graders ranked in the study, only one was American! Yet
there were 58 American first-graders among the bottom
100 and 67 fifth graders among the bottom 100.

*opening helps her
achieve her goal of
creating dissonance—
making the audience
feel uncomfortable
with the level of stu-
dent achievement.*

    As would-be-parents, who will be sending our kids
to school, we want to do something. We want a public
education system that will be the best for our children.
But I think you will agree with me that to get there we
are going to have to increase our commitment to excellence. It's time to make some fundamental changes to
move us toward a system that educates our students. It's
time to think about extending the school year for elementary and secondary schools to 12 months.

*Now the speaker be-
gins to focus on the
goals we set for educa-
tion. Notice how she
only seeks to get us
"to think about" such
a change. She realizes
that an audience is
unlikely to adopt such
a radical departure on
the basis of a single
speech.*

    Now this is not some crackpot idea. It's one that's
been tested in various places in this country. Just what is
"year-around" schooling? A typical year-around program
expands the year to four sessions with about two weeks
off between each session, making for about a 44-week
school year. Why this arrangement? "The year-around
calendar is designed the way people learn—on a contin-
ual basis," said Charles Ballinger, coordinator of the San
Diego County Office of Education. What outcomes are
we looking for in an improved educational setting? Well,
certainly we're most interested in increasing what our
students learn. In addition, I believe we'd all say that
we'd like to see more students motivated to stay in
school. And I think we'd all like to see even better
teaching. Folks, I believe lengthening the school year
would achieve all three of these goals!

*This section is an ex-
cellent example of de-
fusing audience
opposition. Notice
that although the
speaker is using a
problem-solution or-
ganization, there is a
criteria-satisfaction
tone to this section.
Also notice the use of
rhetorical questions to
personalize the infor-
mation.*

    First, with a year-around program, all of your
students are going to learn a lot more. To increase student
learning, we need a year-around program to provide

*Now that she has laid
a groundwork, the
speaker launches into*

enough time to cover information and to provide necessary reinforcement. The current nine-month year just doesn't provide enough time to cover the topics that need to be covered. The nine-month school year is based on an outdated agricultural society. Clarence Schoenfeld, former assistant to the chancellor of the University of Wisconsin Center System and author of *Year Around Education,* said that the critical importance of getting in the crops has dictated for centuries that wars and education start in September and fade in spring. This pattern found ready acceptance in an agricultural America, and it has persisted, even though summer is less of a harvest time than a vacation period. Of course, a nine-month school year also assumes that there is enough time to cover the topics.

the three reasons for supporting such a change. Each of the reasons is clearly stated and generally well supported. Notice the way she uses theSchoenfeld quotation to help increase the vividness of her point.

Yet, in a nine-month year, teachers aren't able to present the material that they need to. Perhaps the classic example of what happens with a nine-month year can be seen by looking at history courses. I know that I didn't learn about World War II or the Vietnam War until I came to college, and I took a history course specifically from the 1920s until the present. And I bet my bottom dollar that many of you have had the same experience. We got to the Great Depression at about the end of May, just before the start of summer vacation, and never got any further in any other class. And I went to what was considered a good school. But the year-around education system would give enough time so that students could finish history to the present time. This same completion of material would be true of other courses as well.

Here we see a good example of the speaker first using personal experience and then adapting to presumed audience experience. This common ground helps her increase audience motivation. At this place in the speech, many in the audience are nodding their heads in agreement.

Part of the problem with the nine-month year is that teachers typically spend more time reviewing from the year before. With a year-around school program, all this would be changed. Jim Melville, a sixth-grade teacher from a year-around program at Orchard Elementary in Utah, said that he spends far less time reviewing. Why? Because children retain more information after a three-week absence, than after a three-month summer vacation. The educational results of the lengthened school year are dramatic. For instance, third-graders at Commack Elementary School gained in reading compre-

Here she uses well-documented evidence to support her point. One strength of this speech is good reasons with generally good supporting material. Although her efforts to build credibility are indirect, they are still effective. Her excel-

hension. After 3.7 months in an extended program, the reading comprehension increased an average of 6.5 months. And the slow-learner group even gained over the control group.

A second major reason for making such a change is that it would increase students' motivation to stay in school. William White, the assistant superintendent of the Jefferson County schools in Colorado, said, "Year-around school virtually eliminated the dropout problem in our high school." This motivation is seen not only in the dropout rate but also in daily attendance. For instance, it's been reported that attendance has improved dramatically in the 65 year-around schools in Los Angeles. Why? Because the students see a light at the end of the tunnel. If students had difficulty with a course in a term, since most schools are on a six-term system throughout the year, they could come back in the second term and retake that class.

A third reason is that a year-around program would improve teaching. More frequent breaks help prevent teacher burnout. As teachers get more periodic vacations throughout the year—most extended-year programs go for 60 days in school then 15 days off school—they are much more capable of dealing with the pressures of school. It helps them knowing that short breaks are coming up and it gives them time to replenish themselves before going back into the classroom. Beverly Cook, a teacher in a year-around school in Los Angeles, said, "On a year-around schedule, I'm a better teacher—I have the energy to give more." And of course an added benefit to this is that teachers' salaries increase with a year-around school system.

Now, I am not saying that adopting a year-around program is going to cure all the ills in our educational system, but it is going to give us a foundation to build from. It's going to help us reform our educational system. It's going to provide enough time to cover all we need to cover. And it's going to benefit our teachers, which will benefit children in the long run. Why haven't we already moved to the year-around calendar? It's educationally

lent information helps to build her expertise, and her tone shows her concern for better education.
After clearly stating the second reason, she provides evidence to show that such a program has lowered the number of dropouts and improved attendance. Although this is a short section, it contains two strong subpoints.

Here she gives information to show that teaching will improve as well. Although the first part of this reason is well supported, the second part about salaries is only asserted. We see another excellent use of quotation in support of her point.

Here she presents a rather cautious conclusion that is in keeping with her goal of getting us to begin considering this proposal. The use of clear reasons, good sound; it will increase motivation. But, as we all know, it is bucking tradition. Still, I think it is an idea whose time has come.

supporting material (including several excellent quotations), and personal language adapted to the audience make this an effective persuasive speech.

Notes

[1]Cicero, *De Orator* V. III, in H. Rackham (trans.) (Cambridge, MA: Harvard University Press, 1960), p. 56.

[2]See W. James Potter and Richard Emanuel, "Students' Preferences for Communication Styles and Their Relationship to Achievement," *Communication Education,* 39 (July 1990), p. 235. They review a number of research articles that show the importance of expressiveness to audience satisfaction.

[3]Delivered in a speech class at the University of Cincinnati. Reprinted by permission of Martha Harris.

Part III

Modules

Part 3 consists of five modules that focus on specific kinds of speech situations. The first three modules explain different types of campaigns. Although you may reach your goal with a single speech, reaching most persuasive speaking goals requires a series of speeches as part of a campaign. The three kinds of campaigns covered in Part 3 are the social action campaign (Module A), the election campaign (Module B), and the sales campaign (Module C). The other two modules focus on refutation and speech writing. In most of your speeches, you will play the role of the advocate, the one who is seeking change. There are times, however, when you will want to oppose change. Module D shows you how to proceed when you want to refute arguments. Finally, there will be times when you are called upon to write a speech for someone else or when you will want to deliver your own manuscript speech. Module E shows you how to write speeches for others and how to prepare such speeches for delivery.

Module **A**

Social Action Campaigning

Heather Johnson, a junior communication major, was concerned that the Department of Communication did not offer a course in cross-cultural communication. When she mentioned her concern to a faculty member, he told her that the course was probably a good idea but that the department didn't have the money to staff a new course. The more Heather thought about it, however, the more she was convinced that the department needed to offer the course to strengthen its interpersonal communication program. She was struck with the reality that if anything was going to be done about it in the near future, she was going to have to take the leadership role. Heather decided that to get the department to act, she was going to have to campaign. Now Heather had to figure out how to get the campaign started.

This scenario is an example of a typical situation in which people attempt to reach their action goal by launching a campaign. Although there are situations where a person can present an idea and get an audience to act on the basis of a single speech, more often than not, efforts to bring people to action are part of social action campaigns. In this module we consider types of social action campaigns and the steps you have to follow to make a social action campaign work. Finally, we conclude the module with a speech assignment that enables you to put what you have learned about social action campaigning into practice and an example of a speech that is part of a campaign.

Planning a Social Action Campaign

Action campaigns vary in size and complexity. Although some social action campaigns may be major projects that involve large numbers of people working together over many months (or even years), other campaigns, like Heather's, may involve relatively small numbers of people, may involve a relatively simple action plan, and may be accomplished within a few weeks. A community campaign to encourage people to support the city's Fine Arts Fund, a community action group campaign to open a neighborhood soup kitchen for the homeless, a marketing organization campaign to get students to attend a job fair, and a campaign to close an X-rated movie theater opened recently in a residential area of the community are all examples of social action campaigns.

Whatever the type and size of social action campaign you anticipate, you need an organized plan of action to be successful. An action plan like the one Heather was initiating should include the following steps.

Setting a Goal

You begin a campaign by identifying a goal. Your goal may first be verbalized as a general idea. For instance, you may start a campaign to improve the quality of public education in your city, or to raise money to support school extracurricular activities, or to help the homeless. Heather's general goal is to improve the department's interpersonal communication curriculum.

Before going very far with your plans, you need to focus on a specific goal. A campaign is not likely to get support unless people know exactly what action they are supporting. The general goal of improving the quality of public education may evolve into the specific goal of campaigning for year-around schooling; the general goal of helping the homeless may evolve into the specific goal of campaigning for opening a soup kitchen. Heather's general goal of improving the curriculum is expressed with the specific goal of campaigning for a cross-cultural communication course.

Analyzing the Target Audience

As with preparing a speech, your next step is to analyze the target audience. A target audience for a campaign is the people who are in a position to bring about a change or action. Identifying a target audience can be more difficult than it originally seems. For instance, for a citywide Fine Arts Fund campaign, the target audience would appear to include everyone in the community. Although that's true in a sense, the fund-raising campaign would likely fail if the campaign was directed equally to everyone. In most campaigns, the target audience is divided into segments. For a fund-raising campaign, the highest priority segment would include a small number of individuals or groups who could contribute large amounts of money—this segment might be expected to give as much as half of all the money collected. The next segment would consist of a larger number of individuals or groups of people who are capable of contributing rather substantial amounts of money—this segment might be expected to give as much as one-third of all the money collected. Then a third segment would consist of the rest of the people in the community. A fund-raising campaign must reach all three audiences to be successful, but each of the three is likely to be approached somewhat differently.

Similarly, Heather may see her target audience as segmented into two groups. The first segment consists of communication majors who need to be mobilized in order to develop the campaign. The second segment, and the group that holds the decision-making power, consists of the department faculty who will vote on her proposal.

Analyzing the Situation

You must also be concerned with the characteristics of the context. Whether your goal is fund raising, curriculum change, or social action, the context includes political, economic, and cultural issues that affect the campaign. Since Heather seeks a curriculum change, she must understand all the factors that come into play in making such changes. Before she makes any speeches, she will have to make sure she knows the political context that outlines the procedure involved in course changes. Likewise she needs to be familiar with any historical or economic constraints that might affect a curriculum decision. If, for instance, the college has a one-year freeze on new courses, Heather's campaign is doomed before it begins.

Developing a Strategy

Just as with preparing a single speech, after you have analyzed your target audience, you prepare a strategy, an action plan. At a minimum, an action plan involves a theme and a procedure. All major campaigns are likely to follow a theme. An early campaign step is to select a slogan that emphasizes the theme for the campaign. For instance, a fine arts funding drive that is emphasizing the theme of how everyone benefits from the arts may create the slogan "Arts Are for All." A procedure includes the actual steps involved in completing the campaign. The steps may include petitioning, polling, interviewing, preparing posters, writing media ads, sending personal letters, conducting door-to-door polls, writing press releases, and giving speeches. For instance, Heather may decide that her campaign focus will be on speeches to mobilize students and persuade the faculty. Her total procedure may involve polling student opinion, preparing a petition, and interviewing faculty. But she will focus on scheduling speeches to the undergraduate student organization, to classes, and finally to the faculty.

Mobilizing Resources

Resources involve both people and money. Even in a small campaign a person can't do everything alone. In Heather's campaign to get a course started, she will need the backing of communication majors. She will have to speak at the undergraduate student organization meeting. She will then have to mobilize members of that organization to help get student signatures on a petition. To do this, she will have to mobilize individuals to go to classes and get permission to speak to those classes and circulate the petitions.

But suppose she was initiating a campaign to get the university to give a larger share of its athletic budget to women's sports. Since this task would be much larger, Heather would also need to get other people to volunteer to help her in the campaign.

A second aspect of mobilizing resources is getting financial support. Depending on the size of the campaign, Heather might also need to engage in some fund raising. For instance, a campaign to get the city to establish a recycling center would be a much more long-range campaign and would require funds to finance various means of persuasion. In Heather's case, she may decide that little or no outside money will be needed.

Building Your Case

A final, but perhaps most important part of the campaign is to build your case. Regardless of how well organized your campaign, if you can't make a sound case for your proposed action, it will fail. For instance, there is no sense in even beginning a campaign if there aren't good reasons for starting a cross-cultural communication course.

Speeches are often one of the major ways that campaigners make a target audience aware of their case. Usually a campaign originates because there is some problem that will be solved or some need that will be met by the proposed action. The basic case is likely to involve a variation of the traditional problem-solution pattern. Heather's case for a cross-cultural course will include demonstrating a problem or a need for change, and showing that the proposal would solve the problem or meet the need. In outline form, the overall case for a cross-cultural course will answer each of the following questions:

1. Is there a problem created by not having the course? (Is there a need for a course?)
2. Will a course solve the problem or meet the need?
3. Is it practical to begin such a course?
4. Will the benefits of beginning such a course outweigh any problems that it might create?

When you have information that answers these questions, you are in a position to prepare the campaign speeches. Each speech that is given will draw from the pool of information that has been gathered. How much of the information, which reasons, and what kind of an organization you use will depend on the nature of the specific audience to whom the speeches will be given.

Summary

Action campaigns vary in size and complexity. Although some social action campaigns may be major projects that involve large numbers of people working together over many months (or even years), other campaigns may involve relatively small numbers of people, may involve a relatively simple action plan, and may be accomplished within a few weeks.

Whatever the type and size of social action campaign you anticipate, you need an organized plan of action to be successful. You begin a campaign by identifying a goal. Your goal may first be verbalized as a general idea, but before going very far with your plans, you need to focus on a goal.

Your next step is to analyze the target audience. A target audience for a campaign is the people who are in a position to bring about a change or action. In most campaigns, target audience is divided into high-priority and low-priority segments.

You must also be concerned with the characteristics of the context. Whether your goal is fund raising, curriculum change, or social action, the context includes the political, economic, and cultural issues that affect the campaign.

After you have analyzed your target audience, you prepare a strategy, an action plan. At a minimum, an action plan involves a theme and a procedure that includes the actual steps involved in completing the campaign. The steps may include petitioning, polling, interviewing, preparing posters, writing media ads, sending personal letters, conducting door-to-door canvassing, writing press releases, and giving speeches.

The resources you need include both people and money. Even in a small campaign, a person can't do everything alone. Mobilization of resources also means getting financial support. Depending on the size of the campaign, you might need to engage in some fund raising.

A final and perhaps most important part of the campaign is to build your case. Regardless of how well organized your campaign, if you can't make a sound case for your proposed action, it will fail. Usually a campaign originates because there is some problem that will be solved or some need that will be met by the proposed action. The basic case is likely to involve a variation of the traditional problem-solution pattern.

Skill Development Exercises

From a recent issue of *Vital Speeches* select a speech that you believe could have been a part of a social action campaign. How well does the speech exemplify characteristics of a social action campaign speech?

Speech Preparation Exercises

1. Select a course of action that you believe should be taken. Write a campaign plan (including specific goal, target audience, situation, strategy, mobilization of resources, and basic case) that you could follow to gain support for this social action.
2. Prepare a six- to ten-minute persuasive speech that is intended to be a part of a social action campaign. As part of your preparation, complete the following speech plan.
   a. Write your speech goal.
   b. Indicate the three features of your audience analysis that you believe are most significant in drawing conclusions about the audience.
   c. Indicate what you plan to do to build audience interest. Include methods of showing timeliness, proximity, and personal effect.
   d. Indicate what you plan to do to adapt to the knowledge level of your audience, including what background information you have to include to orient them.
   e. In light of the audience's attitude (in favor, neutral, or opposed), what do you plan to do to adapt to that attitude?
   f. Indicate what you plan to do to build your credibility in the speech.
   g. Indicate what you plan to do to motivate your audience.
   h. What organization do you believe is most appropriate for your speech in light of that attitude?

3. What part of the plan do you believe is likely to be easiest to achieve? Most difficult? Explain.

Study Questions

For each of the following, be prepared to give examples in support of your answers.

1. Discuss the steps that must be followed for a campaign.
2. Why is a problem-solution format suitable for a social action campaign speech?

SAMPLE SPEECH PLAN AND SPEECH

A Campaign to Increase Attendance at the 13th Annual Career Forum, *by Nancy Stunkel*[1]

1. *Speech goal.* I want my audience to attend the 13th annual Careers Forum.

2. *Audience profile.* From my analysis of my audience, I believe the most significant factor is education (college juniors and seniors).

3. *Campaign progress.* For the last two weeks posters have been displayed on campus and this week an article is scheduled to appear in the student newspaper. Also this week, one week before the forum, members of the student organization are soliciting invitations to take five minutes of time to give speeches in various classes.

4. *Audience interest.* Since most of my audience members are approaching the time when they will begin a job search, I believe that they are likely to be interested in hearing about a program that is designed to familiarize them with job opportunities. To maintain their interest I will show the poster as a visual aid, and I will focus on the relevance of my information. I will try to show that this information is personally relevant to all class members.

5. *Audience knowledge.* Although a few students will have seen posters in Lindner Hall, most of the audience will be uninformed about the forum. I do not believe the audience will need any special orientation material to understand the reasons I give for attending.

6. *Audience attitude.* At the beginning of the speech I believe my audience will be neutral, largely because they will not have seen the posters publicizing the forum. Once they hear the goal, I believe they will show the usual resistance to attending on-campus activities: they don't have time, they don't need to, they don't want to. Since I believe I will be facing apathy more than negative reaction, I will present the facts and concentrate on motivational efforts.

7. *Credibility.* Early in the speech I hope to build my expertise on this topic. I believe that my being a member of the sponsoring group will raise the audience's perception of my credibility. I plan to emphasize that I am a member of the American Marketing Association, the group that organizes and sponsors this forum. I also plan to speak from past experience of this forum.

8. *Motivational elements.* I'm sure my audience will be apathetic at first, so I plan to gain their attention by developing relevance through the timeliness of the forum and personal need for the information. I will "warn" them that graduation is creeping up on them and that they must soon start looking for a job. I then plan to show them how this forum could be the answer to their problems. In the latter part of the speech I will focus on economic and achievement needs.

9. *Organizational plan.* I plan to introduce my speech with the specific details of the forum and then move on to major benefits for attending the forum. I plan to conclude my speech with a restatement of the specific details because I feel that interest will increase by then.

SPEECH OUTLINE

Speech goal: I want my audience to attend the 13th Annual Careers Forum.

Introduction

I. Graduation is coming closer, and you will soon need to begin looking for a job.
II. Orientation: The Careers Forum will be held on Monday, February 12, from 6:00 to 9:00 in the Great Hall.

Body

I. First, the Careers Forum will allow you to meet representatives of companies.
   A. This allows you to ask questions in an informal atmosphere that would not be appropriate in a formal interview.
   B. This also allows you to gather information about companies so you can get an idea of who you might want to work for.
II. Second, the Careers Forum gives companies the chance to meet you.
   A. If reps like you, they might hang on to your resume.
   B. If you do get an interview in the future, you can show your previous interest in their company.

forum gives you an opportunity to distribute your resume. Now you may think this is just busywork, but if the representatives have even the remotest thought that you might fit in, they'll hang on to your resume. Then, later, they might call you and ask you to apply. After all, companies are always looking for possible recruits. Folks, several people who have attended these forums have turned the opportunity into a job! Moreover, later you might call and ask to speak to that representative. The person may not remember you, but he or she is still likely to have your resume on file. And this can work in favor if there are any openings in the company. Companies like to talk to people who have shown an interest in them. If you do ever schedule an interview with them, they will know that you attended the forum and showed interest in the company.

Third, and perhaps most important, attending this forum gives you good professional experience. Remember, this is a pressure-free situation. Still, you'll have a chance to talk on a professional level to people who have experience in the working world. As a result, you'll find it is excellent experience for you when it comes time to go to a real interview. Remember that oftentimes it's the personal impression you make that can give you an edge over another prospect. The more experience you have in interviewing, the better you're going to be at projecting your qualifications. And this is important because it may be your professional conduct in the interview—how you act under pressure—and not your education or grades in school that actually get you the job. So experience like this will be invaluable to you. In addition, this forum can give you an edge when it comes to learning about the various businesses and industries in the area, information you can use later during a formal interview. Interviewers like it when you are knowledgeable about their company; it tells them that you don't just want any job, but that you want a specific one with that company.

Now remember, the forum is Monday, February 12, from 6 to 9 P.M. in the Great Hall. It's for all students. You don't need a written invitation. Just show up; there's no fee. Now if you're not sold yet, let me leave you with

She continues to build motivation by pointing out how attending can lead to consideration. Still, the point would be even stronger if she had been specific about people who got jobs—or at least interviews—as a result of attending.

The third reason is a clearly stated and extremely practical reason for attending the forum. Students recognize the pressure of an on-site interview. The more actual experience they can get, the better. And again, the point is that attendees gain invaluable benefits with very little cost. I wish the speaker would have used more personal experience. She had an excellent opportunity to build credibility but didn't take advantage of it.

The conclusion reviews the main ideas of the speech. She stresses that every-

a word of advice from Nancy Pressler, a national representative of the American Marketing Association, who said, "The key to getting the job that you want is to have business contacts." This career forum can give you these business contacts. It just might help you get your foot through the door into the future.

thing has been done to make attending easy. Throughout the speech the motivation based on costs versus rewards is excellent. Moreover, each reason serves as an excellent incentive. This speech is an excellent part of a campaign to increase attendance at the forum.

Note

[1]Delivered in a speech class. Reprinted by permission of Nancy Stunkel.

Module **B**

Election Campaign Speaking

> Good evening. My name is Chris Hoskins. I'm a candidate for president of the student body. I'm here to tell you a little about myself and my ideas about what the university should be doing in the next few years to meet the needs of all students.

So begins one of many speeches Chris Hoskins will make in his campaign for student body president.

In nearly every organization individual members have the option to run for election to various offices. Election campaign speaking, and the election campaign itself, is a different kind of speech situation from the social action campaign. In this module we look at the election campaign context and the content requirements of campaign speaking. We conclude the module with a speech assignment that enables you to put what you have learned into practice and a speech that is appropriate for an election campaign.

Election Campaign Stages

The following stages of election campaigning (surfacing, legitimation, promotion, and analysis) are adapted from a *communicative functions* approach to presidential campaigning developed by Judith Trent and Robert Friedenberg.[1]

Surfacing

A candidate *surfaces* by making himself or herself known as a candidate for office. The surfacing stage involves the person "looking and sounding" like a candidate. In this stage people test their ideas in the public forum and attempt to promote their image.

In this surfacing stage, people usually hire or appoint a campaign manager. Sometimes people serve as their own campaign manager, but if the campaign is likely to be either long or complex, a separate campaign manager is a necessity. A campaign manager will be indispensable in the activities that begin in the surfacing stage.

Platform. Perhaps the most important aspect of the surfacing stage is to prepare your platform—that is, to determine the issues that you are going to speak to and the position you are going take on those issues. To capture the attention of the electorate, you are going to have to have a clear position on the issues. It is in this stage of the campaign, before you are immersed in the hustle and bustle of promotion, that you want your positions clearly articulated.

Scheduling. In running for any position, you have to be in the right place at the right time to give speeches that will do you the most good. Although a campaign manager is responsible for scheduling, in a small campaign, like the one for student body office, you will likely be responsible for your own scheduling.

You have to be invited to speak by the groups who represent your target audience. For instance, if you are running for fraternity president, you will need to speak only to members of your fraternity; if you are running for dean, you will want to speak to the departments in your college that will be voting; if you are running for city council, you will want to speak to as many organizations in your district as possible.

In campaigns that require appearances before several organizations, your campaign manager will send letters asking for invitations to speak or asking people to host a small reception or coffee hour. As you get name recognition, invitations are likely to come faster than you can fill them, but in the early stages of the campaign you will have to take the initiative.

A typical letter tells who you are, what you are running for, your recognition of the key issues of concern to the constituents, the request to speak, and the means of getting you on the schedule.

Press Releases. In public campaigns you will want press releases that publicize your stand on key issues. Since advertisements cost money, candidates need to get as much free publicity as possible. As you say and do things that are "noteworthy," your manager will prepare statements and send them to the various print and electronic media.

Legitimation

Once you have surfaced as a candidate, you need to begin to legitimize your campaign by seeking key endorsements and getting financial support. Legitimation means establishing yourself as a force to be contended with. Many people will surface as candidates, but until they develop a power base, they are not likely to be taken seriously.

Getting endorsements from important segments of your target audience is vital to this step. In a city council race, you need endorsements from your political party and from influential groups of people such as the city education association; in a student body president campaign, candidates seek endorsements from various student organizations.

In addition to gaining endorsements, you have to gain a financial base. In a political election, endorsement of a political party is also likely to include some monetary support. But in any kind of election, candidates are likely to need to solicit contributions from other kinds of groups and significant individuals. In a student body election, for example, a candidate may be able to get the necessary small amount of funding from a campus social organization.

Promotion

The major goals of promotion are to develop a personal identity, to build your credibility, and to build a case for your support. It is during the promotion stage of the campaign that your speech making is most important. For instance, in an election for city council, each candidate and the major supporters will give countless speeches to audiences of various sizes under a variety of circumstances during the six-month period before the election. Think of the campaign as an educational process—one in which you educate the community about yourself or your candidate.

Analysis

When the campaign is over, win or lose, you analyze the campaign to determine where you went right and where you went wrong. You then use the knowledge you gained for strengthening future campaigns for the same or for other types of office.

Issues in Your Campaign Speeches

Although your campaign goal may be cast as a proposition of policy, "I want my audience to vote for me [my candidate] for student body president," much of the emphasis of the speech will be on showing why you or your candidate is the best. To do so you must show that you or your candidate meets the criteria for "best candidate." In your planning, then, you will be concerned with the following two questions:

1. What are the criteria for establishing a "best candidate"?
2. Do the facts show that the candidate meets these criteria?

Although there are many criteria that can be considered in determining that you are the best candidate, three of the most important are personal character, qualifications, and goals or platform.

Personal Character. Today more than ever we hear people lamenting the fact that candidates are running strictly on personality, that "the issues" are buried, ignored, or forgotten. And although there may be some truth to such an assessment, the fact is that personal character (not just personality or image) may be more important than content issues. Why? Mostly because issues change, but a person's character does not. During any candidate's tenure of office the issues that were prominent at the time of election may disappear and new issues may emerge. For instance, if you run for office on the platform that you will support legislation in favor of a plan of waste recycling, when that issue is resolved (perhaps even during your first few months in office), you'll still be in office and your constituency will still expect you to work in their behalf. As a result, members of an electorate are often more interested in the quality of the person, for if the person proves to have principles and good ideas, that person is likely to be able to handle any issue. As a result, it is important for an electorate to know what kind of a person you are. Through your campaign you must do everything possible to stress your personal characteristics.

Qualifications. Qualifications include a person's professional expertise. The electorate is looking for a candidate who understands the office. Your record as a leader, your knowledge of the working mechanism of the position, and your personnel skills are all important. Office and leadership are, or should be, synonymous. And communication skills are a major part of leadership potential. Although some people get elected without leadership qualities, they are unlikely to make much of a mark while they are in office. In your speeches you must identify your leadership skills and cite instances when policies were established as a result of your leadership. Also of importance is knowledge of the working mechanism of the position. Although you never know all that an office entails until you have been elected, if you are running for city council, chairperson of the board, or student body president, the electorate wants some sense that if you are elected you will be able to get things done. Likewise, since every office holder will have a working team, personnel skills are also important.

Platform. Few candidates get elected on personal character and qualifications alone. Constituencies like to have some idea of the *kind* of leadership the candidate will provide, so you must have a strong, well-thought-out platform of goals. The subject of platform brings up the "campaigner's dilemma": if I say what I really believe, I can't get elected; if I say what I need to say to get elected, I'm not being true to myself. Like many dilemmas, this one proves to be false. The extraordinary candidate can be straightforward in explaining positions on issues because he or she can state even unpopular positions in ways that show sensitivity to the beliefs of the constituency.

In your speeches, then, you must focus on what you plan to accomplish in office. Whatever your goals, however, you can't discuss them all in detail in every speech. A candidate should have a master outline of arguments in favor of various goals. Then in speeches you focus on one or two of the issues that are particularly important to you and to the *specific audience.* Over the course of your campaign you will cover all of your plans.

Knowledge of all the issues is also important to prepare you to answer questions that you are likely to get after your formal speech. If you are really well prepared on all issues, you can give good answers to those questions.

Your Election Campaign Speech Plan

The special feature of your speech plan for a campaign is that although you have the same goal for every speech—getting people to support you or your candidate—the campaign will be composed of many speeches. This is why it is especially important to have a strong master outline of arguments, for in each speech you may focus on different arguments depending on the nature of the audience and their immediate concerns. The question is: How can you best show your character, your qualifications, and your goals for each of the many audiences you will face?

Your campaign speech plan will include your speech goal; the factors that you believe are particularly significant in making predictions about your audience; your strategies for getting and maintaining interest, orienting your audience, adapting to audience attitude, maintaining or increasing your credibility, and motivating your audience; a justification for the organizational pattern; and a complete outline.

Summary

The election campaign is a situation somewhat different from the action campaign. The major stages of the election campaign are surfacing, legitimation, promotion, and analysis. A candidate surfaces by making himself or herself known as a candidate for office. The surfacing stage involves the person "looking and sounding" like a candidate. In this surfacing stage, people usually hire or appoint a campaign manager. A campaign manager is indispensable in helping prepare the platform, schedule appearances, and prepare press releases.

Once you have surfaced as a candidate, you need to begin to legitimize your campaign by seeking key endorsements and getting financial support.

The major part of your promotion is to develop a personal identity, to build your credibility, and to build a case for your support. It is during the promotion stage of the campaign that your speech making is most important.

When the campaign is over, win or lose, you analyze the campaign to determine where you went right and where you went wrong. You then use the knowledge you gained for strengthening future campaigns for the same or for other types of office.

The issues in an election campaign include qualifications, experience, and platform. Audiences want to know what kind of a person they would be putting in office. Qualifications include a person's professional expertise. The electorate is looking for a candidate who understands the office. Record as a leader, knowledge of the working mechanism of the position, and personnel skills are all important. Constituencies like to have some idea of the kind of leadership the candidate will provide, so goals must be strong and well thought out.

Skill Development Exercises

1. From a recent issue of *Vital Speeches* select a speech that you believe could have been a part of an election campaign. How well does the speech exemplify characteristics of an election campaign speech?
2. Listen to a candidate for office make speeches to two different audiences.

In what ways were the speeches the same? In what ways did they differ? Does the speaker seem to understand the importance of audience adaptation? Explain.

Speech Preparation Exercises

1. Indicate an office for which you would like to run. Write a campaign plan that you could follow to increase your chances of gaining that office.
2. Prepare a six- to ten-minute persuasive speech that is intended to be a part of an election campaign. As part of your preparation, complete the following speech plan.
   a. Write your speech goal.
   b. Indicate the three features of your audience analysis that you believe are most significant in drawing conclusions about the audience.
   c. Indicate what you plan to do to build audience interest. Include methods of showing timeliness, proximity, and personal effect.
   d. Indicate what you plan to do to adapt to the knowledge level of your audience, including what background information you will have to include to orient them.
   e. In light of the audience's attitude (in favor, neutral, or opposed), what do you plan to do to adapt to that attitude?
   f. Indicate what you plan to do to build your credibility in the speech.
   g. Indicate what you plan to do to motivate your audience.
   h. What organization do you believe is most appropriate for your speech in light of that attitude?
3. What part of the plan do you believe is likely to be easiest to achieve? Most difficult? Explain.

Study Questions

For each of the following, be prepared to give examples in support of your answers.

1. What are the key features of "surfacing"? Why is surfacing so important to a candidate?
2. What can a candidate do to fulfill the legitimation steps?
3. Why are the personal characteristics of a candidate especially important in a campaign speech?
4. Why does a candidate need a good platform?

SAMPLE SPEECH PLAN AND SPEECH

A Campaign to Elect Reggie Williams, *by Ronald Cushing*[2]

1. *Speech goal.* I want my audience to vote for Reggie Williams.

2. *Audience profile.* As I look at my audience, I believe the most significant factors in reference to this proposition are age (early 20s) and education (soon to be college graduates).

3. *Audience interest.* Since members of the audience will be voting soon, I predict that their interest in hearing about candidates should be reasonably high. To maintain interest, I plan to open the speech with a story about how Reggie Williams has overcome personal tragedy and passed up scholarships to pay his own way to Dartmouth. This should nullify the "stupid jock" stereotype as well as get the audience more interested in Reggie Williams.

4. *Audience knowledge.* Although I believe everyone in the audience will know about Reggie Williams as a football player, I believe that I will have to stress information about Reggie Williams as a community servant.

5. *Audience attitude.* Since many people have a negative image of an athlete as politician, I predict that my audience may be slightly negative. However, because they are college students with open minds, I believe they will listen to arguments on Williams's behalf. Additionally, some of the students may already support one of the other candidates. It will be my job to show them that Reggie Williams is the best candidate to support.

6. *Perception of speaker credibility.* I plan to build my credibility by demonstrating that I have talked with Williams and have a good grasp of what he wishes to accomplish. However, the audience may believe that I am supporting Reggie Williams solely because he plays football, and they know I am a sports nut. To build my credibility I will focus on Williams's positive traits such as his character, intelligence, and desire to serve the community.

7. *Motivational elements.* I think my best strategy is to work with the audience's knowledge of Williams's sports strengths and show how they transfer to the political arena. I hope to develop a great deal of personal identification. In addition, I hope to show that Reggie Williams's plans are consistent with the values of the audience.

8. *Organizational plan.* Because I see the audience as uninformed and slightly negative, I will go with a kind of criteria-satisfaction plan.

SPEECH OUTLINE

Speech goal: I want the audience to vote for Reggie Williams.

Introduction

I. This speech is about a man who has never taken the easy way out.

II. This is the story of Reggie Williams.

Body

I. Reggie Williams is well qualified.
 A. Reggie Williams has been a strong force in the community.
  1. He has been involved with over 100 service organizations during the last ten years.
  2. He is a two-time winner of the NFL's Man of the Year Award for community service.
 B. Reggie Williams has council experience.
  1. He has been a council member for $1^1/_2$ years.
  2. He has learned while he has been in office.

II. Reggie Williams has well-defined goals for the community.
 A. He wants to assure that the drug awareness education program gets better support.
  1. The program offers classes on drug education.
  2. The program makes counselors available to students.
 B. He wants to increase funding of arts projects in order to stimulate community cultural and educational development.
 C. He wants to strengthen procedures for awarding contracts for downtown reconstruction.

Conclusion

I. He is a concerned community leader.

II. He has a plan of action.

Sources

The Cincinnati Enquirer, Monday, October 16, 1989, p. A8 (staff).
The Cincinnati Enquirer, Sunday, October 22, 1989, Special Election Section, p. 2 (staff).
Interview with Reggie Williams, October 24, 1989.
"Reggie Williams: A Man for All Seasons," published by Hamilton Projects.
"Reggie Williams: A Leader and a Role Model," published by Reggie Williams Campaign Committee, Inc., 1989.

Read the following speech aloud. Then analyze it on the basis of organization, reasoning and evidence, motivation, and speaker credibility. After you have read and analyzed the speech, refer to the analysis on the right.

Speech

There's a story I'd like to tell you about a man who as a child had a severe speech impediment. He was believed to be a slow learner. Doctors discovered that the reason he had these problems was because he was 40 percent deaf in both ears. Determined to overcome his handicap, he worked every day for three years with a speech therapist to relearn the mechanics of speech. It is this kind of dedication that enabled him to excel in football. Upon graduating from high school, he turned down scholarships to major colleges where he could not only play football but also get his education for free. He decided to go to Dartmouth University where he would have to pay his own tuition. Why did he do this? Because he wanted to get the best education he possibly could. Upon graduating with honors from Dartmouth, he was given virtually no chance to even make an NFL team, much less succeed in the league.

Fourteen years later, he is still starting for the Cincinnati Bengals. Over this time period he became very committed to community service. In the last ten years, he has worked with over 100 service organizations. His intelligence, community leadership, and education resulted in his unanimous appointment to city council in 1988. I don't know about you, but this is the story of the type of man that I would like to elect to help lead our city. This is, of course, the story of Reggie Williams. Reggie Williams is one of 20 candidates who you can vote for to become a member of city council.

I think we're all looking for the same basic criteria in a city council candidate—a person who is well qualified, a person with experience, and a person with a solid platform. I think you'll see that Reggie Williams meets all three of these criteria.

The first reason I believe you should vote for Reggie Williams is that he is qualified for the job. And when you're looking at a candidate's qualifications for a public office, you need to look at two things: personal characteristics and the experience necessary to excel in the office.

Analysis

The speaker begins with a narrative. Although most of the people in the audience are well aware of who he is talking about, the narrative approach serves the purpose of filling in some background information that both builds credibility for the candidate and begins a line of motivation.

In this second part of the introduction, he moves to the present. By the end of the introduction, he is into his persuasive appeal. In this final part of the introduction, he lists the criteria. They are presented in a way that is designed to achieve a "yes" response—the audience is likely to be responding, "Yes, that's what we want in a candidate."

Here he states the first reason and clarifies its two subdivisions.

To excel in city council the candidate must be community service oriented. Reggie Williams's commitment to community service is unequaled by any candidate. As I stated in the opening, over the last ten years, he has been involved with over 100 service organizations. He goes beyond just getting his name associated with these organizations. He is heavily involved in developing and managing projects he personally believes in. I'm sure all of you remember last year at this time the barrage of "Just Say No" commercials and the "Just Say No" rap song featuring Reggie and other Cincinnati Bengals. That was his idea. He wrote the song and the commercial. He saw to the distribution of the commercial and the record and made sure that the proceeds went to the drug education program. It is this type of commitment to community service that has resulted in Reggie's receiving numerous local and national awards, including winning the NFL's Man of the Year Award—twice! This award is given to the player who does the most good for the community in which he lives. Reggie Williams loves to serve Cincinnati.

In this section, he gives a great deal of supporting information. The personal characteristics are well developed. Phrases like "I'm sure all of you remember" help to personalize the information.

In addition to having the personal characteristics needed to excel in the office, Reggie Williams has the experience. He has been a council member now for a year and a half. During an interview Reggie was gracious enough to grant me, I asked him how he thought his experience stacked up against that of some of the other council members. His reply was that a year and a half ago when Ken Blackwell took a job in Washington, the members of city council unanimously decided that he was the best person to fill the position. And now that he has the experience of the day-to-day workings of the council, coupled with his years of experience as a community servant, he believes he has all the experience he needs to do a great job.

Even though the speaker is able to show that Williams's backers believe he has the necessary experience, he needs to be more specific about what Reggie Williams did in his year and a half.

If you're like me, regardless of a person's experience or desire to serve the community, you are not going to give them your vote until you know what kinds of goals the person wants to accomplish in office. Reggie Williams has set three main goals for himself. The first is assuring that the drug resistance education program now

This is probably the most completely developed of the three reasons. In the first part of the reason he does an excellent job of

being implemented in some of our schools gets the funding it needs to expand so that more of our kids may benefit from it. This drug resistance education program offers classes on drug education and it provides counselors for the kids to talk to. I'm sure some of you can remember back to high school and know some people, maybe even some good friends, who could have benefited from such a program. As future parents whose children can certainly benefit from the program, and as concerned citizens, this is a goal we can all identify with.

The second goal of Reggie Williams is to encourage financial support for the arts. This goal includes making the much talked about entertainment center a reality. As part of the center he advocates a museum and a theater that would show international, critically acclaimed films, films that don't otherwise make it to Cincinnati because they are not big box-office draws. As students who are are striving to improve our own education and become more diverse ourselves, this is also a goal we can identify with.

A third goal of Reggie Williams is to get legislation passed that will aid in development projects to improve the quality of our downtown, projects that will bring more housing, retail space, and entertainment to our city. The goal of this legislation is to prevent problems like those that have occurred with the Fountain Square West project. The end result would be more businesses and jobs. Students like ourselves who are getting degrees could benefit from this. We'd have more retailing and housing to choose from and we could all certainly benefit from the added entertainment. Reggie Williams has goals to make Cincinnati a better community.

There is no one label that can describe Reggie Williams. He is a football player. He is a community leader, a public servant, and a concerned citizen. He wants to continue his 14 years of unequaled community service as a member of the city council. He has the experience. He has the personal characteristics. He has the goals to make Cincinnati a better community. Very soon you will be going to the polls to select the nine

showing Williams's devotion to the drug program. Again in this section we see examples of the speaker personalizing the language.

At this time in Cincinnati many people have been anxious about the city council's failure to pursue support for an entertainment center and to expedite completion of other downtown projects that are on the drawing board. The speaker does a good job of showing how Williams stands on these issues and what he intends to do about them.

Good summary-type conclusion to draw the points together. In the last sentence he picks up on a slogan that has been associated with the Cincinnati Bengals football people who will form Cincinnati's city council. As you're weighing and considering each of the candidates, I want you to keep just one last thing in mind: Who dey, Who dey think could make a better councilman than Reggie Williams—nobody!

team, of which he
was a part for so
many years.
This speech could be
a valuable part of
Williams's election
campaign.

Notes

[1]Judith S. Trent and Robert Friedenberg, *Political Campaign Communication: Principles and Practices* (New York: Praeger, 1983).
[2]Speech delivered in a speech class at the University of Cincinnati. Reprinted by permission of Ronald Cushing.

Module **C**

Sales Campaign Speaking

Good afternoon, my name is Gale Ashworth and I represent the O'Cedar Company whose parent company is Dracket. I'm here today to introduce you to a new product which I feel especially qualified to endorse.

So begins Gale Ashworth's sales speech to a group of buyers for the Cincinnati market.

Selling can take place in a one-on-one, a small-group, or a one-to-many public speaking context. Sometimes the salesperson initiates the first contact. For instance, a door-to-door salesperson comes to your house to try to sell you magazines. Often, however, the consumer initiates the first contact. A company may form a committee to look into purchasing a new computer system. The committee then invites vendors to demonstrate their products.

Although this module features the one-to-many public speaking format, much of what we say is relevant to any sales context. The speech context usually provides the speaker with an uninterrupted segment of time for the presentation. But even in a situation where the potential customer can break in with questions, the methods and procedures for preparing the speech are much the same. Many companies provide training programs to teach new salespeople how to give their "pitch" from a set script. Then salespeople learn to vary the script for different circumstances.

192

In contrast to your role in a social action campaign or an election campaign, you are unlikely to initiate and develop a sales campaign. More likely, your speech is an integral part of a long-range corporate campaign that is already in progress. Nevertheless, in this module we briefly consider the stages of the product sales campaign. Then we focus on the characteristics of the salesperson and elements of the sales speech. We conclude with a student speech plan, outline, and sales speech.

Planning a Sales Campaign

Sales campaigns are built on the assumption that through promotion buyers will move from one stage of receptivity to another. Many discussions of the stages of marketing use the image of the "staircase."[1] In this analysis we consider this staircase as having four steps (various authors suggest as few as four and as many as seven steps). The steps are: creating product awareness, stimulating acceptance and preference, triggering the purchase, and reinforcing purchase patterns or reevaluating failure.

Marketers understand that potential buyers are likely to be at different levels on this staircase. For instance, the marketing of fax machines to businesses involves a different set of communication problems from the marketing of a new brand of breakfast cereal. Since people already buy, eat, and enjoy breakfast cereals, the potential consumer does not have to be sold on cereal as a viable breakfast. In contrast, when fax machines were first being marketed, the seller had to explain the function of the product, how it worked, why it was practical, and why it was better than such known means as overnight mail.

Creating Product Awareness. At the bottom of the marketing steps are potential buyers who are unaware of the existence of the product or service. Thus, the first step involves creating product awareness. The emphasis is not on selling or even on a knowledge of the product, but on becoming aware of the product. Speeches given in this stage often focus on creating images of the product and its name. For instance, if the product is a fax machine, in this stage speakers might discuss the miracle of sending letters via the telephone. They would explain that the machine that accomplishes this miracle is called a fax machine.

Stimulating Acceptance and Preference. The next step is often referred to as the knowledge or information step. The advertiser attempts to stimulate the potential buyer to accept the value of the product and select it over other similar products. Speeches given in this stage attempt to show the potential buyer the nature of the product and suggest appropriate uses for the product.

After people are aware of what the product can do, speeches in this stage also might focus on why this product is better than similar products or better than other ways of achieving the goal. In the early stages of a fax campaign, people would be encouraged to see exactly how a letter is sent via the fax. They would also be shown that a letter sent this way is of high quality. Speeches given later in this stage show why a fax is better than overnight letters, the prevailing means of quick delivery before faxing was introduced.

Triggering the Purchase. The third step on the staircase involves triggering the purchase—getting people to buy. The emphasis in this stage is on motivation. For a fax machine campaign, emphasis would be on comparative costs, showing the company how it could own or lease a fax machine that pays for itself. Additional incentives would be announced—extension of warranty, lifetime guarantee, rebates, discounts, and so on.

Reinforcement or Reevaluation. The final step involves reinforcement. Often people think of the purchase as the final step, but after a company has gotten initial purchases, it needs to continue to reinforce the product. If a product is successful, lookalikes may appear to offer the same quality or even greater advantages. If the product is not reinforced, it may eventually fail. On the other hand, if the product has failed, the failure needs to be reevaluated so that the same mistakes will not be made again.

In the typical sales campaign, a tremendous burden falls on the salesperson. Although advertising paves the way for a company to familiarize its potential customers with the product, in a majority of cases it is the salesperson who actually cinches the sale. And often whether the sale is made depends on that salesperson's presentation. In the remainder of this module we consider the characteristics of an effective salesperson and the methods of making an effective sales presentation.

Characteristics of the Effective Salesperson

Since a reality of sales is that if you sell yourself, you sell your product, credibility may be the salesperson's most significant selling point. Especially when products have relatively similar features, customers purchase from the salesperson with whom they feel most comfortable. I know several people who felt such loyalty to a salesperson that they continued to buy from that particular person even when that person changed companies.

The following are some of the qualities that customers find particularly important to a salesperson's credibility.

Knowledgeability about the Product or Service.   Probably the number one characteristic of outstanding salespeople is that they know what they are talking about. In one study of top salespeople who were chosen based on selling records alone, in every case these superior salespeople were found to be genuine experts in the products they were handling.[2] Expertise is often measured by how well the salesperson can respond to customer questions. When questions are well answered, customer confidence increases; when questions are not answered to customer satisfaction, customer confidence nosedives. One reason why veteran salespeople are often among the sales leaders in their companies is that they have been with the company long enough to know the ins and outs of the product.

What marks a salesperson as knowledgeable? To be well prepared to sell your product, you must have a firm grasp of its features and benefits.[3]

A *feature* is some characteristic that distinguishes the product. For instance, a feature of a particular piece of furniture may be that it is solid wood (no veneer), or stain resistant, or hand finished. Any product has many features that give it a distinctive character. From a sales presentation people want information on features that give a product an edge over the competition.

A *benefit* is an edge or an advantage that a feature of the product has for the customer. For instance, as a result of certain features of the product, a customer may gain such benefits as higher profit, greater convenience of operation, better performance, and safer performance.

How do features and benefits correlate? If a computer features an operating system that allows the operator to get from place to place in a document faster, then the operator accrues the benefit of a savings in time.

In the early stages of planning your speech, it is often a good idea to make a feature-benefits inventory. List the features of your product that are unique or special. Then list the benefits that the customer will get from your product as a result of these features.

Although some product information is relatively easy to get, some of the most important information requires creative approaches. Certainly the first source of information about your product is the material printed by the manufacturer. Companies publish a variety of sales manuals and literature. If you work directly for the company, they will see to it that you have all of this material. If you are working for another agency that is selling products from several companies, then you must make sure that you receive all the information that a company supplies about its product.

Reading should not be limited to material from the producing company. For most products you can find some kind of evaluation. For consumer products, you can get test results from *Consumer Reports* and *Consumer Bulletin.* Magazines related to certain product lines also conduct tests. For instance, automotive magazines routinely have test results of new and used cars. Likewise, computer magazines have test results of computers and computer hardware and software systems.

A second way of getting information is to visit the production facility. Although this is not always practical, it can be very beneficial.

A third way is to get hands-on experience. Needless to say, you should never try to sell a product that you have not worked with enough to know its strengths and weaknesses.

Sensitivity to the Needs of the Consumer.   Top-selling salespersons care for the needs of their clients. Think of yourself as providing a service for your client or customer. The client or customer has specific needs to be met, and you have the service or product to meet those needs. For instance, before top-selling real estate agents show houses to customers, they find out exactly what kinds of houses their customers are looking for. They take time to learn the kinds of features that are wanted, they probe to find which of these features are a necessity and which are not, and they find out how much a family can afford to pay. Then they begin to show homes that seem to fit those needs. We often hear stories of the salesperson who is master of the hard sale—the person who can sell air conditioners to people who live in igloos. Although the hard sell works in some businesses where no return sales are expected (or sought), customers are often resentful of hard sell tactics.

Enthusiasm for the Product or Service.   As we said in Chapter 9 on presentation style, enthusiasm is infectious. When we see that a salesperson gets a real joy out of selling the product, our confidence in the person and product goes up as well. If we sense that the salesperson is "only doing a job," we begin to wonder whether that person cares enough to do the most for us. Enthusiasm is a sign of the salesperson's confidence in the product.

Ethical Sales Practices.   Too many people correlate the profession of sales with con men—unscrupulous, unprincipled people who will do anything for a sale. Although there are salespeople who fit the stereotype, the great majority of salespeople understand fully that ethics and sincerity are not only good character traits, but they are also good business. I'm reminded of a waiter I had recently who, when I ordered a menu item that was supposed to be a house specialty, said, "That's usually one of our best dishes, but it's really not good this evening; may I suggest the lamb instead?" When I got my meal and it was excellent, the amount I was planning to tip rose considerably. Customers are always on the lookout for salespeople they can trust. Successful salespeople show their products well and stand by what they sell.

Articulate Communicators. The better you have learned your communication skills, the better salesperson you are. People enjoy talking with a salesperson who is articulate. We become suspicious of people who stumble for the right word, are vague and imprecise, and show a general inability to communicate effectively.

Effective salespeople tend to be extroverts—people who are outgoing and talkative. Keep in mind that there is a line between being outgoing and talkative and boisterous and loudmouthed. Just as we feel very comfortable with a person who is easy to talk with, we become uncomfortable with one who we perceive as domineering.

Finally, we expect a salesperson to fit our preconceived notion of the "ideal salesperson." Often this includes how a person looks and acts. We expect a salesperson to dress and behave appropriately.

Building Your Case

The goals you write for sales speeches will be action statements, such as "I want the administration to purchase Macintosh II computers for all departments," "I want the school system to purchase World Book Encyclopedias for all school libraries," or "I want the class to buy my line of hypoallergenic cosmetic products."

Since a sales speech provides a solution to a perceived need or want, the *issues* are similar to those for any policy speech. Let's review them and see where they differ in emphasis.

1. *What are the needs of the consumer? (What are the goals that the person or the company is trying to meet?)* The consumer has needs that must be met. Sometimes these needs are already apparent to the consumer. For instance, a company that is experiencing a problem with its software system is likely to be in the market for a new system. In this case the salesperson knows the needs the company expects a new system to meet. Sometimes the consumer is unaware of its needs or believes that its needs are already being met. For instance, a company may have accounting needs that are currently being met with older technology. In this case the salesperson must convince the company that its needs are not really being met.

2. *Does this product meet the needs of potential consumers?* A successful product must meet the specific needs of the potential customer. It is with this issue that you focus on the features and benefits of your product that are designed to meet the consumer's needs. An effective way of convincing the consumer that your product will satisfy the needs is to demonstrate it. In one-on-one sales, you

can involve the consumer in the demonstration. In a one-to-many presentation, you can conduct the demonstration.

3. *Is the product practical for the consumer?* A consumer may like your product but may perceive it as impractical at this time. For instance, a new software system might save the company time because of easier use and faster operation, but the consumer may believe that the initial startup costs are far more than the company could save over time by adopting the new product. To meet the issue of practicality, a company often offers such incentives as discounts, rebates, free training, extended warranties, or reduced-cost service contracts to the consumer. You need to know what leeway you have to offer additional incentives for buying the product.

Summary

In contrast to your role in a social action campaign or an election campaign, you are unlikely to initiate and develop a sales campaign. More likely, your speech will be an integral part of a long-range corporate campaign that is already in progress.

Sales campaigns are built on the assumption that through promotion, buyers will move from one stage of receptivity to another. At the bottom of the steps are potential buyers who are unaware of the existence of the product or service, so the first step in the staircase involves creating product awareness. The next step is often referred to as the knowledge or information step. The advertiser attempts to stimulate the potential buyer to accept the value of the product and select it over other similar products. The third step on the staircase involves triggering the purchase—getting people to buy. The emphasis is on motivation. The final step involves reinforcement. Often people think of the purchase as the final step, but after a company has gotten initial purchases, it needs to continue to reinforce the product. If a product is successful, lookalikes may appear on the market to offer the same quality or even greater advantages. If the product is not reinforced, it eventually fails. On the other hand, if the product has failed, the failure needs to be reevaluated so that the same mistakes will not be made again.

In the typical sales campaign, a tremendous burden falls on the salesperson. Whether the sale is made depends on that salesperson's presentation, and credibility may be the salesperson's most significant selling point. Probably the number one characteristic of outstanding salespeople is that they know what they are talking about. To be well prepared to sell your product you must have a firm grasp of its features, characteristics that distinguish the product, and its benefits, edges or advantages that the features give the product for the customer. The first source of information about your product is everything the maker has written about it and any test results that are reported in consumer magazines. You can also get information by visiting the production facility and by getting hands-on experience.

Top-selling salespersons care for the needs of their clients and they are enthusiastic in their presentation. Finally, they are ethical in dealings with their clients.

Since a sales speech provides a solution to a perceived need or want, the *issues* are similar to those for any policy-type speech. In your speeches you must be able to identify consumer needs, show how the product meets those needs, and give the consumer incentives to show that purchasing the product is practical.

Skill Development Exercises

Look for a television commercial in which an on-camera spokesperson advocates a product.

1. Identify the features or benefits of the product. How are they explained? Is the explanation convincing? Why?
2. What is the basis of the spokesperson's credibility? Is the basis justifiable? Explain.

Speech Preparation Exercises

1. Indicate a sales campaign for which your speech could be a part. Explain the role of your speech in that campaign.
2. Prepare a six- to ten-minute persuasive speech that is intended to be part of a sales campaign. As part of your preparation complete the following speech plan.
   a. Write your speech goal.
   b. Indicate the features of your audience analysis that you believe are most significant in drawing conclusions about the audience.
   c. Indicate what you plan to do to build audience interest. Include methods of showing timeliness, proximity, and personal effect.
   d. Indicate what you plan to do to adapt to the knowledge level of your audience, including what background information you will have to include to orient them.
   e. In light of the audience's attitude (in favor, neutral, or opposed), what do you plan to do to adapt to that attitude?
   f. Indicate what you plan to do to build your credibility in the speech.

    g.   Indicate what you plan to do to motivate your audience.

    h.   What organization do you believe is most appropriate for your speech in light of that attitude?

3. What part of the plan do you believe is likely to be easiest to achieve? Most difficult? Explain.

Study Questions

For each of the following, be prepared to give examples in support of your answers.

1. What are four essential steps of a sales campaign?
2. What are ways of getting product knowledge?
3. What are the differences between features and benefits?
4. What differentiates ethical from unethical sales practices?

SAMPLE SPEECH PLAN AND SPEECH

A Campaign to Sell O'Cedar's Easy Reach Scrubber, *by Gail Ashworth*[4]

1. *Speech goal.* My goal is to persuade supermarket distributors to order the O'Cedar Easy Reach Scrubber.

2. *Interest.* My audience will have a general interest, since they are looking for products that they can sell in large numbers. I believe that as I discuss what O'Cedar can do for them, their interest will be increased. I hope to boost interest by demonstrating the scrubber.

3. *Knowledge.* Although my audience will be familiar with cleaning brushes and sponges, they will not be familiar with this particular product. As a result, I will need to spend time familiarizing them with the features.

4. *Attitude.* Since my audience is interested in stocking new products that are likely to make money for them, they are likely to have a reasonably open mind. At the same time, they are likely to be a little cynical; every sales representative is likely to suggest that his or her product is the best thing since sliced bread. To meet this neutral but perhaps cynical attitude, I hope to rely on well-documented information.

5. *Credibility.* Since O'Cedar has an excellent reputation, I believe my audience will anticipate a useful product. During the speech it is up to me to maintain O'Cedar's reputation and build my own credibility. In the speech I hope to develop my expertise and familiarity with cleaning products. I also hope to show that my own arthritic condition makes me particularly credible for demonstrating the easy-to-use features of the product.

6. *Motivation.* Instead of just citing features, I will demonstrate them. I believe that the rather dramatic demonstration of features will have some motivating effect. Then I want to emphasize the incentives that O'Cedar will provide for those distributors who stock the product during this introductory period.

7. *Organization.* My organization will follow a comparative-advantages or benefits pattern.

SPEECH OUTLINE

Speech goal: I want to persuade supermarket distributors to order the O'Cedar Easy Reach Scrubber.

Introduction

I. Easy Reach is an innovative, unique product produced by a reliable, reputable company.

II. Easy Reach has features that are not available in any other product.

Body

I. The Easy Reach Scrubber is innovative.
- A. The handle is specially designed.
  1. It has a specially designed 22-inch handle that allows you to reach high or low places with virtually no stretching or bending.
  2. The comfort grip handle fits the hand and is textured for a sure grip.
  3. The handle has a hanger hook for easy storage.
- B. The sponge head is flexible.
  1. It swivels 180 degrees, making it possible to reach all bathroom surfaces.
  2. The back plate bends to clean contours of bathroom surfaces.
- C. The sponge itself is specially engineered.
  1. The white dimpled surface gives you strong cleaning action without marring or scratching.
  2. The sponge holds 23 times its weight in water.

II. O'Cedar is now offering special incentives.
- A. O'Cedar helps give you a head start with its national advertising sendoff.
  1. We will offer an outstanding $13 million national annual spending campaign during the introductory period.

2. The 30-second commercials will air on daytime and prime time syndication.

B. O'Cedar will offer you special pricing at this time.

1. You will get a $1.32 per case allowance on each case purchased during this introductory period.
2. You will get a $4.00 display allowance.

Conclusion

I. The Easy Reach Scrubber has innovative features that can't be matched.

II. O'Cedar is providing incentives that make this the time to buy.

III. O'Cedar really does make your life easier.

Read the following speech aloud. Then analyze it as a sales speech on the basis of organization, reasoning and evidence, motivation, and speaker credibility. After you have read and analyzed the speech, refer to the analysis on the right.

Speech

Good afternoon. My name is Gale Ashworth, and I represent the O'Cedar Company whose parent company, as you may know, is Dracket. I'm here today to introduce you to a new product which I feel especially qualified to endorse. I've cleaned a lot of bathrooms in my day, and I'll tell you, as a fully qualified "domestic engineer" I've never seen a bathroom and tile cleaner that has as many innovative ideas as our new product called Easy Reach. At first glance this may not look much different from some other bath and tile cleaners you have stocked. But looks are deceptive. This single product has seven features that other products of its kind just can't duplicate.

Let's start with the handle. First, notice that Easy Reach has a specially designed 22-inch handle that allows you to reach high or low places with virtually no stretching or bending. Since most showers have tile that extends over the head of the normal-sized person, you are not tall enough to reach the ceiling of that shower. With Easy Reach you are—and one of the reasons it's

Analysis

Notice how the speaker uses humor in the opening while subtly building her credibility. She acknowledges that the product looks similar to others, but she then announces that it has seven distinct features. Since she knows that the audience will be interested in a product of merit, she begins to place her emphasis on features and benefits.

In this part of the speech she moves through the product in a spatial order, beginning with the handle. She takes her time to show each of the three

called "Easy Reach" is because it is so easy to reach with. Second, notice the comfort grip handle. See how nicely it fits the hand. *And* it is textured for a sure grip that keeps it from slipping out of your hand as you clean. Third, notice that the handle comes with a hanger that enables you to hang it on the shower or on the towel rod, or on one of those nails you've driven into the back of the door for your robe. A nifty little addition, right?

features that make the handle unique.

Next, look at the sponge head. What makes this sponge head special? First, notice that it swivels a full 180 degrees, making it possible for you to reach all bathroom surfaces. You can reach the sides of the bathroom and the shower, as well as the sides of the bathtub. Also notice that the back plate is flexible so that it will clean contours of bathroom surfaces. Let me demonstrate this flexibility for you. [Here she displays a model of a bathtub.] When you stand here, this side of the bathtub is easy to reach with any cleaning implement. But as you are well aware, the other side is nearly impossible to reach and really get clean without bending over and breaking your back. But watch how the Easy Reach works. Notice how it conforms in size, it reaches all the way over to the other side, and it swivels to get into corners. Folks, at this time Easy Reach is the only product of its kind that gives you this flexibility.

From the handle she moves to the other key part of the Easy Reach, the scrubber. Since she can't fully demonstrate the scrubber, she uses a model that gives the audience the idea of the value of the sponge's flexibility. The way she demonstrates the use of the scrubber helps the audience see what she is talking about.

These features are especially useful for those people who have arthritis or lower back problems and find stretching, bending, and turning extremely difficult. In fact, as a result of these features Easy Reach has won the endorsement of the American Society for Aging and testimonials by *Mature Plus* magazine. Not only older people have difficulty cleaning the bathtub, however; younger people do as well. I myself have an arthritic arm. I have difficulty doing this job and it's not a lot of fun; sometimes it's difficult and at other times it's really excruciating. I use this product—I like it. I find it really does a nice job and it really does make my life easier.

Here she develops motivation by showing how this scrubber will meet the needs of large numbers of the population—both the elderly and younger people with physical handicaps. Furthermore, she builds credibility for the product by giving the endorsement.

Now let's look at the sponge itself. First let's consider the ease of mind this particular sponge gives: this white dimpled sponge that will not harm porcelain, fiber glass, or tile. It gives you a strong scrubbing effect

In this section she focuses on the unique aspects of the sponge and places special em-

without marring or scratching. In addition, this sponge has a tremendous capacity. It may look like your ordinary everyday sponge, but it's not because it holds 23 times its weight in water. Let me repeat that—it holds 23 times its weight in water! This means you get lots of cleaning, scouring, and rinsing. The white dimpled scrubbing sponge surface cleans off soap scum better than regular sponges. Moreover, the sponge is totally pliable and it bends completely around.

From what I've shown you so far, you can see that Easy Reach is by far the best cleaning product of its type on the market. Other products may have one or two similar features, but no other product has all that Easy Reach has: there are scrub brushes with long handles, but they don't swivel; they are not designed specifically to allow the human body to reach difficult-to-reach places, and they don't have a sponge with anywhere near the capacity.

OK, so you're sold on the product, but you're still not sure the market will support the product. Let's look at the numbers. There are 86.5 million families with at least one bathroom in the United States. Fifty-five percent of women surveyed by Homemakers Institute of America say they clean their bathroom once a week. Now here's the good news: 71 percent of our test market said they probably would or definitely would buy the Easy Reach Scrubber for their bathroom. So there's no question that you have a real market for the product.

But I'm not done yet. During this introductory period we are also offering your company the unique opportunity to provide this product to your consumers. To start with, we are willing to offer you a $1.32 off each six-pack case of Easy Reach Scrubbers *and* a $4.00 rebate on the display stand and rack to hold your Easy Reach Scrubbers. Also, if you buy now, you'll have the power of the O'Cedar advertising budget behind you. During this introductory time period, O'Cedar will be spending $13 million in 30-second television spots at various times throughout the day, including prime time.

Now, how can you go wrong? You're buying a product from O'Cedar, a company that is a reputable,

phasis on the capacity.

Here we see good use of repetition.

In this short section she briefly summarizes the major features that make Easy Reach unique.

At this point, she has made a good logical case for the Easy Reach. Now she moves to the next stage, assuring the buyers that there is a market for the product. There is good statistical analysis in this section.
This is a good effort to move listeners to the buying stage. To stimulate her audience to make an order now, she outlines the incentives.

Notice how she reinforces the point that

recognizable home product company that's been in business since 1949. It has survived these 50 years because it has provided the household cleaning market with many new innovative ideas. And Easy Reach is the newest in this long line of innovative products. Let's review. Easy Reach is a bath and tile scrubber that represents one innovative idea after another: a 22-inch handle with a comfortable grip and a hanger for easy storage, a sponge head that swivels and conforms in size, a sponge surface that cleans without marring or scratching, and capacity that is without equal. Moreover, O'Cedar is providing television advertising that will reach an enormous market plus rebates on cases you buy as well as on your display cases. Most of all, we are offering you the opportunity to present the public with a product that helps them accomplish a mundane chore in a much more comfortable manner. I hope you will consider purchasing the Easy Reach Scrubber. And just remember, "O'Cedar really does make your life easier."

buyers are purchasing a solid company name as well as a specific product. Here she reviews the seven unique features that she mentioned in the introduction. Her clear presentation of sound reasons and good support give the speech a good logical base. She does an excellent job of dramatizing the features. Her language style throughout the speech helps to make this an effective sales speech.

Notes

1. See, for instance, William Zikmund and Michael D'Amico, *Marketing*, 2d ed. (New York: John Wiley & Sons, 1986), p. 483.
2. Frederic A. Russell, Frank H. Beach, and Richard H. Buskirk, *Textbook of Salesmanship*, 10th ed. (New York: McGraw-Hill Book Company, 1978), p. 73.
3. Robert Seng, *The Skills of Selling* (New York: Amacom, 1977), p. 22.
4. Delivered in a speech class at the University of Cincinnati. Reprinted by permission of Gail Ashworth.

Module **D**

Opposing Persuasive Arguments

When you are confronted with a speech that makes a claim and you disagree with that claim, you can sit quietly and fume, or you can take issue with the reasons and evidence in support of that claim. The goal of this module is to give you the expertise to refute arguments when you believe that they are faulty or not in the best interests of the audience.

The first part of this module defines refutation, the next part considers critical evaluation of arguments, and the third part shows how to use the results of critical evaluation in refutation. The module concludes with a speech assignment that enables you to put what you've learned into practice and an example of a speech that is designed to illustrate refutation.

Refutation Defined

Some people believe that they are refuting a speech when they give a persuasive speech "on the other side." But, if a person gives a speech with three reasons in support of abolishing capital punishment and you reply by giving a speech with three reasons in support of capital punishment, your speech is not necessarily refutation. *Refutation* is the process of proving that a reason or some evidence, is false, erroneous—or at least doubtful. If someone argues that capital punishment should be abolished because it is not a deterrent and you argue that capital punishment *is* a deterrent, your statement and the supporting evidence you present are direct refutation.

Sometimes refutation is a small segment of a speech. Suppose you are giving a speech in support of donating money to the United Way. To counter an audience belief that the United Way distributes its money to agencies more for political reasons than for need, you might plan to save a small portion of your speaking time to refute that argument. At other times, refutation may be the basic method for the entire speech. Suppose you just heard a colleague argue that the company ought to invest a large portion of its pension plan in real estate, a proposal you think is very risky. Under those circumstances, you might reply to the proposal with an entire speech of refutation. In either case, learning to refute is an important skill for any responsible citizen to acquire.

Critical Analysis of Speech Arguments

To critically analyze a speech argument, you must have an accurate representation of that argument. When you evaluate written sources, the entire argument is on paper in front of you. To evaluate an oral argument, however, you need to outline the argument carefully to preserve its essence. After you have outlined an argument or a series of arguments, you can begin to examine the reasoning used.

Outlining Arguments

Good outlining requires that you get the key material down on paper accurately. Keep in mind that a good outline is not a transcription of the entire argument. For a persuasive argument, an outline contains the reasons presented in defense of a claim and the grounds used in support of the reasons with notations of whether the grounds are documented.

Let's look at an abbreviated written version of an oral argument:

Public schools have been criticized during the past few years, but the accomplishments of some schools in the city show that public schools are capable of high levels of achievement. Park Hills, a public school on the west side, is an excellent example. Three years ago Park Hills raised its standards in all academic courses. It forced its students to work much harder to achieve good grades. According to an article in the June 26 issue of the *Post,* this year Park Hills had three National Merit scholars, more than in any year in its history. Moreover, student SAT scores were up 20 points from student scores just three years ago. Linden, a public school on the east side, is another example. Four years ago Linden began increasing homework assignments and now requires two hours per evening of homework as well as three major papers a year from all students. According to that same *Post* article, this year Linden had 85 percent of its graduating class accepted to college, up 30 percent from four years ago.

The following is the kind of outline you would write to analyze the argument.

I. Public schools are capable of high levels of achievement.
   A. Park Hills (example)
      1. Raised standards in all courses (How?)
      2. Forced students to work harder for grades (What does this mean?)
      3. Three National Merit scholars—more than ever
      4. SAT scores up 20 points in three years (What were scores in other years?)
   B. Linden (a second example)
      1. Two hours of homework per night
      2. Three papers a year from all students (Compared to what?)
      3. 85 percent of graduates accepted to college—up 30 percent in four years

Determining the Basis for Refutation

Once you have the substance of the speech (or argument) written in outline form, you can begin to test the grounds and the reasoning. Refutation starts with anticipating what the opposition will say. For any controversial issue you should know the reasons that are likely to be presented on either side. If you have anticipated the reasons your opponent is likely to use, you are in a much better position to reply. If the opponent talks for very long, you should probably take some notes; you do not want to run the risk of being accused of distorting what your opponent really said.

You can base your refutation on amount of support, quality of support, or reasoning. If the opposition's case is built on assertion with little or no supporting evidence, you can refute the argument on that basis. A better method, however, is to attack the quality of the material. If sheer amount of evidence was the most important criterion in proving a point, the person with the most material would always win. However, there is often no direct relationship between amount of material and quality of proof. For example, a statement by a judge who has studied the issue of individual rights to privacy would be worth far more than several opinions on the rights to privacy from athletes, musicians, or politicians who have not studied the subject.

Evaluating Evidence

For every bit of evidence that is presented, you should ask the following questions:

1. *Is the evidence fact or opinion?* As we said earlier, fact is usually worth more than opinion, and expert opinion is worth more than inexpert opinion.

2. *Where does the evidence come from?* This question involves both the people who offered the opinions or compiled the facts and the book, journal, or source in which they were reported. Just as some people's opinions are more reliable than others, some printed sources are more reliable than others. That something appeared in print does not necessarily make it true. If data come from a poor source, an unreliable source, or a biased source, no reliable conclusion can be drawn from them, and you should refute the argument on that basis.

3. *Is the evidence recent?* Products, ideas, and statistics often are obsolete as soon as they are produced. You must ask when the particular evidence was true. Five-year-old evidence may not be true today. Furthermore, an article in last week's news magazine may be using five-year-old evidence.

4. *Is the evidence relevant?* You may find that the evidence has little to do with the point being presented. This question of relevancy may well lead you into the reasoning process itself.

Evaluating Reasoning

Although attacks on evidence are sometimes effective means of refutation, the form of refutation that is most convincing is an attack on the reasoning from the evidence. Each argument presented in a persuasive speech is composed of at least three elements: (1) evidence or grounds from which a conclusion is drawn, (2) the conclusion itself, and (3) a stated or implied link that takes speakers from their evidence to the conclusions they have drawn. In order to refute the reasoning, first check whether the reasons prove the proposition and are supported; then identify the method or methods of reasoning and assess their validity. As we showed in Chapter 5, you ask different questions depending on the argument.

Let's briefly review the questions that you should be prepared to ask for each type of reasoning. When the speaker has reasoned from example, you question the number and typicality of the instances and whether negative instances were accounted for. When the speaker has reasoned from analogy, question the similarity of the subjects and whether any dissimilarities have been omitted. When the speaker has reasoned from causation, question whether data are sufficient to bring about the effect, whether some other data may have caused the effect, and whether the relationships between cause and effect are consistent. When the speaker has reasoned from sign, question the number of signs, the relationship of the signs to the conclusion, and the omission of contradictory signs. When the speaker has reasoned from definition, question the criteria and whether the subject meets the criteria. And when the speaker has reasoned from authority, question the credibility of the source.

Special Fallacies in Reasoning

As you study the oral arguments you oppose, you may discover fallacious ways in which speakers have tried to reason. Let's consider five of the most common fallacious reasoning patterns.

Hasty Generalization. Recall that one of the most common forms of argument is by example or generalization. Likewise, one of the most common thinking fallacies is the *hasty generalization,* which results from a shortage of data. Conclusions from hasty generalization fail to meet the test of sufficient instances cited. In real-life situations, people often make generalizations based on only one, or at most a few examples. For instance, in support of the argument that the U.S. population believe that drugs (marijuana, cocaine, and heroin) should be legalized, a person might cite the opinion of two of his neighbors. Yet, that sample is neither large enough nor representative enough. In a speech, an argument may sound more impressive than it is, especially if the speaker dramatizes the one example. But you can refute the argument as a hasty generalization.

If a speaker presents a generalization with no supporting examples or with only one or two unrepresentative examples, you may attack the argument on that basis alone.

Questionable Cause. Another common thinking fallacy, *questionable cause,* is marked by the failure of an argument to stand because the data alone are insufficient to bring about a particular conclusion. It is human nature to look for causes for events. If we are having a drought, we want to know the cause; if the schools are in financial trouble, we want to know the cause; if the crime rate has risen during the year, we want to know the cause. In our haste to discover causes for events, we sometimes identify something that happened or existed before the event or at the time of the event, and then label that something as the cause of the event. This tendency leads to the fallacy of questionable cause.

Think of the people who blame loss of money, sickness, and problems at work on black cats that ran in front of them, or mirrors that broke, or ladders they walked under. You recognize these as superstitions. They are excellent examples of attributing cause to unrelated events.

Superstitions are not the only examples of questionable cause. Consider a situation that occurs yearly on many college campuses. One year a coach's team has a winning season and the coach is lauded for his or her expertise. The next year the team does poorly and the coach is fired. Has the coach's skill deteriorated that much in one year? It is unlikely. But it's much easier to point the finger at the coach as the cause of the team's failure than it is to admit that the entire team or the program itself is inferior. Examples of this kind of argument are frequent.

If you believe that the data alone are not important or significant enough to bring about the conclusion, then you can question the reasoning on that basis.

Appeal to Authority.   An *appeal to authority* is a fallacy based on the quality of the data. When people support their argument with the testimony of an authority, you can refute it as being fallacious if the testimony fails to meet either of two tests: (1) Is the source really an authority on the issue? (2) Is the content of the testimonial consistent with other expert opinions?

Let us consider cases where the source is not really an authority. Advertisers are well aware that because the public idolizes athletes, movie stars, and television performers, people are likely to accept their word on subjects they may know little about. So when an athlete tries to get the viewer to purchase perfume, the athlete's argument is a fallacy.

Although the fallacy of authority may be easy to recognize in a television ad, other examples may not be so easy to recognize. Economists, politicians, and scientists often comment on subjects outside their areas of expertise; sometimes neither they nor we realize how unqualified they are to speak on such subjects. A scientist's statement is good evidence only in the science in which he or she is an expert. Thus, a geneticist's views on the world food supply may be fallacious, depending on the point he or she is trying to make.

The other test is whether the content of the testimonial is consistent with other expert opinions. Even when an authority states an opinion relevant to his or her area of expertise, that opinion may be fallacious if it is not supported by a majority of other authorities in that field. If a space biologist says that there must be life like our own on other planets, his or her opinion is no more logical proof than any other opinion; it is not even an authoritative opinion if a majority of other equally qualified space biologists believe otherwise. If you look long enough, you can always find someone who has said something in support of even the most foolish statement. Try to avoid the mistake of accepting any statement as valid support just because some alleged authority is cited as the source.

Appeals Based on Statistics.   Fallacies in the use of statistics may be based on the quantity of data, quality of data, or reasoning from data. Statistics are nothing more than large numbers of instances, but statistics seem to have a bewitching force. Most of us are conditioned to believe that instances stated in statistical form carry the weight of authority. The potential fallacies from statistics are so numerous that there is no way I can do total justice to the subject in this short analysis. The old saying, "Figures don't lie, but liars figure," is so applicable to the general use of statistics that you need to be particularly careful with their use. To be safe, you should look at any statistical proof as potentially fallacious. Even statistics that are used honestly and with the best motives may still be fallacious because the clear, logical use of statistics is so difficult.

As you examine arguments supported with statistics, look for the following red flags:

1. *Statistics that are impossible to verify.* If you are like me, you have read countless startling statements such as, "Fifteen million mosquitoes are hatched each day in the Canadian province of Ontario" or "One out of every 17 women in ancient Greece had six fingers." Now, don't go around quoting these—I made them up, but they are no more unlikely than many other examples I have seen. The fact is we have no way of verifying such statistics. How does anyone count the number of mosquitoes hatched? How can we test whether anyone counted the fingers of ancient Greek women? Statistics of this kind are startling and make interesting conversation, but they are fallacious as support for arguments.

2. *Statistics used alone.* Statistics by themselves do not mean much; for example, "Last season the Cincinnati Reds drew about 1.7 million fans to their 70 home games." Although at face value this sounds like (and it is) a lot of people, it does not tell much about the club's attendance. Is this figure good or bad? Was attendance up or down? Often statistics are not meaningful until they are compared with other data.

3. *Statistics used with unknown comparative bases.* Comparisons of statistics do not mean much if the comparative base is not given. Consider the statement, "While the Zolon growth rate was dawdling along at some 3 percent last year, Allon was growing at a healthy 8 percent." This statement implies that Allon is doing much better than Zolon; however, if Zolon's base was larger, its 3 percent increase could be much better than Allon's 8 percent. We cannot know unless we understand the base from which the statistics were drawn.

Ad Hominem Argument. An *ad hominem argument* is an attack on the person making the argument rather than on the argument itself. Literally, *ad hominem* means "to the man." For instance, if Bill Bradley, U.S. senator from New Jersey, the highly intelligent and articulate former New York Knicks basketball player, stated that athletics are important to the development of the total person, an ad hominem argument would be, "Great, all we need is some jock justifying his own existence."

Such a personal attack is often made as a smokescreen to cover up for a lack of good reasons and evidence. Ad hominem, name-calling, is used to try to encourage the audience to ignore a lack of evidence. Make no mistake, ridicule, name-calling, and other personal attacks are at times highly successful, but they are almost always fallacious.

There are many other types of fallacy that I have not covered in this short section. What can you do when you encounter an argument that you cannot identify? Outline the argument, test the data, and test the reasoning link. Even if you are unable to identify the type of argument, you can probably still judge its relative strength or weakness.

How to Refute

Although you do not have as long to consider exactly what you are going to say, your refutation must be organized nearly as well as a planned speech. If you think of refutation as units of argument, each organized in four definite steps, you can learn to prepare and present refutation effectively.

1. State the argument you are going to refute clearly and concisely. (Or, as an advocate replying to refutation, state the argument you are going to rebuild.)
2. State what you will prove. You must tell your listeners how you plan to proceed so they will be able to follow your thinking.
3. Present the proof completely with documentation.
4. Draw your own conclusion. Do not rely on the audience to draw the proper conclusion for you. Never go on to another argument before you have drawn your conclusion.

In the following abbreviated statement, notice how the four steps of refutation (stating the argument, stating what you will prove, presenting the proof, and drawing a conclusion) are incorporated. For purposes of analysis, each of the four steps is numbered.

(1) Ms. Horan has said that buying insurance provides a systematic, compulsory savings. Her assumption is that "systematic, compulsory savings" is a benefit of buying insurance while you are young. (2) But I believe that just the opposite is true. I believe that there are at least two serious disadvantages resulting from this. (3) First, the system is so compulsory that if you miss a payment you stand to lose your entire savings and all benefits. Most insurance contracts include a clause giving you a 30-day grace period, after which the policy is canceled [evidence]. Second, if you need money desperately, you have to take a loan on your policy. The end result of such a loan is that you have to pay interest in order to borrow your own money [evidence]. (4) From this analysis, I think you can see that the "systematic, compulsory savings" is more a disadvantage than an advantage for people who are trying to save money.

Summary

Refutation is the process of proving that an argument or the conclusion drawn from that argument is false, erroneous—or at least doubtful. Sometimes refutation makes up a small segment of a speech. Other times, it may be the basic method for the entire speech.

To critically analyze a speech argument, you must have an accurate representation of that argument in outline form. When you have outlined the speech, you can test the grounds and the reasoning.

You test the grounds by asking questions about source, recency, relevancy, and whether the grounds are fact or opinion. You test the reasoning by asking questions about the warrant for the particular argument, whether it be from example, statistics, analogy, cause, sign, definition, or authority.

In your analysis you also look for such fallacies as hasty generalization, questionable cause, appeal to authority, appeals based on statistics, and ad hominem argument.

Refutation must be handled systematically. You should prepare material on both sides of the proposal, take careful notes of what your opponent says, note your reaction to each argument, plan your procedure, and present your refutation following the four-step method.

Skill Development Exercises

1. From a recent issue of *Vital Speeches* select a speech that you believe includes refutation. How well does the speech exemplify the steps of effective refutation?
2. How successful are the speaker's efforts? Explain.

Speech Preparation Exercises

1. Listen to a speech that establishes or changes a belief such as "The United States should establish mandatory, periodic drug testing for all air traffic controllers" or "The United States should withdraw all troops from Europe." The speech may well be one that has been given during class in an earlier round. Make careful notes of the arguments and evidence in the speech.
2. Prepare a six- to ten-minute refutation speech. As part of your preparation, complete the following speech plan.
   a. Write your speech goal.

   b. Indicate the features of your audience analysis that you believe are most significant in drawing conclusions about the audience.

   c. Indicate what you plan to do to build audience interest. Include methods of showing timeliness, proximity, and personal effect.

   d. Indicate what you plan to do to adapt to the knowledge level of your audience, including what background information you will have to include to orient them.

   e. In light of the audience's attitude (in favor, neutral, or opposed), what do you plan to do to adapt to that attitude?

   f. Indicate what you plan to do to build your credibility in the speech.

   g. Indicate what you plan to do to motivate your audience.

   h. What organization do you believe is most appropriate for your speech in light of that attitude?

3. What part of the plan do you believe is likely to be easiest to achieve? Most difficult? Explain.

Study Questions

For each of the following, be prepared to give examples in support of your answers.

1. What does it mean to refute?
2. What are the essentials of outlining arguments you plan to refute?
3. What are four tests of evidence?
4. What are three major reasoning fallacies?

SAMPLE SPEECH OUTLINE AND SPEECH

Against Legalization of Drugs, *by Lynne Laube*[1]

Speech goal: I want the audience to believe that drugs should not be legalized.

Introduction

   I. According to a recent poll in *Time* magazine, Americans consider drug abuse the most pressing problem in our country.

  II. Legalizing drugs is not the answer.

Body

   I. Advocates argue that legalizing drugs will reduce their costs and allow them to be regulated by the government. I do not believe that is true.

A. The costs of drugs will not be reduced in the long run.
   1. We spend $8 billion annually on fighting drugs compared with $100 billion to pay for the effects of keeping alcohol legal.
   2. Like taxes from the sale of alcohol, tax revenues from drugs will not go to education, but to other areas such as national defense.
   3. Money spent on drugs will not be reduced greatly because of the cost of regulations that will be needed.
B. The environment cannot be controlled.
   1. Selling only certain kinds of drugs will not eliminate pushers. If all kinds are sold, pushers will develop synthetic drugs.
   2. If drugs are sold in prescriptions or in limited quantities, pushers will fill the excess demand.
   3. Selling to people over age 21 does not work for alcohol.
   4. Ads cannot be banned. Anything legally acceptable is socially acceptable.

II. Advocates argue that legalizing drugs will reduce crime caused by them. I do not believe that is true.
   A. Dr. Rosenthal from Harvard says that crime is drug addicts' way of life, not just how they support a habit.
   B. A survey of prison inmates in 1986 showed that 43 percent used drugs daily before they committed their first crime.
   C. Only 15 percent of drug crimes are stealing and killing to get drugs.

III. Advocates argue that legalizing drugs will reduce demand. I do not believe that is true.
   A. Demand for alcohol and cigarettes has risen steadily.
   B. Legalization invites everyone to use drugs.
   C. Drug use has been going down with current laws.
      1. Use by high school seniors is down 13.6 percent since 1982; 48 percent view drugs as a great risk.
      2. General use has gone down 3 percent a year since 1982.

Conclusion

I. We cannot make drugs legal because once we do there is no turning back.
II. Legalization is not a workable solution.

Sources

Church, George. "Thinking the Unthinkable." *Time*, May 30, 1988.
"The Drug Debate." *Mademoiselle*, Nov. 1988.
Gussmann, Vic. "How to Beat Drugs." *U.S. News & World Report*, Sept. 11, 1989.
Kupfer, Andrew. "What to Do about Drugs?" *Fortune*, June 20, 1988.
Nadelmann, Ethan. "Drug Prohibition in the United States: Costs, Consequences, and Alternatives," *Science*, Sept. 1, 1989, pp. 939–946.

Read the following refutation speech aloud. Then analyze it on the basis of organization of refutation, reasoning, and evidence. After you have read and analyzed the speech, refer to the analysis on the right.

Speech

According to a recent poll in *Time* magazine, Americans consider drugs the most pressing problem in our country. It's also the most frustrating problem. It seems like for every drug house the police close down, ten more pop up. Because of this, many Americans suggest that we legalize drugs to solve the drug problem. If it would work, I'd agree wholeheartedly. But rather than solving our current problems, legalizing drugs would just create more. In this speech I want to identify the key reasons people give for legalizing drugs and show that those reasons are fallacious.

One of the reasons you will hear is that legalizing drugs will reduce the costs on society. But I believe legalization would dramatically increase the costs on society. It is true that we do spend billions of dollars a year fighting drugs. As a matter of fact, this year we will spend $8 billion fighting drugs, and that's an awful lot of money. But compare that to the $100 billion a year we spend dealing with the problems caused by alcoholism in our society, the $100 billion a year we spend on problems of lost productivity, lost jobs, and drinking and driving accidents. Now here's the question: Would you rather spend $8 billion a year fighting the problem or $100 billion a year coping with the results of the problem?

Interestingly, those in support of legalizing drugs are aware of these costs. What is their response? They say, we'll legalize drugs and we'll tax them and we'll take the money we get from taxes and we'll put it toward education and treatment programs. But my position on

Analysis

After indicating that drugs are perceived as the major problem in the United States, she states that legalizing drugs would not be the answer. Since a speech of refutation often follows a speech advocating a particular policy or action, the direct approach shown in this introduction is appropriate. She begins with a clear statement of a major point in support of legalization, cost. She does a good job of comparing costs to show that no real savings would occur. In this section we see a problem that crops up throughout the speech. Although she has impressive facts and figures, she fails to document them—a problem that could well hurt her credibility. This is a good use of argument from analogy. In this section, as in other sections of the speech, she does a this point is that a tax will not work because the money gained will not all go to drug programs. Why do I say this? Well, we tax alcohol, and the first thing we find is that the government uses part of the tax money for other programs. The result is that even with a heavy alcohol tax, we do not have nearly enough government-supported treatment programs to meet the problem. Right now an alcoholic can have as long as a four-month waiting period to get treatment. Think of the devastating potential of such a waiting period for a cocaine addict—each time the addict snorts cocaine could be his or her last! So if taxing doesn't provide the necessary treatment for alcoholics, why do people think it will work for cocaine and heroin addicts?

good job of reasoning with us. The way she presents her arguments allows us to follow her thinking easily.

   Another major reason people cite in favor of legalizing drugs is that legalization will reduce crime. When I first heard this argument, I thought it was a good one—legalizing could reduce crime. The problem is, we're assuming that all drug-related crimes are caused by people trying to get the drugs, but that's false. Only 15 percent of drug-related crimes result from people trying to get drugs; the rest are caused by people who are on drugs. Dr. Leonard Rosenthal, a Harvard professor, has said that crime is a way of life for the druggy. A 1986 survey of prison inmates indicated that 43 percent were addicted to drugs. Moreover, they were on drugs daily *before* they committed their first crime. So the problem isn't stopping people from committing crimes to buy drugs; the problem is stopping people from committing crimes after they're addicted. If drugs become legalized, we're more likely to have more addicts and thus more crime.

After a clear transition, she moves directly to refutation of the second key argument. I like the way she admits that an opposing argument sounds logical. Since many in the audience are likely to think the arguments sound logical, this helps her identify with the audience. She then moves on to show the flaw in the logic. She does an excellent job of showing why providing drugs is likely to increase crime.

   A third reason many people cite for legalizing drugs is that the government can control the drug environment if drugs are legal. Proponents argue that if we decriminalize drugs, the government can control them and there will no longer be bad drugs or illegal profits for drug dealers. This would be wonderful if it would work, but it can't. My point is that government cannot control the drug environment. Let's see why not. If the govern-

This is a well-reasoned attack on control of drugs. This section focuses on the

problem of giving social acceptability.

ment legalizes only certain drugs, as many advocates of legalization have suggested, there's still going to be a demand for other drugs—a demand that will be filled illegally. If the government legalizes all drugs, there will still be a market for teenagers and others who don't meet legal requirements. On top of these reasons, legalization will create a double standard. You will have one set of circumstances where the government says that using drugs is all right and another set of circumstances where it isn't. If we legalize it and say it's OK to do it once or twice, how can we not say it's OK to abuse it? How are you going to explain that to people?

Now the final reason that people have for the legalization of drugs is that it will reduce the ultimate demand. If something is legal and you can get it easily, well, you don't want it anymore. That's reverse psychology, but unfortunately it doesn't work. First of all, it hasn't worked to reduce the demand for alcohol and cigarettes. Although alcohol and cigarette use has declined with some age groups, overall people are still buying just as much as they did ten years ago. Moreover, the level of buying among people under 25 has even increased some.

Again she uses comparison to help make her point. And again the point would have been even more powerful if she had cited figures and the source for the figures.

Second of all, if you legalize drugs, it opens up the drug market to people who currently refrain from trying drugs *because* they're illegal. Right now there are still a great number of law-abiding citizens who automatically say, no, I'm not going to buy drugs because they're illegal. Moreover, even if we did want to try drugs, most of us have no idea how to do it. And if we did know how, we'd feel uncomfortable purchasing drugs from street-corner criminals. Most nonusers are not going to take risks to get drugs. But if all we had to do was walk into the local Walgreen's and pick up a packet of drugs, then a major barrier for trying them would be removed. Such legalization would open up the drug environment to a lot of people who would never have considered it.

This is one of her strongest and best discussed arguments. Also note the excellent use of personalization.

If your goal is truly to reduce the demand, then we ought to continue what we're doing, because demand is already going down. Our major efforts have been focused on the youth of America—and we're definitely making headway. A current survey of high school seniors shows

After showing why legalization won't reduce demand, she shows how the present policy is work-

a 13.6 percent decrease in the use of drugs compared to 1982. Forty-eight percent of those high school seniors say they consider drugs a great risk and would not try them. In fact, since 1982 our society as a whole has had a reduction of intake of 3 percent per year. Our solutions to the drug problem are working slowly, but they are working.

ing—albeit slowly. This is a good strategy.

Yes, our drug problem is crazy, and we get very frustrated at times, but legalizing drugs is not the solution. And if your thought is, What would it hurt to give legalization a try? remember, we can never go back. Recall that we tried prohibition of alcohol, but it didn't work. Let's not legalize currently illegal drugs.

Although she makes a good point here, her conclusion is rather abrupt. In general, the speech shows good refutation form and good argument. The major weakness, as I said earlier, is failure to document the good evidence.

Note

[1]Presented in a speech class at the University of Cincinnati. Reprinted by permission of Lynne Laube.

Module **E**

Speech Writing: Preparing and Delivering Manuscripts

Throughout this textbook I have recommended that you prepare your speech using the outline method and that you deliver the speech extemporaneously. At times, however, the situation may call for you to prepare a complete manuscript for yourself or for someone else to read. In this module I focus on two issues: (1) preparing a manuscript for someone else to read and (2) delivering a speech from manuscript.

Rationale for Speech Writing

Since the fifth century B.C. in ancient Greece speech writers have earned money by writing speeches for others. Still, many people see "ghost writing" as a rather nasty, perhaps even immoral act. But perhaps more than ever before, the use of speech writers is now the norm for campaign and corporate speakers.[1] When people don't have the time, the inclination, or perhaps the talent to construct speeches for themselves, they turn to others to write for them.

U.S. presidents, governors of states, chief executive officers of major corporations, and college presidents all face the challenge of being called upon to give formal speeches for so many occasions that the luxury of being able to personally compose a speech for each is beyond them. Even if early in their careers these people wrote all of their own speeches, when the demands of their office become too much, they turn to others for help. To give an idea of the corporate speech load, it is reported that business executives are likely to give at least 50 speeches a year. Robert J. Buckly, president and CEO of Allegheny International Inc., says he gives as many as 1000 speeches a year![2] Even university personnel use speech writers. A survey of 168 chief executives in higher education revealed that presidents of state colleges and universities give an average of 57 major speeches a year.[3] Because of these tremendous demands, such people are likely to have anywhere from one person to a team of persons who pitch in: Some provide data, some do outlines, and many write complete speeches. Especially in a busy campaign, principal speakers are likely to rely on speech writers.

Even some people who have plenty of time don't have the necessary background or training to prepare their own speeches. As you have learned, good speech preparation is a time-consuming task that requires a high level of skill development. Many people who hold prestigious positions never even had a course in public speaking. According to the results of a study I conducted among people whose speeches have appeared in *Vital Speeches*, the great majority learned to write their speeches through trial and error. As the pages of *Vital Speeches* testify, many of the speeches that are printed are not really well organized or well developed.[4]

Now, let's consider some of the issues involved in writing speeches for others. Then we consider issues that relate to delivering a speech from manuscript regardless of whether the speech you are delivering is your own or was written by someone else.

Writing Speeches for Others

Guidelines for writing speeches for others include most of those that we discussed in Part 2 of this textbook. Major differences or different emphases may be summarized in the following recommendations:

Put Yourself in the Place of the Speaker. One of the first, but often one of the hardest things for a speech writer to do is to put him or herself into the perspective of the speaker. The temptation is great to think of the product as "your speech," but the fact is that you are an instrument—the ideas, language, and point of view are the speaker's. Your job is to help the speaker make the most of his or her opportunity. Yet as Richard Haven, professor at the University of Wisconsin–Whitewater, says about students in his speech-writing class, "My students consistently failed to come to grips with the personal qualities of their speechmaker."[5]

To do this, you have to meet with the speaker, talk with the speaker, listen to speeches that the person has given in order to get a sense how the person thinks and talks. Diana Prentice Carlin, who has written speeches for a variety of individuals from local officials to state governors, suggests that you take notes, tape record, and read what the person has written.[6] Then you can answer such questions as: Is the person's style formal, informal, businesslike, folksy? Does the person favor long or short sentences? Does the person use adjectives and adverbs descriptively? Are there particular words, phrases, and sayings that the person likes to use? What is the nature of the person's personality? Are there words the person has trouble with?

Analyze the Audience.   When you write for someone else, you must still analyze the audience as carefully as you would if the speech were your own. Then as you work on the speech, keep the needs of that audience in mind.

Write for the Ear, Not for the Eye.   You want to be especially careful not to use words that are clear to the eye on paper, but create confusion when delivered. Robert Rackleff, a speech writer, tells this story: "I heard of a speaker introducing a woman. He said, 'She and her entire family have this special something in their genes.' "[7] If you don't understand the problem from reading the sentence, say it aloud.

If Possible, Involve the Speaker in the Process.   As you will find, speakers have different ideas about how much involvement they want or need. The speech writer's involvement varies depending on the speaker and the situation. Sometimes speakers write an outline and the writer fills in the details, develops, and modifies; sometimes the writer consults with the speaker once or twice during the process; and sometimes the speaker and writer carry on a total partnership.

The following are suggestions for an ideal speaker/speech writer relationship.

1. *Meet with speaker.* You should meet with the speaker to determine broad guidelines, such as the speaker's goal for the speech, the specific audience to which the speech will be given, the key points the speaker wants to make, and the kinds of material the speaker wants to use to develop key points.

2. *Write an outline.* With this information in mind, compose a draft of the overall outline. This first outline should include just the main points and a few of the facts and details that might be used to develop the points.

3. *Discuss the outline with the speaker.* At this very important meeting, the speaker approves the structure or makes suggestions for changes. With this information you can feel comfortable writing a more detailed outline from which you compose a first draft.

4. *Write a first draft.* In this draft try to include enough information so that the speech will meet the time limits. Include an introduction and a conclusion. At crucial places in the speech you might want to provide alternate ways of approaching the same point. You might also want to give the speaker a choice on some of the developmental material, especially the material to be used for getting attention (humorous stories, etc.).

5. *Invite the speaker's comments on the draft.* Get the speaker to comment on how comfortable he or she feels with the material. The speaker can say which of the choices he or she favors and give an overall evaluation.

6. *Write a final draft.* (Depending on the importance of the speech and the whims of the speaker, the draft, critique, and rewrite cycle can go through several rounds.) Once the speaker has the final draft in hand, he or she is free to make any changes.

7. *Offer to listen to a rehearsal.* If the speaker has time and if the speech is particularly important, he or she may wish to have a run through. At this time you can also encourage the speaker to speak from an outline, especially if the speech is to be relatively informal and for a small audience (less than 30). If the speaker wants or needs a full manuscript, then prepare one.

Delivering Manuscript Speeches

After you have finished writing your manuscript speech or after you have received your speech written by someone else, you need to practice using it effectively or help the speaker practice. So that the manuscript will be of maximum value to you, I suggest the following tips for preparing it:

```
1. The manuscript should be typed, pref-
erably on a typewriter with print that is
pica-sized or larger. Many computer programs
are equipped to provide typefaces of 10, 12,
or even 14. If so, you can produce copy that
looks much like this paragraph, which is re-
produced in Courier 14.
```

2. For words that you have difficulty pronouncing, you should use phonetic spelling, accents, or diacritics to help your pronunciation.

3. Make marks that will help you determine pauses, places of special emphasis, and where to slow down or speed up. Also make sure that the last sentence on each page is complete on that page to avoid unintended pauses.

4. Number pages boldly so it is easy to keep them in their proper order. You may also find it valuable to bend the corner of each page slightly to help you turn pages easily.

5. You should be sufficiently familiar with the material so that you do not have to focus your full attention on the manuscript as you read. Read over the manuscript at least three times in the final stages of practice. You will discover that even when you are reading you can have some eye contact with your audience. By watching audience reaction, you know when and if to deviate from the manuscript.

6. Make sure to double check that there will in fact be a lectern or speaker's stand on which the manuscript can be placed.

Summary

At times the situation may call for you to prepare a complete manuscript for yourself or for someone else to read. When people don't have the time, the inclination, or perhaps the talent to construct speeches for themselves, they turn to others to write speeches for them.

Four general recommendations for a speech writer are to put yourself in the place of the speaker, analyze the audience, involve the speaker in the process, and write for the ear, not the eye.

An ideal working relationship includes at least seven steps for the speech writer: meet the speaker, write an outline, discuss the outline with the speaker, write a first draft, get speaker comments on the draft, write a final draft, and offer to listen to the rehearsal.

When you deliver a manuscript, have the manuscript typed in large letters, accent difficult-to-pronounce words, mark the manuscript for pauses and places of special emphasis, number the pages boldly, be completely familiar with the manuscript, and make sure a speaker's stand is present.

Skill Development Exercises

1. From a recent issue of *Vital Speeches* select a speech that you believe was a manuscript speech. What is it about the speech that leads you to that conclusion?

2. What features, if any, support the need for manuscript delivery? Explain.

Speech Preparation Exercises

1. Have each person in class choose a speech writer. The speaker should meet with the writer and give vital information on speech goal, audience, and situation. The writer then prepares a speech for that person. The writer and speaker are allowed two consultations during the preparation period.
2. Prepare a six- to ten-minute persuasive speech for your speaker. As part of your preparation, complete the following speech plan.
   a. Write the speaker's goal.
   b. Indicate the features of the prospective audience analysis that you believe are most significant in drawing conclusions about the audience.
   c. Indicate what you plan to do to build audience interest. Include methods of showing timeliness, proximity, and personal effect.
   d. Indicate what you plan to do to adapt to the knowledge level of the audience, including what background information you will have to include to orient them.
   e. In light of the audience's attitude (in favor, neutral, or opposed), what do you plan to do to adapt to that attitude?
   f. Indicate what you plan to do to build the speaker's credibility in the speech.
   g. Indicate what you plan to do to motivate the audience.
   h. What organization do you believe is most appropriate for your speech in light of that attitude?

Study Questions

For each of the following, be prepared to give examples in support of your answers.

1. What factors do you believe are most important in writing effective speeches for others?
2. What characterizes an ideal speaker/speech writer relationship? What can you do, if anything, to ensure this ideal?
3. Under what circumstances would you recommend that the person deliver the speech from a manuscript rather than presenting it from an outline?

SAMPLE SPEECH

Deforestation of Rain Forests, *by Diane Reder*[8]

Read aloud the following speech, which was written for a student environmentalist who wanted to persuade the class to become personally involved in efforts to promote tropical rain forest conservation. Then analyze it as a manuscript speech on the basis of language, organization, reasoning and evidence, motivation, and speaker credibility. After you have read and analyzed the speech, refer to the analysis on the right.

Speech	Analysis
New Guinea, Borneo, Congo, Zaire, Brazil. What do these seemingly remote countries have to do with us? They contain the great rain forests of the world. These rain forests are not only places of unequalled beauty but also places that hold the world's ecosystem in balance, and thus they have an effect on all of us. Yet, in the minute that it has taken for me to talk so far, 25 acres of rain forest in the tropics have disappeared as people in Third World countries cut and burn them, often in an effort to feed themselves. Their gains are only short term, but the loss may affect us all forever. Approximately 31,000 square miles of tropical rain forest, an area that's about the same size as our neighboring state of Indiana, are cut down each year. About one-half the existing rain forest has been cleared over the past 40 years. At the current rate of deforestation, the rain forests of the world will be stripped bare in another 30 years. Today I want to discuss with you the dangers that can result from this destruction of the tropical rain forests of the world and what we can do to control this problem.	*In this opening, the speaker captures our attention by building suspense. Notice how she dramatizes the speed at which the rain forests of the world are being depleted. She concludes her opening by clearly outlining her goals.*
There are two major problems that deforestation can cause. The first danger is the extinction of many species of plants and animals. With temperatures always close to 80 degrees and humidity near 100 percent, the tropical rain forests that equal just 5 percent of the world's land surface are home to half of *all* the world's species of plants and animals. In the Amazon basin alone there are more than 50,000 species of plants and 5,000 different types of fish. In comparison, the whole of North America has only 17,000 plants and Europe has only 300 different types of fish. In Brazil, botanist Ghillean Prance identified 236 species of trees with diameters larger than 2 inches in a similar area. In a typical New England woods, you might find only five or six. And yet these forests are being destroyed at the rate of 25 acres a minute. We could lose more than one-fifth of all plant and animal species in the next few decades.	*In this section she does an excellent job of outlining the abundance of plants and animals. Her description features an excellent use of statistics. Notice how the abundance of the rain forests is shown through comparisons to other parts of the world.*

The implications of the loss of topical plants and animals could be devastating. Let's look at what these losses could mean to medicine alone. Right now, 25 percent of all prescription drugs are derived from plants grown in tropical rain forests. Alkaloidal drugs derived from rosy periwinkle found in Madagascar have revolutionized the treatment of lymphocytic leukemia in children. Scientists at the National Cancer Institute state that 70 percent of the promising anticancer drugs come from tropical rain forests. Heart surgery would not be possible without curare, which is found there. Recent research on the African clawed frog could lead to the production of a whole new family of antibiotics. And the medical potential in tropical rain forests has barely been tapped. Only one in ten of the species has been examined for medicinal use, and yet some species are disappearing every day and many others are in danger of extinction.

In this section she shows the immediacy of the problem. She does an excellent job of showing the potential loss to medicine.

The other major danger in deforestation pertains to the fact that the tropical rain forests play a large part in stabilizing our climate. Large-scale destruction can result in large-scale climatic changes. Because most of the trees are burned in order to speed the clearing process and supply nutrients to the soil, deforestation is adding an additional 1 billion tons of carbon to the atmosphere every year. This, together with the burning of fossil fuels, has increased the concentration of carbon dioxide in the atmosphere by 25 percent. This increase could lead to a global warming of 3 to 9 degrees in the next century. Deforestation in the rain forest then is a major contributor to the growing threat of the greenhouse effect.

Here she moves to the second danger of deforestation. Notice how she relates this problem to the problem of global warming.

In addition to affecting temperature, deforestation can also affect the world's rainfall. In normal conditions, the rain forest returns so much rain to the atmosphere that moisture is recycled many times before it finally flows back to the ocean. When a large number of trees are removed, the rain runs off as much as 20 times faster. If 8 percent of Brazil's tropical rain forest is cut by the year 2000, the average rainfall in the Amazon could drop by 25 inches annually. This could harm the untouched rain forest and disrupt rainfall patterns thousands of miles away.

Notice the good transition to show us that she is still talking about climate. She continues to use statistics effectively in this section.

Before we can think about a solution to the problem, it is necessary to take a look at what is causing it. Although three related causes are frequently cited, they relate to one root cause—devastating poverty. The irony is that the efforts of the people in these areas to eliminate poverty and make a better life for themselves are resulting in destruction of the rain forest, their most important resource. Let's briefly consider the three direct causes.

By far the major cause, according to an authoritative three-year study by the United Nations Environment Program and the Food and Agriculture Organization of the United Nations, is clearing for agriculture, particularly shifting agriculture. Tens of millions of people who live near these forests face critical shortages of fuel and food. The government of Brazil has been encouraging these people since 1970 to cut down the forest for farming. While the burning of the forest provides temporary nutrients to the soil, after a year or two the crops fail and many of the farmers move on, burning more forest. Cattle ranching has been another reason for clearing rain forests. Since the 1960s, a quarter of the Central American rain forest has been felled to give way to cattle pastures. The number of cattle doubled between 1959 and 1979 and yet consumption of beef in that country decreased. Most of the beef went to the United States for fast food hamburgers. The third reason for deforestation is careless commercial logging. Logging accounts for one-fourth of the destruction of Brazilian rain forests and is the main reason in Southeast Asia.

As we have seen, as a result of the complexity of the problems, the solutions to stopping the destruction of the tropical rain forests of Central and South America will not be easy ones. Currently, various world agencies are studying potential solutions. The International Union for Conservation of Nature and Natural Resources met in Costa Rica and concluded that any strategy must include the establishment of protected areas and programs to promote sustainable agriculture for rural populations.

Here she does an excellent job of laying the groundwork for a discussion of the major cause of deforestation. In essence she is suggesting that none of the causes can be eliminated without eliminating the root cause. This is a pretty good analysis of causes. Notice how she shows that none of these actions is really helping the people.

Here she lays the groundwork for solutions, showing that just as the problem is a world problem, so is the solution.

But the point of my speech is that the United States can take leadership in working on solutions. Through its developmental aid programs, our government can promote the preservation and legal protection of threatened and biologically rich forestlands. It can assist in the preparation of conservation strategies and ensure that new development projects funded by American taxpayers and corporations are diverted away from the conservation areas. This country should also promote agroforestry research, projects for production of fuelwood, and policy reform in countries where present laws promote deforestation.

Large American corporations, especially those with interests in Central and South America, can also help with funds and technologies. Corporations have a responsibility not to take advantage of these developing countries that destroy the tropical rain forest land out of a desperate need for money. There is the example of Coke, which bought 200,000 acres of subtropical moist forest in 1985 in the tiny country of Belize, formerly British Honduras, to grow oranges for its Minute Maid subsidiary. In response to Coke's initial development plans, conservation groups organized sit-ins at bottling plants in West Germany, demonstrations in Stockholm, and a letter-writing campaign in the United States. Coke agreed to meet with these groups and eventually offered to scale down the plans dramatically by preserving up to 166,000 acres in their natural state.

But we can't just sit back and rely on government and big business to take care of the problem. We as people of the world have individual responsibilities. There are things we can do as individuals to help. We can start by joining and supporting conservation leagues with our donations. Can financial support of groups really help? Last year, Conservation International, a U.S.-based environmental group, bought $650,000 of Bolivia's external debt from the World Bank for $100,000. In exchange, that country agreed not to touch 3.7 million acres of its natural forests. This novel debt-for-conservation exchange may be a hope for the future. We can also give direct support when the opportunity arises. We have

She begins to show that although nations worldwide must be involved, the United States must play a leadership role.

Notice how she moved from what the government can do to what business and industry can do. This Coke example is a good one because it is specific and because Coke is so familiar to us.

Here she brings the problem home. In this section she begins the most active part of her persuasion. Now she adapts to the audience more directly.

just seen the influence such groups had in Belize. Another example of what the people can do occurred in Nicaragua in June 1987, when President Daniel Ortega, under pressure from environmentalists in his own country and abroad, cancelled an agreement to sell 3200 square kilometers of virgin rain forest to a Costa Rican timber company.

Am I advocating that you have a personal responsibility in a problem that seems to be thousands of miles away? I am. And I have developed a very simple way of helping you carry your personal involvement one step further. I've composed a letter directed to the attention of Senator Albert Gore, an active proponent of the rain forest preservation campaign, and provided you with free addressed, stamped envelopes. All you need to do is either sign the enclosed letter or draft your own based on the model and drop it in the envelope and mail it as you leave this class. Not only can you join conservation organizations and donate to groups that are backing their plans with financial support, but you can also be more active in getting our government to raise the priority level of this problem. The more our government representatives see that we are concerned about global problems that affect all of us so directly, the better the chances that they will frame policies that will enable our nation to lead by example. We need to let our leaders know that the people of America believe that the preservation of the environment is a priority on the agenda and is something that we value.

In this conclusion she moves us to direct action. Notice that by supplying the class with a letter, she has removed one of the major barriers to action. This is a good conclusion. In general the speech is well written. It is well organized, it uses good examples, and it is clear and vivid. The speech would be even better with more direct efforts to raise the credibility of the speaker and more direct audience adaptation in the first half.

Notes

[1]Carol Kleiman, "Speechwriters Join the Corporate Team," *Chicago Tribune*, February 12, 1989, Section 8, p. 1.
[2]Thomas M. Rohan, "Should You Give That Speech?" *Industry Week*, September 17, 1984, p. 90.
[3]" 'In' Box," *The Chronicle of Higher Education*, October 4, 1989, p. A13; and Rohan.
[4]Rudolph F. Verderber, "Analysis of Vital Speakers," unpublished study.
[5]Richard P. Haven, "Combining Arenas: Making the Speech Writing Course Experience More Authentic," unpublished paper delivered at the 1989 Speech Communication Association Convention, San Francisco, November 18, 1989.

[6]Diana Prentice Carlin, "Perspectives of a Speechwriter: from Theory to Practice," unpublished paper presented at the 1989 Speech Communication Convention, San Francisco, November 18, 1989.
[7]Robert B. Rackleff, "The Art of Speech Writing," *Vital Speeches*, March 1, 1988, p. 313.
[8]Written by Diane Reder; reprinted by permission.

Appendix **A**

Research Tools

Truly effective speakers may not know all the information on any given issue, but they should know *where to find* the information they need. This appendix reviews the sources with which an effective speaker must be familiar.

Books

Whether your library is large or small, it is likely to have books on nearly any subject you choose. The card catalog, the index of library books, indexes holdings by title, author, and subject. Today most university libraries and some public libraries have transferred their holdings to computer. For instance, at the University of Cincinnati, the card catalog does not include any books purchased after 1987. On the other hand, the computer data base does not contain many of the older books that the library holds.

Periodical Indexes in Book Form

The *Reader's Guide to Periodical Literature* is a yearly index of articles in some 200 U.S. general-circulation journals. Such familiar sources as *Atlantic*, *Business Week*, *Newsweek*, and *Time* are all indexed.

Education Index, a cumulative subject index to a selected list of some 200 educational periodicals, proceedings, and yearbooks will lead you to material directly or indirectly related to the field of education.

The *Social Sciences Index* and *Humanities Index* are each guides to more than 250 periodicals. These indexes have been published separately since 1974, when the *Social Sciences and Humanities Index* was divided in two. In contrast to the *Reader's Guide*, which indexes popular magazines, these indexes cover scholarly journals. The *Social Sciences Index* includes such journals as *American Journal of Sociology*, *Economist*, and *Psychological Review*; the *Humanities Index* includes such journals as *Modern Language Quarterly*, *Philosophical Review*, and *Quarterly Journal of Speech*.

Encyclopedias

Encyclopedias are books or series of books that cover all subjects from A to Z. The best use of an encyclopedia is to give you an overview of your subject and some useful primary sources. Most libraries have a recent edition of *Encyclopaedia Britannica*, *Encyclopedia Americana*, or *World Book Encyclopedia*.

Statistical Sources

Statistical sources are books devoted to presenting statistical information on a wide variety of subjects. When you need facts and details, such as statistics about population, records, continents, heads of state, weather, or similar subjects, you should refer to one of the many single-volume sources that report such data. Two of the most popular sources in this category are the *World Almanac and Book of Facts* and the *Statistical Abstract*.

Biographical Sources

Biographical sources provide accounts of people's lives. When you need biographical details, from thumbnail sketches to reasonably complete essays, you can turn to one of the many available biographical sources. In addition to full-length books and encyclopedia entries, you should use such books as *Who's*

Who (British subjects) and *Who's Who in America* (short sketches of U.S. citizens) or *Dictionary of National Biography* and *Dictionary of American Biography* (rather complete essays about prominent British subjects and U.S. citizens, respectively).

Newspapers

Consult your reference librarian for information about which newspapers your library indexes. Your library probably holds indexes of your nearest major daily paper and the *New York Times*.

Editorials on File. This collection contains editorials from more than 140 U.S. and Canadian newspaper editorials. Each issue includes about 200 texts of editorials representing different positions on current issues.

Facts on File. This is a weekly digest of U.S. and foreign news published by major newspapers and other print sources. The indexes are quite easy to use. A limitation, however, is that sources of information are not provided.

U.S. Government Publications

The following are some of the government publications that are especially useful for locating primary sources.

United States Code. The code, published every six years since 1926, includes U.S. federal laws. The 11th edition includes 50 content areas such as census, education, and labor.

Federal Register. The register publishes daily regulations and legal notices issued by the executive branch and federal agencies. The goal of the register is to make regulations including executive orders and federal agency documents available to the public.

Monthly Catalog of United States Government Publications. The monthly catalog covers publications of all branches of the federal government. It has semiannual and annual cumulative indexes by title, author/agency, and subject. The catalog contains a user's guide at the front of each volume that helps identify elements of each entry. Nevertheless, you may wish to get your reference librarian to help you in learning to use it.

CIS/Index to Publications of the United States Congress. This index catalogs all the working papers of Congress. It is published monthly and accumulated quarterly and annually. Although this index provides a wealth of information, very few libraries own the complete collection of all documents that are abstracted. Nevertheless, this is an important index with which you should become familiar because it covers all congressional publications except for the *Congressional Record.*

Microfilm Indexes

A new indexing format that is becoming increasingly available in libraries is called Computer Output Microfilm (COM). These consist of rolls of microfilm prepared from a data base and stored in a mechanized reader. These are frequently updated. Although they are quite comprehensive, they usually cover only the preceding three to five years. Two of the most widely used are *Magazine Index,* indexing more than 370 U.S. periodicals, and *Business Index.* Consult with your reference librarian to see which of these special indexes your library has.

Computer Data Bases

A *computer data base* is information that is stored in such a way that it can be retrieved through a computer terminal. Data bases can be searched much more quickly than their print counterparts. I've already mentioned that your library's card catalog is likely to be on computer. Depending on the size of your library, you may also have access to such computerized data bases as ERIC, MEDLINE, BIOSIS, and PsychoInfo. Currently research libraries have access to more than 300 on-line data bases. Through them you can compile bibliographies and view abstracts and even full articles on the computer screen. To access these data bases, you need to work with your reference librarian. Not only will your librarians know which computer bases your library subscribes to, but they also will be able to show you how to access the various data bases.

To show you the potential of a computer search, let's consider a specific example. Suppose you were researching for a speech on alcohol and drug abuse. By starting out using a key word descriptor like "substance abuse," a time span of the last five years, and searches of such indexes as *Reader's Guide, Magazine Index,* and CIS (three of the indexes discussed in this appendix), in a matter of seconds the computer might indicate that thousands of entries exist. By using more descriptive key words such as "cocaine abuse" or "treatment centers," you might generate a more manageable list. Depending on whether you want sources on the screen, complete articles, or abstracts, you could get the results of your search for a cost of between ten and several hundred dollars.

Appendix B

Interviewing for Speech Information

In your search for information to use as evidence in your speeches, you are likely to need to interview a person who is directly involved with your subject. In this appendix I give you suggestions for selecting the best person to interview, defining the purpose of your interview, determining a logical procedure, and conducting the interview.

Selecting the Best Person to Interview

Since you want to use your time as efficiently as possible, you want to make sure that you have selected the person who is best qualified and most able to give you the kind of information that you need for your speech. Suppose you are planning to give a speech on campus substance abuse. To begin with, you need to find out where information on campus substance abuse is kept and who is responsible for collecting and or analyzing those data. In this situation, then, you might determine that the two most obvious places to begin your quest are the office of student affairs and the campus police office. Telephone calls to each of these offices will probably enable you to identify the names of the person or people with whom you need to talk. When you have decided whom you should interview, make an appointment. Do not walk into any office expecting a busy official to drop everything just to talk to you.

Before you actually interview the person on campus who is responsible for collecting substance abuse data, you should do some preliminary research on the topic of substance abuse. You want to be familiar enough with the topic that you are able to ask intelligent questions. Most interviewees are more likely to talk with you if you are informed; moreover, familiarity with the subject enables you to ask better questions. If, for some reason, you must go into an interview uninformed (perhaps there just isn't much written information on the specific topic you are exploring), then at least spend some time thinking about potential aspects of the problem.

Defining the Purpose of the Interview

To make the most of your telephone or in-person interview, you need to explain to your source the goal of your interview. You should be forthright in your reasons for scheduling the interview. If your interview is for a class project, a newspaper article, or a speech, say so. In most cases this means sharing your speech goal. If, for instance, you are considering giving a speech in which you advocate a more direct role for the university administration in the identification and rehabilitation of students who are engaged in substance abuse on campus, you would tell the person that your goal is to determine the role of the university in identifying and rehabilitating of students engaged in substance abuse. Letting the person know your goal gives the person a chance to draw together the kind of information he or she will need to answer questions you will ask in reference to that goal.

Planning the Interview

Good interviewing results from careful planning. A good plan begins with good questions. Write down all the questions you can think of, revise them until you have worded them clearly and concisely, and put them in the order that seems most appropriate.

Good interviews result from a mix of neutrally phrased, open, closed, and follow-up questions. Neutral questions are those for which the person is free to give an answer without direction from the interviewer. An example of a neutral question is: "What kinds of students are most likely to be substance abusers?" There is nothing in the wording of the question that gives the respondent any indication of how the question should be answered. Except in rare instances, your questions should be phrased neutrally.

By contrast, leading questions are phrased in a way that suggests the interviewer has a preferred answer. For instance, "Poor students are more likely to be substance abusers, aren't they?" is a leading question. In most situations, leading questions are inappropriate because they try to force the person in one direction and tend to make the person defensive.

Open questions are broad-based questions that ask the interviewee to provide whatever information he or she wishes to answer the questions. Open questions range from those with virtually no restrictions, such as "What can you tell me about student substance abusers?" to those that give some direction, such as "What are major characteristics of student substance abusers?" The purpose of the open question is to encourage the person to talk, allowing the interviewer an opportunity to listen and to observe. Through the open question the interviewer finds out about the person's perspectives, values, and goals. Keep in mind, however, that because open questions take time to answer, the interviewer can lose sight of the original purpose.

Closed questions are narrow-focus questions that require very brief answers. Closed questions range from those that can be answered yes or no, such as "Are males more likely to abuse alcohol than females?" to those that require only a short answer, such as "What tend to be the most frequently abused substances by college students?" By asking closed questions you can control the interview; moreover, you can obtain large amounts of information in a short time. On the other hand, the closed question seldom enables you to know the reason behind a certain response, nor is the closed question likely to yield much voluntary information.

Follow-up questions are used to get more information about a subject area. Although follow-up questions may be planned ahead if you can anticipate possible answers, often they are composed as the interview goes along. To ask good follow-up questions, you must pay close attention to what the interviewee is saying. Some follow-up questions encourage the person to continue ("And then?" "Is there more?"); some probe into what the person has said ("What does 'frequently' mean?" "What were you thinking at the time?"); and some plumb the feelings of the person ("How did it feel to get the award?" "Were you worried when you didn't find her?").

The major purpose of follow-up questions is to motivate a person to enlarge upon an answer that appears inadequate. Follow-up questions are often necessary because interviewees may be purposely trying to be evasive, because their answers may be incomplete or vague, or because they may not really understand how much detail you are looking for.

When you list your questions, leave enough space between them to fill in answers as completely as possible. It is also important to leave enough space for answers to follow-up questions. Some interviewers try to conduct the entire interview spontaneously. Even the most skilled interviewer, however, requires some planned questions to ensure coverage of important areas. The order and type of questions you need depend somewhat on what you are hoping to achieve in the interview. How many primary questions should you plan? The answer, of course, depends on how much time you have for the interview. If you have 30 minutes, about ten questions is a reasonable number. Why ten? A 30-minute interview would give about three minutes per question. Remember, for some of your questions you need one or more follow-up questions to get the information you want. If most of your questions are closed, then you can ask more than ten. Keep in mind that you never know how a person will respond. Some people are so talkative and informative that in response to your first question they answer every question you were planning to ask in great detail; other people will answer each question with just a few words—you will need many follow-up questions to draw them out.

In the opening stage of the interview you should plan to ask some questions that can be answered easily and that show your respect for the person you are interviewing. In an interview with the campus official in charge of collecting data on chemical abuse, you might start with such questions as "What caused the university to begin gathering data on substance abuse?" or "How did you get involved in the substance abuse data-gathering program?" The goal is to get the interviewee to feel at ease and to talk freely. Because the most important consideration in this initial stage is to create a positive communication climate, keep the questions simple, nonthreatening, and encouraging.

The body of the interview includes the major questions you have prepared. A good plan is to group questions so that the easy-to-answer questions come first and the hard-hitting questions that require careful thinking come later. For instance, the question "What do you do with repeated abusers?" should come near the end of the interview. You may not ask all the questions you planned to, but you don't want to end the interview until you have the important information you intended to get.

The following is an example of a question schedule you might construct to interview the campus official in charge of gathering data on chemical abuse:

BACKGROUND

1. What are the responsibilities of your office?
2. What motivated your office to begin collecting this information?
3. When did you begin collecting substance-abuse data?

PROCEDURES

4. What methods do you use to get data?

5. How cooperative are students and student organizations in supplying data?
6. What kinds of problems do you face with confidentiality?

RESULTS

7. What are the substances that students are most likely to abuse?
8. What have you discovered to be the major causes of substance abuse on campus?
9. What appears to be the extent of substance abuse on campus?

PLANS

10. Does the university have any master plan for combating the problem of substance abuse on campus?
11. What means, if any, does the campus have for rehabilitating students who are substance abusers?
12. At what point are substance abusers suspended or dismissed from the university?

Conducting the Interview

The most difficult part of interviewing is to conduct the interview in a way that maintains a positive communication climate. Yes, you want to ask "tough" questions, but this can be done without offending the interviewee.

First, of course, you want to be courteous during the interview. You should start by thanking the person for taking the time to talk to you. Remember, that person has nothing to gain from the interview. Try to develop a good rapport, encourage the person to speak freely, and be patient at all times. Most of all, respect what the person says regardless of what you may think of the answers.

Second, listen very carefully. At key places in the interview you should paraphrase what the person has said. A *paraphrase* is a sentence that states in your own words what you perceive to be the idea or feeling the person has communicated. Paraphrasing gives you the chance to make sure that you have heard the answer correctly. For instance, after the person has finished an answer, you might say, "If I've heard you correctly, you're saying that even though there is some campus abuse of cocaine, alcohol is abused far more by college students."

Third, either record the interview or take notes. If you believe that the interview will contain a great deal of factual or controversial material, it is usually a good idea to ask permission to record it. Before the interview begins, ask the subject if he or she objects to tape recording the interview. If the person objects, don't argue; put your recording device away and rely on careful notes. If the person okays recording, make sure that your machine is working properly and that it is set to go. A subject is going to lose faith in you if you fiddle with your recording equipment for several minutes. The advantages of recording an interview are that you can concentrate on the interview and that you have a verbatim record if the material turns out to be controversial.

Even if you plan to record, you may still wish to take notes. Take as few notes as possible during the interview itself, but as soon as the interview is over, take time to fill in the gaps while material is still fresh in your mind. Be very precise in writing down facts and figures. If you plan to quote the subject, you might read back the material you have quoted to make sure that it is correct. If you know shorthand, great—if you do not, you are going to have to develop a kind of shorthand using abbreviations. Some interviewers like to use a separate page for each major question so that later they have room to fill in detail and add personal observations relating to the items of information.

Fourth, keep the interview moving. You do not want to rush the person, but when the allotted time is ending, you should call attention to that fact and be prepared to conclude.

Fifth, make sure that your nonverbal reactions—facial expressions and gestures—are in keeping with the tone you want to communicate. Maintain good eye contact with the person. Nod to show understanding. And smile occasionally to maintain the friendliness of the interview. How you look and act is likely to determine whether the person will warm up to you and give you a good interview.

Finally, if you are going to use direct quotes in your speech, you should offer to let the person hear what you are going to say; this is a courtesy. Although this practice is not followed by many speakers, it may help to build and maintain your own credibility.

Author Index

Subject Index